DAILY GUIDANCE
from Your
ANGELS

∾ By Doreen Virtue ∾

DAILY GUIDANCE
from Your
ANGELS

365 Angelic Messages to Soothe,
Heal, and Open Your Heart

DOREEN VIRTUE

HAY HOUSE, INC.
Carlsbad, California • New York City
London • Sydney • Johannesburg
Vancouver • Hong Kong • New Delhi

Published and distributed in the United States by: Hay House, Inc.: www .hayhouse.com • *Published and distributed in Australia by:* Hay House Australia Pty. Ltd.: www.hayhouse.com.au • *Published and distributed in the United Kingdom by:* Hay House UK, Ltd.: www.hayhouse.co.uk • *Published and distributed in the Republic of South Africa by:* Hay House SA (Pty), Ltd.: www.hayhouse.co.za • *Distributed in Canada by:* Raincoast: www.raincoast.com • *Published in India by:* Hay House Publishers India: www.hayhouse.co.in

Editorial supervision: Jill Kramer • *Design:* Tricia Breidenthal

Library of Congress Cataloging-in-Publication Data

Virtue, Doreen.
  Daily guidance from your angels : 365 angelic messages to soothe, heal, and open your heart / Doreen Virtue.
    p. cm.
  ISBN-13: 978-1-4019-0771-6 (hardcover)
  ISBN-10: 1-4019-0771-7 (hardcover)
  ISBN-13: 978-1-4019-0774-7 (tradepaper)
  ISBN-10: 1-4019-0774-1 (tradepaper)
  1. Angels--Miscellanea. I. Title.
  BF1623.A53V565 2006
  133.9'3--dc22   2006007444

Hardcover: **ISBN 13:** 978-1-4019-0771-6 • **ISBN 10:** 1-4019-0771-7
Tradepaper: **ISBN 13:** 978-1-4019-0774-7 • **ISBN 10:** 1-4019-0774-1

16 15 14 13   8 7 6 5
1st printing, September 2006
5th printing, March 2013

Printed in the United States of America

CONTENTS

INTRODUCTION

No matter where I am in the world or what's on my schedule, I begin each day by reading an inspirational book and then meditating and praying. I adopted this healthy habit many years ago to ensure that my first thoughts of the day were positive.

In the beginning, I let myself skip an occasional morning of reflection, but I always noticed that my day wasn't as fun or satisfying. Whenever I devoted time to my uplifting practice, I was always rewarded with a magical day, new opportunities, and a deep sense of fulfillment. Now I wouldn't even think of neglecting my morning ritual.

This book is a way for you to connect with your guardian angels' loving energy on a daily basis. Ideally, you'll read one entry each morning before you begin your day. You can read the pages in their numbered order, or just let the book fall open to whichever message is best for you at the time.

Each page contains a practical, down-to-earth message from the angels to help you have a wonderful day—and you'll probably also hear or feel your own angels' guidance as you're reading. Every day they'll suggest an action or focus for you to take that will bring you more peace and happiness. The daily message is then followed by a thought or prayer, which you can use as a helpful way to connect further with your angels. Say it out loud, write it down, or just think of it throughout the day—do what feels most natural to you, since the angels can always hear you. Don't worry if you forget or don't have time to follow the angels' suggestions for that day. The most important step is to absorb their loving energy by reading their words.

Although this book is geared toward morning meditations, you can benefit from it anytime, day or night. I suggest keeping it on your bedside table or desk so that you can refer to it whenever you need a comforting boost from above.

I personally learned a great deal from the messages that the angels dictated for this book. Many of them contain profound teachings, as well as suggestions for beneficial ways to approach the day. God and the angels want us to lead happy and healthy lives, and they're available to all of us every moment of every day. My prayer is that you'll allow heaven to help, guide, and love you. Reading this book is one way for that prayer to be answered.

— **Doreen Virtue,**
Laguna Beach, California

∽∾

Know That We're Always with You

*Y*ou're never alone, especially in your time of need. We're next to you continuously, sending you supportive and healing energy and awaiting your requests for help. A mere thought on your part—even a passing one—sends us into action on your behalf.

Listen in stillness for our guidance, which comes upon wings to your heart, mind, and body. Our messages always speak of love. We view you as you truly are: a completely lovable and magnificent being of light.

We can see solutions to every seeming problem. We're happy to guide you through the dark places in your life and then back into the light, and we're able to help you feel good about yourself and your experiences. We can assist you in making decisions and finding answers.

We're your angels . . . we love you unconditionally and eternally. As you read these words, we're right by your side, for we're with you always.

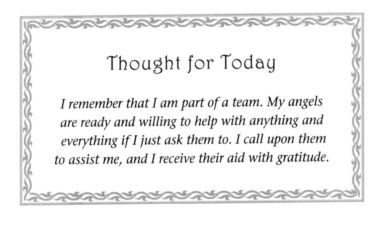

Thought for Today

I remember that I am part of a team. My angels are ready and willing to help with anything and everything if I just ask them to. I call upon them to assist me, and I receive their aid with gratitude.

2

Take Frequent Breaks

Anxiety creates a restlessness that makes it difficult for you to focus and concentrate. At times, your mind and body feel as unsettled as the churning sea.

These feelings spring from a search of peace, without knowing where it is or how to find it. It's a relentless outward quest for perfection and a desire for control that's founded on the longing for serenity. But since peace is God, what you're really craving is a connection with the Divine.

You need a respite from intense situations. Ironically, you created these stressful circumstances because you believed they would bring you tranquility, or at least a diversion from anxiety.

Everything that you're craving is waiting for you in the quiet moments when you close your eyes, breathe, and calm your body and mind. This is where God is and where peace resides . . . this is what you yearn for.

Take frequent breaks, closing your eyes and breathing deeply throughout the day (and especially during difficult situations, or whenever you feel anxious). And remember that we hold your hand through all matters, calm and chaotic. Since we're entirely peaceful, you can lean on us and "borrow" our serenity whenever you choose. Your peacefulness pours cooling liquid upon raging fires, bringing about harmonious solutions to all apparent problems.

Peace is the answer to any question you have today . . . just peace.

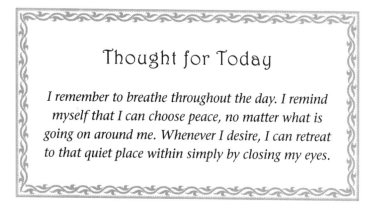

Thought for Today

I remember to breathe throughout the day. I remind myself that I can choose peace, no matter what is going on around me. Whenever I desire, I can retreat to that quiet place within simply by closing my eyes.

3

Dedicate This Day

*Y*ou can set the tone of your day by dedicating it to a specific intention, lesson, or theme that you'd like to experience. For example, you may devote yourself to having warm and loving relationships; seeing the beauty within you, all others, and every situation; taking excellent care of yourself; making good money in meaningful ways; or something else that's personally significant for you.

By offering a dedication each morning, your soul casts a signal outward to the universe—like an angler throwing a large net—attracting situations along its theme, just as you've asked. Dedications are a potent way for you to understand just how powerful you and your decisions are.

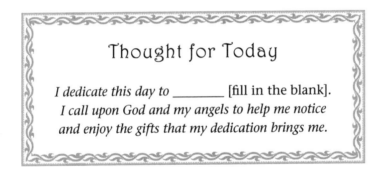

Thought for Today

I dedicate this day to _____ [fill in the blank].
I call upon God and my angels to help me notice
and enjoy the gifts that my dedication brings me.

4

Set Your Dials Up High

You have the ability to regulate your energy, moods, finances, and many other areas of your life. Just as you'd adjust the temperature in your house or refrigerator by changing the settings, you can do the same with yourself.

Imagine that you have a switch within you like your home heating system, which corresponds to something in your life that you'd like to improve. By picturing yourself turning the knob upward (as you would do to control the room temperature), you send an important signal to the universe.

By setting your dials up high, you take charge of the situation. You decide what's acceptable, and you firmly fix your intentions in that direction. Your crystal clear decisions bring about action faster than any amount of money could buy for you. These choices are worth more than a college degree or other earthly measure of success.

Clearly decide what you want, and crank up your dials today in the direction of your desired outcomes.

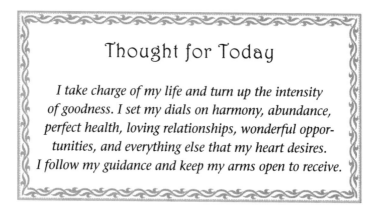

Thought for Today

I take charge of my life and turn up the intensity of goodness. I set my dials on harmony, abundance, perfect health, loving relationships, wonderful opportunities, and everything else that my heart desires. I follow my guidance and keep my arms open to receive.

Pamper Yourself

*Y*ou deserve to receive wonderful treatment, extra-special care, great gifts, and other forms of pampering from the world. The price for all of this indulgence is your gratitude, which is the sweet energy wave that carries these offerings to you and all others.

It's now time to work on joyously accepting the bounties in your life. True acceptance means guiltless gratitude founded on the knowledge that as you receive, you allow others the pleasure of giving. To only give without taking is to block the everlasting abundance. And since you can't dam up an eternal flow, your refusal to receive simply puts a barrier around you. The current then goes around you and extends to others—it seems to skip you. You may feel ignored by the universe, yet this action actually stems from *you*.

Through the process of pampering yourself, lift any blocks you have with respect to receiving. Indulge yourself today . . . and every day.

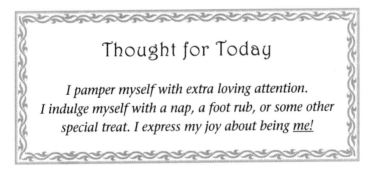

Thought for Today

I pamper myself with extra loving attention.
I indulge myself with a nap, a foot rub, or some other
special treat. I express my joy about being <u>me</u>!

6

Extend Kindness

One caring deed performed each day can elevate your energy, causing you to ride on a cushion of gratitude from those who receive your kindness. When you act compassionately, you're literally directing your power outward, like a beam of light that supports and uplifts the other person. When that individual then extends appreciation back toward you, you then become elevated on a ray of very powerful energy. So each time someone thinks of you in a grateful way, *your* spirits are also raised. You may even notice a lift in your mood or a warm feeling in your heart as the other person sends gratitude your way.

Performing a thoughtful deed each day is an investment in your own ascension and elevation in spiritual growth. You, therefore, are actually extending the kindness to yourself. It's a situation where everyone wins.

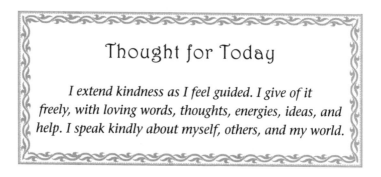

Thought for Today

I extend kindness as I feel guided. I give of it freely, with loving words, thoughts, energies, ideas, and help. I speak kindly about myself, others, and my world.

Be Honest with Others

*F*orthrightness is a term coined to describe the action of moving forward ("forth") into rightness. The energy of this honesty moves your life in a positive, healing direction. That's why another word for honesty is *directness*.

This powerful force overcomes health, financial, and psychic blocks, as well as other imbalances in your life. It sends a huge wave of healing energy that envelops everyone involved, even those who disagree with, or are threatened by, your truth.

It's doubly important for you as a healer to be honest with others. Your truthfulness keeps you healthy and balanced, but it also helps your clients trust you (as they can feel your level of integrity). Bottling up *your* feelings to spare someone else's is a disservice to yourself and all others. It entangles the energy waves, sending crossed signals out into the universe that interfere with your clear manifestations.

We can help guide your words and actions to soften your honesty and to help others hear your truth with love. Be straightforward with other people today, and allow yourself and your energy to be direct and forthright.

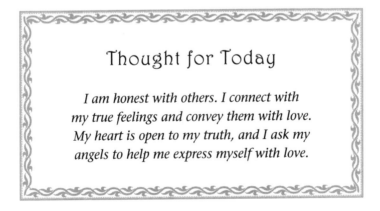

Thought for Today

I am honest with others. I connect with my true feelings and convey them with love. My heart is open to my truth, and I ask my angels to help me express myself with love.

8

Have Patience with Yourself

You're learning and growing every day, even when you're not consciously aware of your progress. As you later look back on this period of your life, you'll understand how the pieces fit together. You'll see the blessings and lessons that you gained from this time period.

Sweet one, you're much too hard on yourself at times! You've come such a long way, and yet you chastise yourself for not going fast or far enough. So this day our message for you is to have patience with yourself and the process of life. All things are Divinely timed—just as a rose unfurls its petals at precisely the right moment, so too does your life progress along a perfect timeline. If you were to force the flower to bloom by prying apart the petals with your hands, it would soon wither away . . . and so it is with your life.

The more patient you are with the process of progression, the more you open the energetic doorways for your good to come to you. Give us any anxieties that you may feel about time, and allow us to transport you to the eternal energy where magic happens.

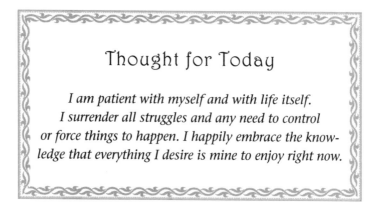

Thought for Today

I am patient with myself and with life itself.
I surrender all struggles and any need to control
or force things to happen. I happily embrace the know-
ledge that everything I desire is mine to enjoy right now.

Forget about Time

The measurement of time allows for precise interactions on a physical level. It has the opposite effect, however, on the nonphysical levels. Your soul time-travels great distances whenever it reaches a saturation point on the earthly plane. Those are the moments when you feel bored or distracted, because your soul is coming from far away.

You can overcome boredom and feel more focused by freeing yourself from measuring time. In this way, you're aligned with your soul instead of your body. When you become overly concerned with temporal reality, your body becomes focused on one dimension and your soul upon another. You experience "time constraints" when your physical and spiritual selves are out of sync with one another.

Free yourself from these limitations today. Instead of worrying about the clock, set clear intentions for your timeliness. Affirm that everything will flow smoothly for you at just the right moment—and it will.

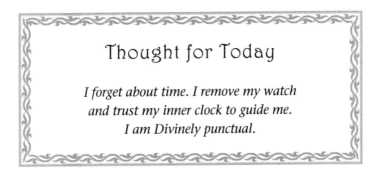

Thought for Today

*I forget about time. I remove my watch
and trust my inner clock to guide me.
I am Divinely punctual.*

10

Release with Love

If your desires aren't materializing as quickly as you want, ask yourself:

- *Am I trying too hard to make something happen?*
- *Do I have underlying fears that my dreams won't come true?*
- *Do I have fixed ideas about how my desires will materialize?*
- *Am I blaming someone for this situation (including myself)?*

Any "yes" answers indicate a need to let go and surrender your wishes to God, the Infinite Supplier. When you clearly state your dreams and then release them to the universe, they can come true very quickly.

Today we want to work with you in relinquishing your desires. Some people believe that surrender is the same as apathy, and that releasing means "I no longer care about this dream." Yet the reverse is actually true: The more you value a desire, the more important it is to deliver it to the universe; otherwise, your concern may invite a parade of anxiety, which could march all over your dream and smother the life force out of it.

We'll help you release with love today, and we'll reassure you that the Infinite Mind is already supplying you with your needs (even if those provisions aren't yet apparent to you).

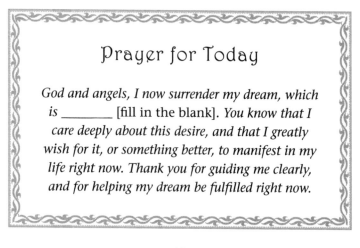

Prayer for Today

God and angels, I now surrender my dream, which is _____ [fill in the blank]. You know that I care deeply about this desire, and that I greatly wish for it, or something better, to manifest in my life right now. Thank you for guiding me clearly, and for helping my dream be fulfilled right now.

11

Let Go

When you wish to control situations or people (including yourself), it's simply a sign of fear and distrust. Have compassion when this tendency shows up in yourself or someone else. Know that you or this other individual simply needs reassurance that the universe is orderly and trustworthy.

Nurturing, soothing love is the remedy for these issues. After all, the person who tries to have power over everything often feels out of control. We can help and intervene by surrounding the entire situation with our clear-eyed vision of a desirable outcome.

If your trust has been shaken and you feel the need for ironclad guarantees, lean upon our unwavering faith—we can refuel your own with our unlimited supply. You see, we know that everything will turn out well for you, and that love and Divine order are completely in charge. The more you're aware of this truth, the more peaceful you'll feel. And with peace comes the knowledge that everything truly *is* under control.

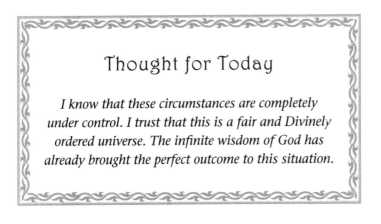

Thought for Today

I know that these circumstances are completely under control. I trust that this is a fair and Divinely ordered universe. The infinite wisdom of God has already brought the perfect outcome to this situation.

12

Know That You're a
Blessing to the World

We're right by your side day and night, without interruption. We send you waves of love at each moment, like the continuous rays of the sun. Our love for you is ongoing and nonstop, because we always see your true perfection.

You're a shining, Divine being who has remarkable gifts of great joy, wisdom, and tremendous compassion. Everyone benefits from your presence on this planet, because you also radiate love throughout each day.

You're a blessing to the world in so many ways, some of which defy earthly logic. Suffice it to say that your existence on this planet is very much appreciated.

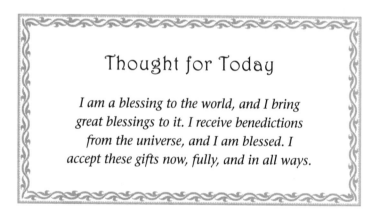

Thought for Today

I am a blessing to the world, and I bring great blessings to it. I receive benedictions from the universe, and I am blessed. I accept these gifts now, fully, and in all ways.

Take One Step at a Time

*Y*ou have beautiful dreams and intentions, all of which are manifesting as you read these words. Don't let the size of your ambitions overwhelm you . . . they're definitely achievable, as long as we work closely together.

Today we ask that you do the following: Decide that you definitely desire something, know that you deserve it, feel that its manifestation is possible, give us permission to help you, follow your guidance, and allow good to come to you. When you do these things, we will absolutely steer you toward actions that bring your dreams into material form.

Every great aspiration consists of many small steps, so focus on taking one step in the direction of your dream right now. We'll support you with guiding messages, which you'll receive as a strong feeling, a vision, a thought, words, or other signs. The faster you follow your guidance, the more quickly your dreams will come true.

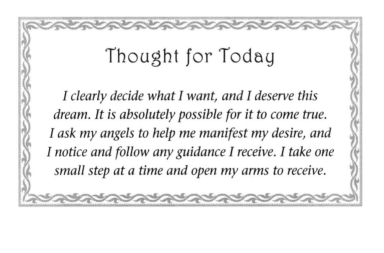

Thought for Today

I clearly decide what I want, and I deserve this dream. It is absolutely possible for it to come true. I ask my angels to help me manifest my desire, and I notice and follow any guidance I receive. I take one small step at a time and open my arms to receive.

14

Find Light in the Darkness

When the sun sets, the world seems a little dimmer and colder. Yet that's the time when the sun's rays and colors are most visible and noticeable. And so it is with your own life: Whenever your thoughts or moods feel darkened, the light shines even brighter within and around you.

Imagine a gorgeous sunset inside of you right now in glorious shades of yellow, orange, pink, and purple; and experience its radiating warmth and beauty. Feel your inner sunset growing larger and brighter, illuminating you from the inside and all around you.

The more you see this glow, the more your life, mood, and energy level brighten. We're next to you right now, shining with God's love for us all. Lean upon our light whenever you wish, and we'll guide you to find and benefit from the radiance that always shines within you.

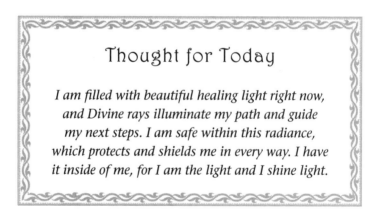

Thought for Today

I am filled with beautiful healing light right now, and Divine rays illuminate my path and guide my next steps. I am safe within this radiance, which protects and shields me in every way. I have it inside of me, for I am the light and I shine light.

Stay True to Yourself

As a sensitive person, you perceive what others want and you wish to please them. Today we'll work on developing healthy limits, or those where you retain your helpful nature while staying true to yourself.

You're overjoyed when you can aid someone to be healthier and happier—this is the expression of your higher self and part of your life's purpose, and we encourage this beautiful aspect of you. Our duty as your angels is to guide you through situations where you feel resentful. This happens when you're too tired or busy to give assistance, but you do so anyway. It also occurs in relationships where you feel that you give far more than you receive (including joy or satisfaction). These are examples of circumstances in which constructive boundaries can enhance your health and happiness.

Whenever someone asks you for help, your intuition and body will guide you as to the best response. If you sense any negativity about the situation, this is a time to hesitate before saying yes. During this pause, call upon us: Pour your heart out about your various thoughts and emotions with regard to the situation. We'll help you clarify your decision and feel good about either saying yes or no to the request for help.

By staying true to yourself, you keep your energy high and clear, and you provide inspirational role modeling for other healers and helpers. Integrity toward yourself is a gift to the world.

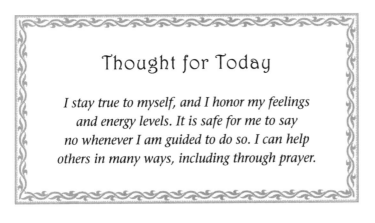

Thought for Today

*I stay true to myself, and I honor my feelings
and energy levels. It is safe for me to say
no whenever I am guided to do so. I can help
others in many ways, including through prayer.*

16

Know That You Are Divine

We come to you today to remind you of your Divinity. You're a holy being, born of the Creator in an atmosphere of complete love and purpose. Your eternal soul was personally created and blessed by God.

A lot of thought and caring went into your creation. You were made intentionally—that is, your entire being was carefully planned and well thought out. Everything about your true self is perfect! Remember your Divinity throughout the day, and honor your holiness in all of your actions.

Know that everyone is part of your holy family. See that sanctity within yourself and all others, and your day will truly be Divine.

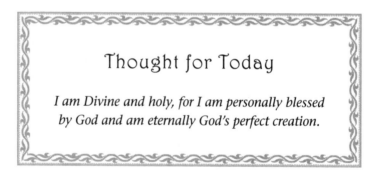

Thought for Today

I am Divine and holy, for I am personally blessed by God and am eternally God's perfect creation.

Send Love Ahead of You into the Day

*Y*our energy of love is so powerful that it can heal anything, including your future. This morning, hold the intention of sending caring energy into the day that you're about to experience. Spread love into each of your future minutes, thoroughly coating the moments with healing power.

This loving energy will then wait for you, ensuring that every second is lifted to its highest potential. You're safely cushioned by love all throughout the day.

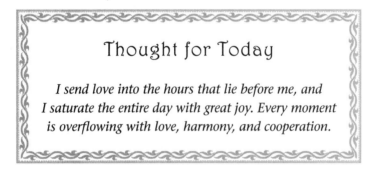

Thought for Today

I send love into the hours that lie before me, and I saturate the entire day with great joy. Every moment is overflowing with love, harmony, and cooperation.

Cast Positive Words into Your Future

Just as you can send loving energy into your future—where it will sit and wait for you, adjusting every situation to its highest potential—so can your utterances. As you already know, each word you speak, think, or say has powerful effects . . . it's the equivalent of a sales order requesting what you'd like to experience.

Today choose words that reflect what you truly desire. Form every one from that loving being within who truly cares about you and the world. Cast positive speech into your future as a gift to yourself. And just like finding something valuable that you'd hidden long ago and forgotten about, the fruits of your past expressions will embrace you in times to come.

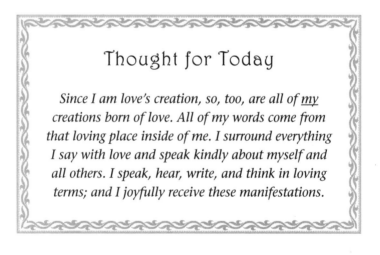

Thought for Today

Since I am love's creation, so, too, are all of __my__ creations born of love. All of my words come from that loving place inside of me. I surround everything I say with love and speak kindly about myself and all others. I speak, hear, write, and think in loving terms; and I joyfully receive these manifestations.

Say Loving Words to Yourself

The words that you use to describe yourself deeply affect your sense of self-love and self-worth. These include what you think, say, write, and even joke about yourself.

You're in a caretaker role with regard to yourself. Much like a mother or father raising a baby, you have responsibilities and obligations to your own self. Your self-parenting duties include speaking lovingly and gently to and about yourself, just as you would to your own infant.

Today use only beautiful terminology to describe yourself. This doesn't mean that you're boastful—you're simply reflecting your Divine nature. When you use beautiful words, you speak the truth. This elevates you to the highest energy possible, where miracles and instant manifestations occur.

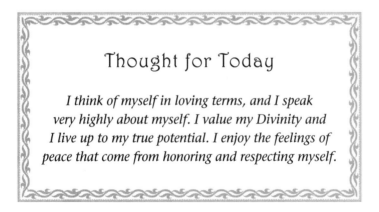

Thought for Today

*I think of myself in loving terms, and I speak
very highly about myself. I value my Divinity and
I live up to my true potential. I enjoy the feelings of
peace that come from honoring and respecting myself.*

Allow Angels to Help You

*Y*ou're our beloved one; and we take great interest in your care, happiness, and peace of mind. When you're upset, we stand even closer to you and embrace you with our affection. Even when you feel all alone or misunderstood, we're with you, loving you steadily.

We're your teammates, who are constantly ready to receive whatever you throw our way. When you coordinate your efforts with us, we can go even farther together. This means keeping open lines of communication at all times, especially when you feel upset or need support.

When you allow us to help you with everything, you'll see evidence of the depth of our love for you. It's so big that it exceeds the capacity of words to express it. Yet when you allow us to demonstrate our devotion, you'll feel it.

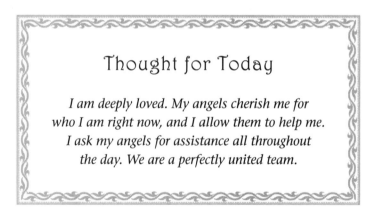

Thought for Today

*I am deeply loved. My angels cherish me for
who I am right now, and I allow them to help me.
I ask my angels for assistance all throughout
the day. We are a perfectly united team.*

Teach Peace by Example

When others see you at peace, they're reminded of the value of tranquility—that is, you inspire *them* to be at peace. Since you attract those who seek serenity, they will end up asking for your help with their own endeavor.

In everything you do, you're always teaching, so today let your lessons be about peace. Take steps to stay centered, such as closing your eyes, praying, breathing deeply, spending time outdoors, and so forth. These time investments keep your harmonious embers burning brightly.

Thought for Today

I center myself all throughout the day. I call upon my angels to assist me in radiating peace wherever I go, and all who see me are blessed with peace as well.

Find the Gift Within Painful Situations

There's no value or virtue in hanging on to pain of any kind. The merit comes in how you lift yourself out of the suffering, like an aircraft ascending above a cloud layer. Suffering carries a message that's demanding your attention—ignoring or masking it isn't the solution, as it will just find another avenue of communication.

Today we work with you in acknowledging the gift that your anguish has brought you, and then in compassionately releasing it. Whether the painful feelings arise from a relationship, a financial situation, a loss, worry over a loved one, or an imbalance in the body, the method is identical.

Right now, breathe in deeply and direct your consciousness toward the challenging area. Quiet your mind as best as you can, and then ask to discover what gift lies within the painful situation. There's always some hidden blessing, such as your learning patience, compassion, forgiveness, strength, and so on.

Once you acknowledge the gift within the hurt, it no longer needs to scream for your attention. It has delivered its message and can now retreat. As this "messenger" leaves, the peace that's always resided within you becomes more apparent. This is the basis for solutions to any seeming problem.

Together, we release the painful situation to God, trusting that it's resolved on the spiritual plane but knowing that it's manifesting now on the physical level as well. We open our arms to the gift of peaceful resolution, healing, and miracles.

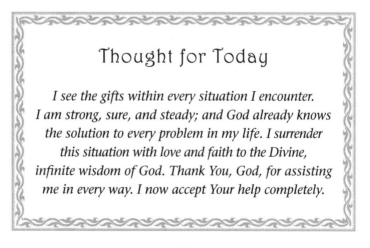

Thought for Today

I see the gifts within every situation I encounter.
I am strong, sure, and steady; and God already knows
the solution to every problem in my life. I surrender
this situation with love and faith to the Divine,
infinite wisdom of God. Thank You, God, for assisting
me in every way. I now accept Your help completely.

Enjoy True Intimacy

A "heart connection" with another person is one of life's great pleasures. It's the gift of true intimacy that each of you gives to the other—and it's true of every type of relationship, be it family, friendship, or love.

We angels share this sort of bond with you, even if you're unaware of our presence in your life. We're intimately connected with all of your emotions, thoughts, and actions. Because we cherish you unconditionally, our love for you never wavers. At each moment, it's as steady and strong as at the next.

Seek out moments of true intimacy with another person (or with us) today. Begin this connection by looking into each other's eyes and speaking the truth that you feel in your heart. Feel the elevated energy that comes from speaking from a place of truth. That is a heart connection . . . true intimacy.

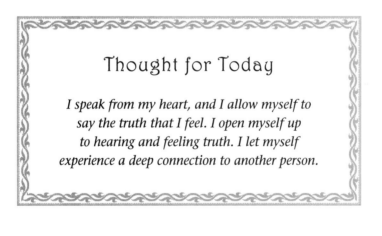

Thought for Today

I speak from my heart, and I allow myself to say the truth that I feel. I open myself up to hearing and feeling truth. I let myself experience a deep connection to another person.

Be Gentle with Yourself

Beloved one, you have a sensitive soul and a feeling heart, so please treat yourself with gentleness. While you're not in any way fragile, you deserve the respect that compassion affords. Just as you would hold a beautiful dove with tender care, we ask you to extend the same treatment toward yourself.

Take your time today and don't rush or push yourself—easy does it. You're God's precious child, and you deserve the rich rewards of gentleness.

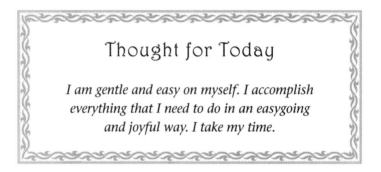

Thought for Today

I am gentle and easy on myself. I accomplish everything that I need to do in an easygoing and joyful way. I take my time.

Remember Your Magnificence

*Y*our soul is Divinely magnificent in all ways. You shine God's light radiantly upon the planet, even when you're unaware of this gift that you bring.

Your greatness is continuously assured, regardless of what's going on around you. No opinion of you—except one of pure and unconditional love—reflects your eternal truth. You're a beautiful example of God's handiwork, completely perfect and a joy to behold.

Today we'd like you to remember your Divine perfection and call upon it to support you. See that same holy ideal within everyone you encounter, and you'll find that all of your relationships are elevated to profoundly joyous experiences.

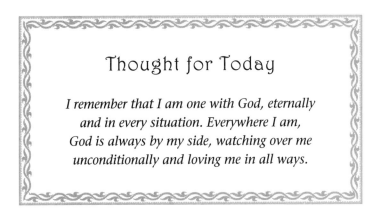

Thought for Today

*I remember that I am one with God, eternally
and in every situation. Everywhere I am,
God is always by my side, watching over me
unconditionally and loving me in all ways.*

Call Upon Angels for Help

If you find yourself fretting about material conditions such as money, work, home, or possessions, please remember that there's another way. The same energy expended on anxiety can instead be spent on prayers and affirmations—tools that bring about solutions and very real help.

The moment you get signals that you're worrying (feeling afraid, for instance, or a tightening in your stomach or jaw), stop and call upon us for help. We'll remind you that all of your needs are provided for every step along the way. We'll soothe you and help clear your mind so that you can receive the intuitive guidance that will ease the situation.

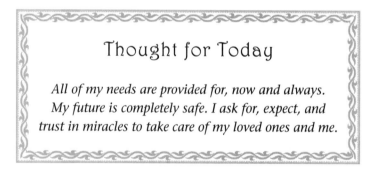

Thought for Today

All of my needs are provided for, now and always.
My future is completely safe. I ask for, expect, and
trust in miracles to take care of my loved ones and me.

Hold Nothing Back from Yourself

*Y*ou have many important inner conversations, many of which you're completely unaware of. Sharing with yourself is vitally important, so what would you like to admit to yourself right now? Sometimes it's just a matter of giving yourself the opportunity to practice self-honesty.

Some of your emotions may worry, frighten, or intimidate you, so you keep them from your conscious awareness. You may be ashamed of your feelings, yet admitting them to yourself is important for happiness and healing. (You don't need to act upon these emotions, but it *is* important to admit them to yourself.) In doing so, you'll understand the reason why they arise, and you'll gain compassion for yourself.

Self-honesty is the cornerstone of self-awareness, which, in turn, is the foundation of self-love. When you know who you are, you can better accept yourself. Have the intention today of eavesdropping upon your own inner conversations; and try to keep a sense of humor, compassion, and love toward them. Hold nothing back from yourself, and candidly converse about every topic, airing your deepest feelings—and then take the risk of expressing them through writing, singing, dancing, or some other creative outlet.

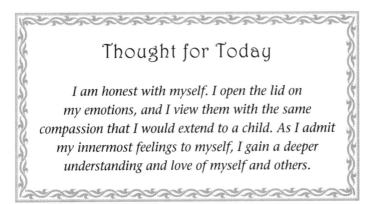

Thought for Today

*I am honest with myself. I open the lid on
my emotions, and I view them with the same
compassion that I would extend to a child. As I admit
my innermost feelings to myself, I gain a deeper
understanding and love of myself and others.*

28

Say Good-bye to Guilt

Guilt occurs when you blame yourself for a troubling situation. It's a heavy burden to carry, as well as being unhealthful and unhelpful. Guilt differs greatly from a sense of responsibility: *Guilt* involves anger, shame, blame, and judgments; while *responsibility* relates to love, sharing, and positive action.

Today we angels lift the burden of self-reproach from your shoulders. Breathe deeply while we unshackle you from the effects of blame, and see yourself in heaven's light of complete forgiveness. Any mistakes have been like children who awkwardly run into each other—in truth, you're innocent and guiltless. And as you live freely and joyously, you bring great blessings to many lives, including your own.

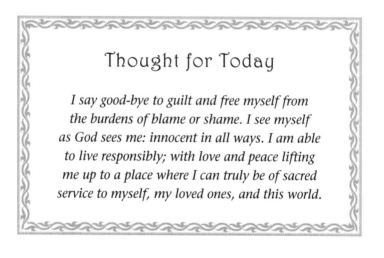

Thought for Today

I say good-bye to guilt and free myself from the burdens of blame or shame. I see myself as God sees me: innocent in all ways. I am able to live responsibly; with love and peace lifting me up to a place where I can truly be of sacred service to myself, my loved ones, and this world.

Know That You Can Do Anything!

*Y*our abilities and power are unlimited, so you can do anything that you set your mind (and heart) to. Approach each situation lightheartedly: Simply focus on your goal as if it's already being manifested in material form.

Whatever you desire, simply affirm that it's already so—this includes behaviors and actions. For example, instead of saying, "I wish I would work out more," set your sights on knowing that you already do. See and feel yourself as highly motivated to exercise, and as actually enjoying the experience. Give thanks that your fitness habit is already in place.

The same goes for anything else you desire. See and feel yourself as patient, prosperous, healthy, happy, enjoying your work and relationships, and everything else that you wish for.

The term *Spirit* is rooted in the words *inspire* and *aspire,* and when you aspire to something, you're inspired by Spirit! You're supported by this eternal force, that same one that you share with God, the angels, and every person on the planet.

You, as Divine Spirit, can do anything!

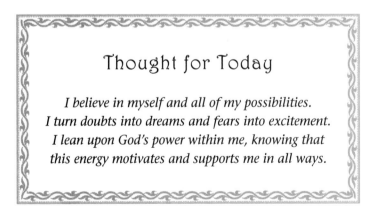

Thought for Today

I believe in myself and all of my possibilities.
I turn doubts into dreams and fears into excitement.
I lean upon God's power within me, knowing that
this energy motivates and supports me in all ways.

Talk to Angels

We hear and answer all of your prayers and requests for help. Even though you may not yet see or feel our presence, we're right here beside you now.

When you talk to us, you open the doorways of angelic connection. The more you talk to us, the more you're aware of us. It doesn't matter which way you communicate—whether through written, spoken, or silent words . . . we hear any discourse you direct our way.

We always respond to you, and at first you may feel our answer in your heart or think it in your mind. These are real messages from us, sent to you on the wings of pure, unconditional love.

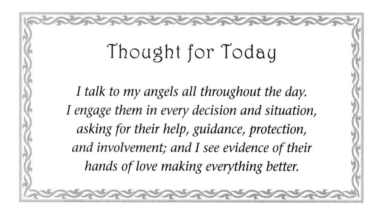

Thought for Today

I talk to my angels all throughout the day.
I engage them in every decision and situation,
asking for their help, guidance, protection,
and involvement; and I see evidence of their
hands of love making everything better.

31

Give Your Worries to God

When you hold your worries inside, they fester within a closed container, growing darker and larger until they haunt you with incessant stress. So instead of bottling up these concerns, give them to God!

The infinite, Divine wisdom of God contains every solution. Even seemingly hopeless situations are worked out peacefully as you hand them over to heaven, for within every possible problem, a resolution has already been created.

In the world of Spirit, there are no actual problems—everything is peaceful, harmonious, and healed. When you turn your mind heavenward, you tap in to this truth and experience it for yourself. Every worry or difficulty is a reminder to turn to heaven's love . . . it's an opportunity for you to choose peace and serenity in place of stress and tension. You're part of a glorious team of angels and other loving beings who come instantly to your assistance the moment you allow their intervention.

Let this be the day when you surrender all of your cares to God. Don't wait a moment longer to release every shred of fear or doubt to heaven's waiting arms.

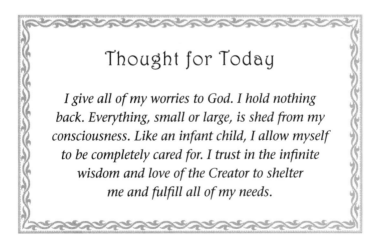

Thought for Today

I give all of my worries to God. I hold nothing back. Everything, small or large, is shed from my consciousness. Like an infant child, I allow myself to be completely cared for. I trust in the infinite wisdom and love of the Creator to shelter me and fulfill all of my needs.

32

Use Loving Words

The words that you speak about yourself, other people, and situations in your life are like putting in an order at a restaurant: They determine what you receive in return. When you speak thoughtfully, your life is filled with loving, harmonious experiences. When you speak harshly, negative energy is the result.

Today make it a point to choose only loving words as you speak. Notice how previously troubling situations shift in response. We can help you with this process, reminding you to see the best in everyone and everything. In this way, greatness comes to *you!*

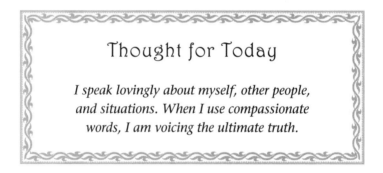

Thought for Today

I speak lovingly about myself, other people, and situations. When I use compassionate words, I am voicing the ultimate truth.

33

Polish the Jewels Inside Your Thoughts

In everything you do, you're eternally supported. At times you may not feel this way, believing that you're struggling within a lonely void. You may feel as if heaven has abandoned you and your prayers have gone unanswered, yet the universal energy holds you up by outpicturing all of your thoughts and feelings. Many times we watch idly by while you make choices that we wouldn't wish upon you—however, your free will dictates that you receive everything you think about. That's because you're a creator, and you continually generate whatever you're contemplating.

Upon your request, we angels are available to guide you toward an enjoyable pattern of creation. Call upon us to polish the jewels inside your thoughts and feelings, for within every fear or worry is a shining energy of love. We can guide you to consciously create experiences that bring high joy and blessings.

Today be aware of your amazing power of manifestation. Know that in everything you think and feel, the entire universe is fully supporting you.

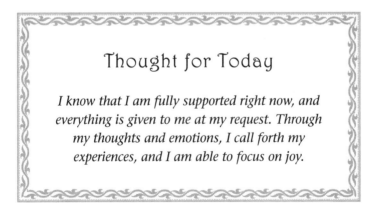

Thought for Today

I know that I am fully supported right now, and everything is given to me at my request. Through my thoughts and emotions, I call forth my experiences, and I am able to focus on joy.

Know That Angels Are Right Here

Heaven isn't some faraway place—it's a dimension that exists all around you. Therefore, at times you will feel our presence or see evidence that we're right here beside you.

We move as you do and stand next to you always. Although we'd never interfere with your free will, we're poised to help at every moment . . . all you need to do is ask.

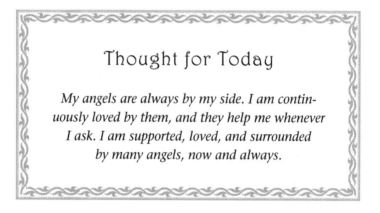

Thought for Today

My angels are always by my side. I am continuously loved by them, and they help me whenever I ask. I am supported, loved, and surrounded by many angels, now and always.

35

Turn Negativity into Positive Energy

Worry, anger, resentment, and the like are called "negative emotions" because they drain away time and energy—that is, their negativity refers to their energy direction. Conversely, since feelings such as joy, elation, and hope increase your power levels, they're called "positive."

Worry is so commonplace that it's essentially a normal human habit. Yet its effects are undesirable, including stress, tension, aging, addictions, sleeplessness, and time consumption. And the same is true for all negative emotions.

You can transform these feelings into positive ones by remembering this: Usually anxiety is the basis of a negative emotion. It's a fear of losing something or someone, or having it withheld from you. It's an affirmation that some power other than yourself is in control.

What if, instead of succumbing to worry, you stopped and prayed for help instead? The effects of your prayer can rapidly stop the cause of your distress, bring you real and lasting assistance, and transmit positive energy to you.

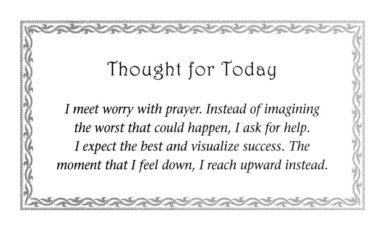

Thought for Today

I meet worry with prayer. Instead of imagining
the worst that could happen, I ask for help.
I expect the best and visualize success. The
moment that I feel down, I reach upward instead.

Enjoy True Safety

*Y*our intuition guides you through all situations safely, provided that you listen to it. We're your backup source of protection, and we vigilantly watch out for your well-being. We signal you if danger lurks, helping you better hear your sixth sense.

Feel safe, knowing that your angels and intuition will warn you if trouble lies ahead. You'll receive strong and unmistakable signals if you need to use caution or take action. Until then, relax in the knowledge that you're protected . . . we have you covered.

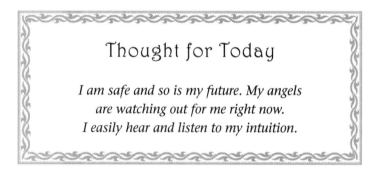

Thought for Today

I am safe and so is my future. My angels
are watching out for me right now.
I easily hear and listen to my intuition.

Notice Beauty

There's infinite beauty within and surrounding you at all times. It holds great power, which you can tap in to and benefit from. As you notice this beauty, it immediately lends you its energy. You may find it in nature's colors, in your interactions with others, or in human creations. You might also notice it in the way that experiences synchronistically line up so that you can see the Divine order in everything that happens to you.

You're a being of great beauty. You take our breath away with your glowing inner light, your loving intentions, and the radiant blessings you bring to others! This shines in your smile, face, posture, actions, and heart.

Dedicate today to beauty. As you keep it in mind throughout the day, you'll automatically spread it wherever you go. This force purifies your thoughts, emotions, and intentions, as you realize that it's Divine—and that everyone and everything is part of one beautiful Spirit.

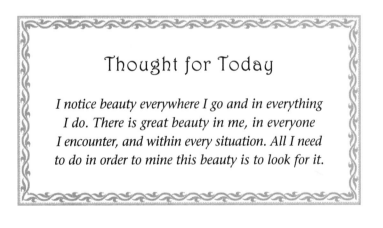

Thought for Today

*I notice beauty everywhere I go and in everything
I do. There is great beauty in me, in everyone
I encounter, and within every situation. All I need
to do in order to mine this beauty is to look for it.*

Enjoy New Friendships

We angels are your companions because we see your wonderful qualities, and many people would also enjoy getting to know you and becoming your friend.

To attract wonderful acquaintances, develop and display the qualities that you desire in a friend. Use positive and uplifting words that are attractive to the people around you. In order to *have* friends, be one to others.

We'll guide you in all of your relationships, including bringing new friends to you.

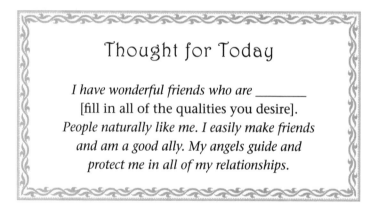

Thought for Today

*I have wonderful friends who are _____
[fill in all of the qualities you desire].
People naturally like me. I easily make friends
and am a good ally. My angels guide and
protect me in all of my relationships.*

Know That You Deserve Good in Your Life

*Y*ou're loved as much as every one of God's creations, yet sometimes you feel as though you're less than other people. These opinions are echoes of fear and not true descriptions of yourself. The fact is that God desires only the best for you, just as any loving parent wishes great experiences for their offspring. You deserve good things just as much as any other person is worthy of support, love, and care.

When you receive, you fill the well of blessings that allows you to help others. Your receptivity also fulfills God's wish to give to you. By letting yourself receive, you tune in to the universe's music, which steadily pulsates harmonious gifts for everyone.

You're entirely lovable and guiltless. You haven't done anything wrong, and there's nothing wrong with you. You're an innocent, precious, and much-loved child of God. Give yourself over to good today . . . open your arms, receive, and say "Thank you."

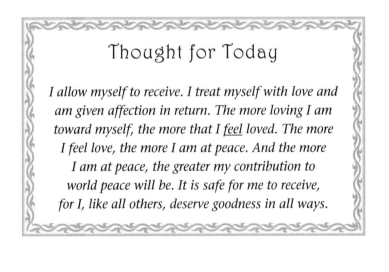

Thought for Today

I allow myself to receive. I treat myself with love and am given affection in return. The more loving I am toward myself, the more that I feel loved. The more I feel love, the more I am at peace. And the more I am at peace, the greater my contribution to world peace will be. It is safe for me to receive, for I, like all others, deserve goodness in all ways.

Take a Chance

What's your secret wish that you'd like to manifest into form and reality? Perhaps you fear disappointment, so you're reluctant to admit your innermost desire or take action toward its fulfillment.

Beloved one, we're supporting you and your aspirations. Take a chance and allow yourself to dream—imagining that your desire is fulfilled—and *do* something to help make it come true.

What you do is secondary to the simple act of moving in the direction of your deepest desire. Whether it's making a telephone call, writing, researching, affirming, or anything else you feel drawn to, the energy you expend will set the universe into motion on your behalf.

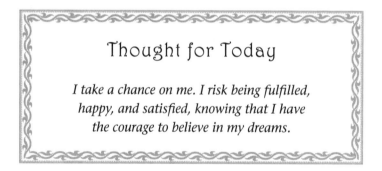

Thought for Today

*I take a chance on me. I risk being fulfilled,
happy, and satisfied, knowing that I have
the courage to believe in my dreams.*

Breathe Deeply

*B*reath is the bridge connecting the spiritual and physical worlds. Your respiration carries your spiritual sustenance into your physical self, which feeds your soul, mind, and body.

Deep breaths are akin to taking a holiday, which is why they're called "breathers." Become aware of your breathing, and deepen it right now. Pause between inhalation and exhalation, delighting in the deliciousness of the air.

Fill your life with fresh air: Spend time in the country, place live plants in your home and office, or invest in an air purifier. Keep in mind that the environment near running water (including your shower or bathtub) is filled with powerful molecules that support your health and happiness.

Make it a point today to stay aware of the rhythm and rate of your breathing. If you experience stress, be sure to inhale deeply. The oxygen relaxes your body, invigorates your energy levels, and leads to creative insights and solutions.

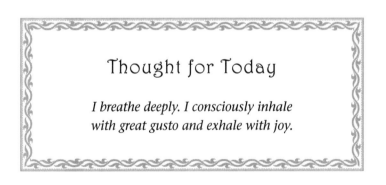

Thought for Today

I breathe deeply. I consciously inhale
with great gusto and exhale with joy.

Dream Big

*Y*our imagination is the place where your future experiences are constructed. You're like the chef who chooses and controls what's placed into a creation, no matter what the outside influences or circumstances are.

What would you like to cook up in your mind? This decision has a direct bearing on your future experiences. Naturally, you'd prefer to have happy encounters—but do you truly understand that you can ensure their occurrence?

This is the day to take charge of your world and envision whatever elaborate and exotic future you desire! We'll guide you, and help you guard against placing unwanted elements into the mix, so dream big today. Whether it's planning a comfortable and quiet experience or one that's more challenging, make choices that truly mirror your innermost feelings.

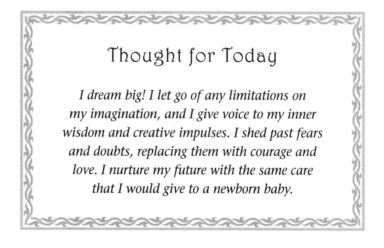

Thought for Today

I dream big! I let go of any limitations on my imagination, and I give voice to my inner wisdom and creative impulses. I shed past fears and doubts, replacing them with courage and love. I nurture my future with the same care that I would give to a newborn baby.

Tithe

The energy of this planet is twofold and can be summarized by a simple illustration of giving and receiving. The force of the former is magnificent to behold, extending your light outward so that its embers burn more boldly and brightly, similar to adding fuel and oxygen to a fire. The power of receptivity is cooler, yet equally beautiful to witness, evoking the feeling of blue light on snow and ice. It draws sustenance inward, where it can be gratefully utilized, before spreading energy outward again through the process of giving. Both forces help one another—that is, you need to give in order to receive, and vice versa. This cycle is woven so deeply into the fabric of physical existence that to boost the flow of what you're receiving, you simply need to increase your giving.

Tithing is the ancient tradition of contributing 10 percent of your income to a cause of your choice, yet it means so much more energetically, for you can give in many ways. If you long for more time, then volunteer your hours helping others. If you desire more clothing, furniture, or other material goods, then donate similar items to charities or individuals in need. If you'd like more money, then make a financial donation as you feel guided.

Bestowing gifts jump-starts the abundance that's always pulsating throughout the physical universe. It goes to work immediately for all who move with these natural cycles. Give with great joy today—not for the purpose of receiving, but for the pure enjoyment of life's inherent rhythmic flow.

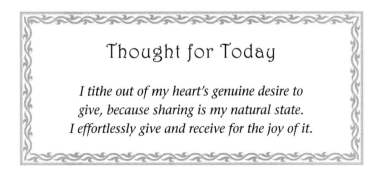

Thought for Today

I tithe out of my heart's genuine desire to
give, because sharing is my natural state.
I effortlessly give and receive for the joy of it.

Call Upon Archangel Michael

All angels are powerful, just as all humans are, and Archangel Michael is revered as being especially strong because he chooses to shine purely and reflect the Creator's great energy. His purpose is as large as his stature. He lends you his strength during those times when you've momentarily forgotten your own power. His deep love envelops you protectively, shielding you from any manifestations of fear.

Call upon Michael to stay by your side today. Ask him to give you strength and courage, especially when you consider pursuing your deepest desires. He can help you walk safely through the doorway of life changes.

Speak to Michael about any fears, doubts, or insecurities you may have. He'll sweep them away and fan the flames of your inner fire, showing you the energy and power that eternally resides within you.

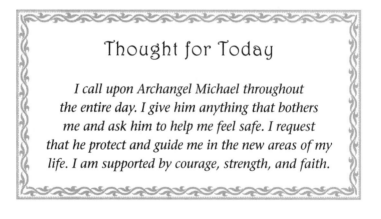

Thought for Today

*I call upon Archangel Michael throughout
the entire day. I give him anything that bothers
me and ask him to help me feel safe. I request
that he protect and guide me in the new areas of my
life. I am supported by courage, strength, and faith.*

45

Open Your Heart

*Y*ou were made out of love by a caring Creator. Everything about you is based in love, and feeling it means that you're aware of your own self. You encounter God when you experience love, but to do so, your heart must be open—which may seem difficult or dangerous if you've closed yourself off for protection against emotional pain.

We angels can help you open up in a way that feels safe and secure. Go at your own pace with us as your steady guides and we'll sweep away old pain and resentment as we guide you to trustworthy situations and relationships. All we need is for you to stay in close communication with us, telling us about your wishes and emotions. (Although we already know what you're feeling, we can't act on your desires without your consent.)

An open heart is God's most beautiful creation, because it reflects heavenly love on Earth.

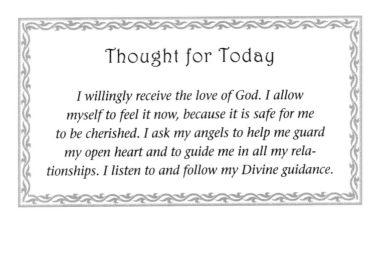

Thought for Today

I willingly receive the love of God. I allow myself to feel it now, because it is safe for me to be cherished. I ask my angels to help me guard my open heart and to guide me in all my relationships. I listen to and follow my Divine guidance.

Call Upon Archangel Raphael

Since Raphael's aim is focused on healing, his energy has a curative effect. You can also focus your intention in this way, as can anyone else who wants to project a therapeutic presence. Simply affirm and pray daily that you can serve as a healing agent for others, and it becomes true. This is because your output matches your input—in other words, what you pray and intend for yourself is what shows up in your energy field and experiences. This is the basis of all healing.

You can also call upon Raphael to increase your resolve to mend yourself and others. If your faith wavers or your mind wanders into negativity, he can remind you of your purpose. This archangel can also guide and direct you in all activities and aspirations that promote well-being.

Today, call upon Raphael to soothe and ease your mind. He can calm any worries you have about illness, finances, relationships, or other areas of your life. And as you regain a peaceful mind-set, healing will dawn on your horizon.

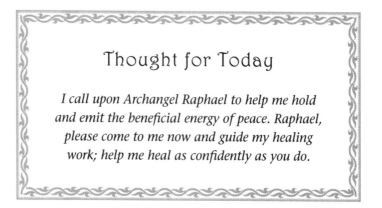

Thought for Today

I call upon Archangel Raphael to help me hold and emit the beneficial energy of peace. Raphael, please come to me now and guide my healing work; help me heal as confidently as you do.

Thank the Universe

The universe is the unfolding and never-ending energy of the Divine, magnified in every life-form. You are an extension of this power and a perfect reflection of God's brightness.

Your gratitude exists on the same wavelength as the universe, so it connects you to this flow and ensures that you'll continue to have experiences that inspire your thankfulness.

Today, create a list called "Thank you, Universe!" which contains everything you're grateful for. Make this an ongoing project that you add to regularly. Read the list whenever you want a pick-me-up, and your gratitude will elevate you once again.

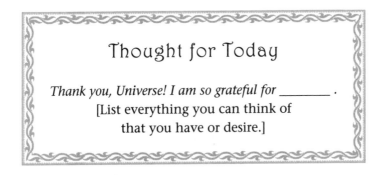

Thought for Today

Thank you, Universe! I am so grateful for _____ .
[List everything you can think of
that you have or desire.]

Work with Archangel Azrael

Azrael brings relief from suffering and gladdens hearts that are darkened by sorrow. He gives heaven's light to every spirit he touches, and his simple presence can be enough to help a grieving person regain faith in a brighter tomorrow.

Azrael needs human helpers to deliver his messages of hope. Because those who are grief stricken sometimes can't pick up on the voices from the realm of Spirit, they need to hear Divine messages from humans. You can act as an earthly angel by asking Azrael to guide your interactions with those who are sad or dispirited. He'll speak through you, saying just the right words, accompanied by high healing energy.

Today call upon Archangel Azrael, and work with him to lift the energy of those in need. He'll cleanse the residue of grief from your own heart and then team up with you to illuminate others' as well. Azrael reminds you that happiness is holy, and that the best way to honor those who have passed on is to enjoy your life.

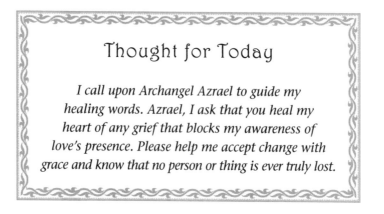

Thought for Today

I call upon Archangel Azrael to guide my healing words. Azrael, I ask that you heal my heart of any grief that blocks my awareness of love's presence. Please help me accept change with grace and know that no person or thing is ever truly lost.

Know That You Are Valuable

*Y*ou are God's miracle in human form—the living embodiment of Divine love and will. Is it any wonder that angels are assigned to be by your side, like the guards at Fort Knox? You are valuable, beloved one, and cherished beyond compare. We angels know your true essence, and it's entirely perfect.

You are a golden child sent to Earth because your very existence and breath manifests love upon this planet. Every kind thought, word, or action on your part has healing effects.

You are valuable not only to God and us, but to everyone else as well. On a soul level, every person knows that you are here for a worthwhile purpose. Even if someone doesn't show understanding or appreciation of you on the surface level, that individual's spirit knows your worth.

Every one of God's children is a priceless miracle—and that definitely includes you.

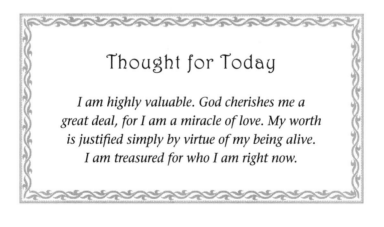

Thought for Today

I am highly valuable. God cherishes me a great deal, for I am a miracle of love. My worth is justified simply by virtue of my being alive. I am treasured for who I am right now.

50

Connect with Archangel Ariel

Since Ariel oversees nature and the environment, she shares similar attributes with the fairies. She's demure yet powerful—feminine in her gracefulness and strength, and magical in her ability to make wishes appear in material form.

Ariel helps reignite wondrous awe and utter faith, much like what you enjoyed in childhood. She shows you how belief in the Divine is now a conscious decision that lets you escape from the rigid thinking that may thwart your efforts upon manifestation.

Today, call upon Ariel to reawaken your sense of childlike wonder and awe. After you do so, allow yourself to follow your inner guidance to dance, sing, or play, as these actions will spur the progression of your dreams.

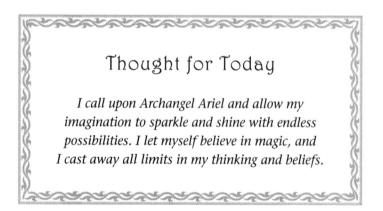

Thought for Today

I call upon Archangel Ariel and allow my imagination to sparkle and shine with endless possibilities. I let myself believe in magic, and I cast away all limits in my thinking and beliefs.

Feel the Angels' Love

We're sending you love as you read these words. Tune in to your breathing and body, and notice the tender emotions that you receive with each inhalation. You're drawing in our love, taking it into your body to warm, balance, and heal you.

Today we'll send you this feeling all throughout the day. If you lose awareness of our presence, that's okay. Just know that we're here when you need a boost or some reassurance.

Every breath you inhale is inscribed with all our love . . . *feel* it.

Thought for Today

I notice the warm, loving feelings inside of me. I inhale deeply and sense my angels' caring presence. I think of them often and allow myself to feel happy and joyful.

52

Connect with the Nature Angels

The beings overseeing the plant, mineral, and animal kingdom are known as *fairies, elementals,* and *nature angels,* and they're as solid and real as you are. Like you, these creatures have important roles. Chiefly, they ensure harmony and sustenance within what you call "nature," and they can help *you* grow and thrive as well.

They bring a spirit of adventure and playfulness to the planet, which you can tap in to simply by spending time outdoors, among plants, or with animals (domestic or wild). Since these spirits reside on the earth, they're compassionate listeners and helpers with material matters. They're happy to assist you with issues involving love and money, for example.

The elementals can sense when a person sincerely desires to support nature's causes by engaging in recycling, kindness toward animals, and the like. These actions engender the nature angels' favor, and once this is gained, it will earn you many rewards.

Spend time with these angels today. Give your relationship an opportunity to develop, as you would with new human acquaintances, and you'll grow to trust, help, and love each other over time. As you become closely associated with the elementals, you'll begin to share their lighthearted and magical outlook toward life, which is a healthy approach indeed!

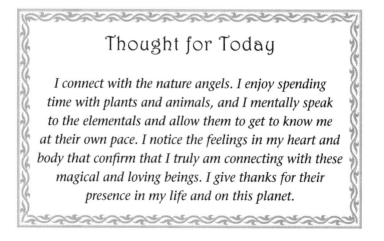

Thought for Today

I connect with the nature angels. I enjoy spending time with plants and animals, and I mentally speak to the elementals and allow them to get to know me at their own pace. I notice the feelings in my heart and body that confirm that I truly am connecting with these magical and loving beings. I give thanks for their presence in my life and on this planet.

53

Simplify

What's one thing that you'd change about your life to make it less complicated? Notice the first answer that enters your mind, and know that we angels can help you turn this into reality. You really can have a simpler life and still meet your financial responsibilities while fulfilling your desires.

Focus upon simplicity today. Ask yourself if there's an easier way to approach each situation. Shed the belief that struggle is a necessary component of life, and open your arms to doing things in a harmonious manner. We'll help you meet this goal if you'll only ask.

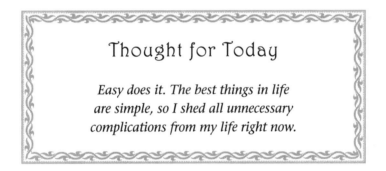

Thought for Today

Easy does it. The best things in life are simple, so I shed all unnecessary complications from my life right now.

54

Shake Up Your Routines

Although routines are comforting, they can also blind you to life's variety. Habitual patterns dull your senses to anything out of the ordinary. Awaken your awareness, and feel extra alive by shaking up your regular activities.

Have fun by creatively changing everything today. Exchange your usual schedule, your normal eating habits, and your accustomed manners for novel ways of doing things. You may feel awkward as you try something new, but you'll also have the exhilaration of exploring fresh ways to live. You'll probably return to some of your comfortable routines, yet you'll very likely incorporate fresh approaches as well. In other words, through the process of experimentation, you may discover wonderful new ways to live.

One reason why holidays and vacations are so invigorating is that they involve the exploration of new places, people, food, and leisure activities. You can create this same energy by changing things up right now.

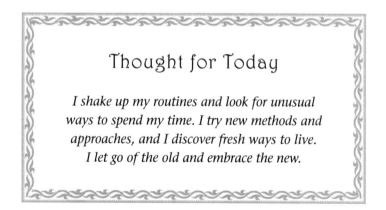

Thought for Today

I shake up my routines and look for unusual ways to spend my time. I try new methods and approaches, and I discover fresh ways to live. I let go of the old and embrace the new.

Hearing Our Messages

We always answer your questions and prayers. Usually we communicate with you quietly through energy transfers that you pick up as feelings. But if we find that you aren't hearing our messages, we'll deliver them to you in less subtle ways.

Today we'll communicate with you through the physical world. Notice the underlying meanings in what people say to you as well, as in conversations or songs that you overhear. You'll know the information that comes from us, as your heart will resonate with its truth.

Our missives travel upon the energy of love from our heart to yours. Trust the impressions you receive that encourage you to live lovingly—those are our messages to you.

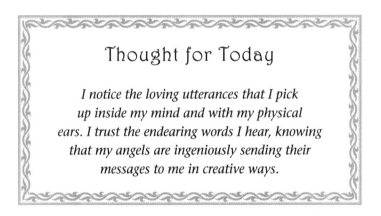

Thought for Today

I notice the loving utterances that I pick up inside my mind and with my physical ears. I trust the endearing words I hear, knowing that my angels are ingeniously sending their messages to me in creative ways.

Surrender Your Cares

*Y*our cares are too heavy a burden to shoulder by yourself. Imagine a large white silk sheet spread out before you, and place all of your worries onto it. Then roll up the sheet and hand it to us. When you're done, notice the lightness that you feel.

We'll take your cares heavenward. Once they're moved to a higher plane, your outlook will be uplifted as well. This new perspective will help you think clearly and creatively, allowing you to attract and manifest all the good you desire.

Instead of wrestling with mind-clouding cares and strains, give them all to us. As a united team who works with precision by your side, we can never undermine your free will. We can, however, allow you to exercise your highest ideals.

Let this be your last day of needlessly and single-handedly carrying burdens. Allow us to take the weight completely from your shoulders and lift your mind and heart to the light.

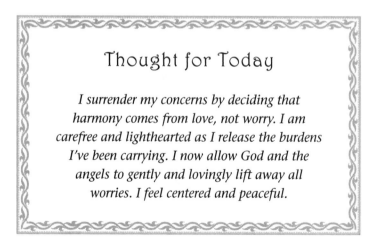

Thought for Today

I surrender my concerns by deciding that harmony comes from love, not worry. I am carefree and lighthearted as I release the burdens I've been carrying. I now allow God and the angels to gently and lovingly lift away all worries. I feel centered and peaceful.

Know That You've Already Won

When you see an advertisement saying that you may have already won a jackpot, your body becomes activated with excitement. Yet such words are true: You *have* already won!

Every prize imaginable in this life is yours, so there's no need for you to search any longer. You're already the winner, and you claim your prizes through affirmative thinking and positive emotions. Imagine what it feels like to swim in a sea of your manifested desires. Retain that sensation, along with your gratitude, and it shall be done.

You're a winner through and through. The more you know this fact, the more you *live* it.

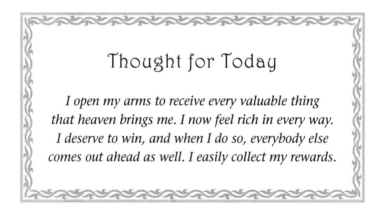

Thought for Today

I open my arms to receive every valuable thing that heaven brings me. I now feel rich in every way. I deserve to win, and when I do so, everybody else comes out ahead as well. I easily collect my rewards.

Give Your Imagination Free Rein

The inner world of your imagination is like a clear, deep lake fed by the rivers of your emotions, physical feelings, experiences, and thoughts. It's the meeting ground for your reactions to life.

You may have heard derogatory references to the imagination that call it "invalid" or "unreal." Yet it is your God-connection headquarters, allowing you to wander far from your physical senses and explore other realms. Your imagination pieces together the seemingly impossible and illogical until it brings about new creations.

Have no worries that your mental explorations could mislead you, for true imagination is borne upon the wings of angels. It's pure and childlike in the very best sense. It's also untamed and unrestricted—even when you try to retrain your creative self, it's constantly at work during dream time and moments of peaceful contemplation.

Allow the world of your fantasies to run free, and notice its ingenious creations. They're gifts from Spirit that are conceived and incubated mentally and then born into material reality. When you unleash your imagination, you liberate yourself . . . and you're then able to live without limits and soar.

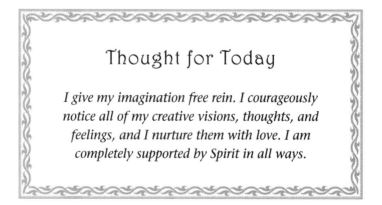

Thought for Today

I give my imagination free rein. I courageously notice all of my creative visions, thoughts, and feelings, and I nurture them with love. I am completely supported by Spirit in all ways.

Meditate

Approach meditation with ease and as a joyous escape—after all, you practice this activity naturally during moments of daydreaming or lucid awareness. Be unconcerned with rules or guidelines lest this become a chore of drudgery. Instead, allow your mind to quiet itself at its own pace, and compassionately let your body slow down of its own accord—this is meditation. It's a time when your mind is completely connected to your heavenly home. Think of it as hooking up to a fuel station, where you're filled with energy, ideas, and tranquility.

There are countless ways to calm your mind, and as we just mentioned, you shouldn't burden yourself with worries about your specific method. *That* you meditate is more important than how you do so. Closing your eyes and breathing deeply is one technique, as is sitting in front of an altar or relaxing outdoors in nature.

The words *meditate* and *medicate* share the same root for good reason, since they're both approaches to health. Meditation is your free and portable healing agent whose only side effects are peace of mind and rejuvenation. Approach it as you would a delicious meal, for it's a true spiritual banquet. Enjoy your tranquil moments today in the spirit of feeding your needs and desires.

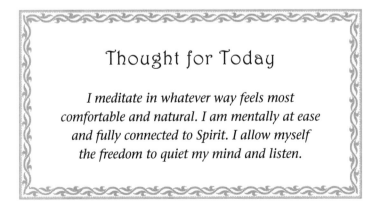

Thought for Today

I meditate in whatever way feels most comfortable and natural. I am mentally at ease and fully connected to Spirit. I allow myself the freedom to quiet my mind and listen.

60

Pray

Prayer means communing with the Divine through dialogue. It's your method of conveying your hopes, dreams, and wishes to the spirit world, where we angels love to assist you. You don't need to tell us what you desire, for it's apparent to all who are attuned to you. However, Divine decree states that you must give us the signal that you're approachable and amenable to receiving help. That's all we wait for, and then our assistance is yours.

Prayer can help you clear the air within yourself during times of confusion or indecision. It's a process of self-reflection and honesty in which you let your guard down and admit your deepest feelings and desires.

Although we already know your true feelings, this is a means of communing with Spirit—especially your higher self—with a deep sense of acceptance. This allows you to bring your shadows to the light, where you discover that there's nothing to fear.

Prayer is an act of surrendering, asking for help, and being open to receiving assistance. This receptivity allows the Great Light to come streaming into your consciousness, where your thoughts and emotions are lifted to higher levels.

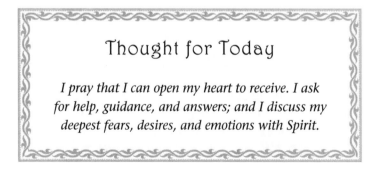

Thought for Today

I pray that I can open my heart to receive. I ask for help, guidance, and answers; and I discuss my deepest fears, desires, and emotions with Spirit.

# 61

Stretch Yourself

Today we'll work with you on stretching yourself as a means of further opening up to delicious information, feelings, and activities. The focus will be on flexing your body at regular intervals, as well as your imagination.

Stretching involves reaching, which has an overall effect of encouraging you to arrive at new heights in both experiences and energies. It also shakes up your routines, helping you access fresh ideas.

This is a day to expand your imagination and think of ordinary situations in novel ways. Come up with new methods for getting dressed, working, and relating to other people. Allow your imagination free rein, and stretch your body and mind with great joy.

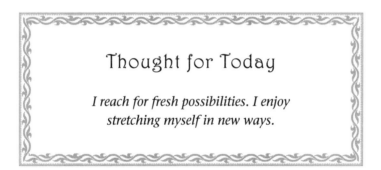

Thought for Today

I reach for fresh possibilities. I enjoy stretching myself in new ways.

Give Time to Your Priorities

*Y*ou have dreams, activities, and relationships that are meaningful to you. They matter a lot, and you feel happy thinking about them . . . they are your *priorities*. When you nurture them, you're not only more cheerful, but you feel more positive about yourself. It's an act of self-care to devote time to what you value.

Despite appearances to the contrary, you really are in charge of your schedule. You can give attention to whatever you choose, and we angels will keep interruptions away and help ensure that your responsibilities are met.

Acknowledge any fears and insecurities that trigger procrastination, and know that they're perfectly natural and normal emotions that merely represent a resistance to happiness and nothing more. Lovingly laugh at your concerns, and then move ahead with your beloved dreams.

Even spending a few moments on what's important to you can elevate your mood, self-esteem, and energy levels. Devoting time to your priorities then becomes a healthy new habit that you develop gradually, so have patience with yourself if you occasionally backslide on your way to giving them your full attention.

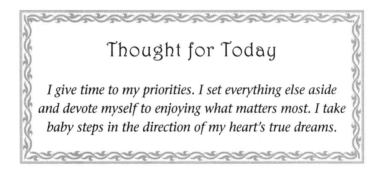

Thought for Today

I give time to my priorities. I set everything else aside and devote myself to enjoying what matters most. I take baby steps in the direction of my heart's true dreams.

63

Enjoy Love Day

It's Love Day! We angels have dedicated today to honoring this emotion. To commemorate the occasion, put your focus on caring. For instance, note examples of affection, express your feelings to your friends and family, and act kindly toward yourself and all others.

Experience the many ways in which this quality shows itself, in all of its various colors and forms. Revel in this celebration, and know that you play an important role in making every day one of love.

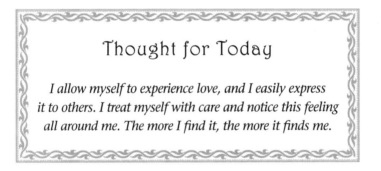

Thought for Today

I allow myself to experience love, and I easily express it to others. I treat myself with care and notice this feeling all around me. The more I find it, the more it finds me.

Acknowledge Your Inner Genius

*Y*ou have a genius inside of you, a wise and knowing self who enjoys learning, teaching, and intellectual stimulation. Focus today on caring for this being within.

Make it a point to learn something new, such as a word, skill, song, or technique. Congratulate yourself on this experience, feel the joy that your inner genius exudes, and know that this brilliance is *you!*

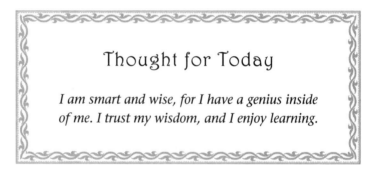

Thought for Today

I am smart and wise, for I have a genius inside of me. I trust my wisdom, and I enjoy learning.

65

Sing

The music within your soul desires freedom. Your inner melody doesn't care whether you sing off-key or forget the lyrics—it merely wants to be expressed aloud so that it can float upon the air and join the other musical notes in the universe.

Song allows you to convey deep emotions that exceed the boundaries of mere words. Even if you feel bashful about your abilities, give yourself permission to sing today. Add your voice to the music you play on your stereo, or go a cappella (without accompaniment). Hum in the shower, with your friends, or to yourself—the form isn't important. What *does* matter is the act of expressing yourself musically.

Think of this as yoga for your soul, an opportunity to stretch yourself, and a reflection of your innermost spirit. Notice the tunes that you're attracted to, as their words, melodies, and sentiments all contain messages for you.

Know that we angels thank you for your musical contribution to the world's positive energy waves.

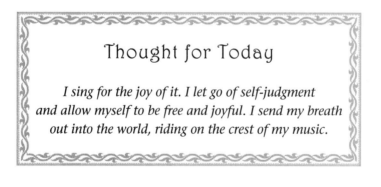

Thought for Today

I sing for the joy of it. I let go of self-judgment and allow myself to be free and joyful. I send my breath out into the world, riding on the crest of my music.

Dance

When you move your body, you elevate more than your heart rate; you also lift your mood and energy levels. You become more playful and alive; and with your heightened spirits, your power grows, too. This force, which you always possess and share with every individual, allows you to consciously manifest your dreams into existence.

Make time to dance today. Turn on some music and begin swaying, letting yourself spontaneously express yourself with physical movements. If you're shy about your body, then try it alone—but with practice, your enthusiasm about the healing effects of this art form will become something that you'll want to share with others. This is the reason why so many ancient cultures revere this activity as a sacred custom central to their spirituality.

Dancing helps you regain a connection to your Divine physical essence. Your body is an extension of your being, and it's important to honor it with your awareness. Your movements bring your consciousness forward in a very pleasant way. You'll learn that you're graceful, attractive, and elegant—qualities that the Creator endowed you with long ago. Recapturing the knowledge of these gifts helps you shine even more brightly.

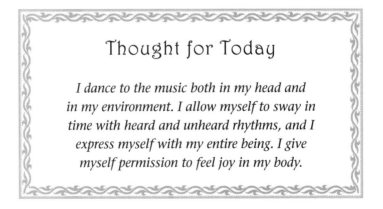

Thought for Today

I dance to the music both in my head and in my environment. I allow myself to sway in time with heard and unheard rhythms, and I express myself with my entire being. I give myself permission to feel joy in my body.

Clear Away Clutter

Your inner drive for orderliness comes from your inherent knowledge of energy flow. You can feel the difference when you're in a clean room versus a messy one, sensing the effect of disorder in your closet, desk, garage, cupboards, or other areas. Organization is a way of streamlining your thought processes so that it's not an uphill battle to get dressed, find a paper, or fix something to eat.

However, there's a flip side to this in which some people become so fixated on order that they lose their spontaneity. In such cases, tidying up is a delay tactic to avoid working toward their life purpose and happiness. There should be a balance between enjoying and *needing* organization.

Energy streams through physical structures in much the same way that water and air flow. When there are too many objects in an environment, that power is obstructed. The effects of this blockage include physical fatigue, difficulty concentrating, increased appetite, and slow manifestations.

We give you all this background information to help motivate you to clear the clutter in your home or other areas of your life. Even a minor change such as cleaning out a closet, straightening a desktop, or giving away one unwanted item will provide benefits. As your energy increases through these small efforts, you'll find that you have the time and initiative for larger projects.

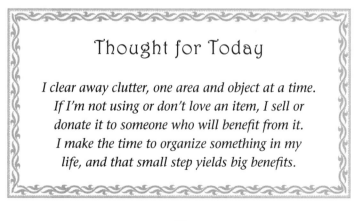

Thought for Today

I clear away clutter, one area and object at a time.
If I'm not using or don't love an item, I sell or
donate it to someone who will benefit from it.
I make the time to organize something in my
life, and that small step yields big benefits.

68

Do Something Out of the Ordinary

Imagine what you'd like to do if all things were instantly possible. Well, guess what? Anything *can* happen, and this is as good a day as any to seize every opportunity. We angels can guide you and support your actions so that you can jump right in and enjoy extraordinary activities.

What would you like to do today? Take a moment to notice everything that comes to mind in answer to this question. Then decide on one pursuit, and take action in the direction of your choice without delay.

Give yourself permission to do something outside your routine today. The new perspective you'll gain will help you see your entire life with fresh eyes, and you'll benefit from a renewed appreciation of everything and everyone around you. Approaching the unfamiliar will also teach you about the hidden talents and strength you possess—and this may be a catalyst for wonderful new possibilities!

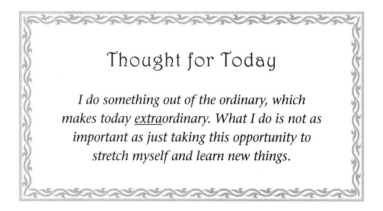

Thought for Today

I do something out of the ordinary, which makes today <u>extra</u>ordinary. What I do is not as important as just taking this opportunity to stretch myself and learn new things.

Let It Come to You

Instead of struggling to attain your desires, relax and let everything come to you. You don't have to strain to find what you're looking for—simply hold a clear vision that it's already yours, keep faith that it will come to you easily and effortlessly, and follow any guidance you receive.

Today, let go of old approaches to fulfilling your needs. Be like the smart angler who uses the proper bait (in this case, your crystal clear thoughts), casts a line into the lake (corresponding to the act of giving your desires to Spirit), and patiently waits to be rewarded.

Determine what it is you want . . . and realize that as long as you're searching for that item, you're sending out a signal that you don't have it. So thank the universe, and feel grateful for the fact that you've already received your wish. This process will yield the manifestation of your desire, often in a way that exceeds your expectations.

Write a detailed description of what you want today, and sign it with a "Thank you." Fill your heart with feelings of gratitude—and enjoy the quick response that you receive from the universe.

Thought for Today

I let things come to me. I cast my desires before me, allowing them to return to me in material form. I feel gratitude before and after my wishes come true.

Plant a Seed

A plant is a wonderful symbol of your life! The way the tiny seedling sprouts beneath the soil and pushes up to follow the light mirrors so many aspects of your own development.

That's why we're guiding you to plant a seed today—literally. Purchase a packet of them at the market, or use one from a fresh fruit or vegetable. Before you put your seed in the earth, bring to mind a new project that you intend to begin. Hold the seed in your hand, and infuse it with prayers both for you and the plant. Then ceremoniously place it into soil.

Nurture both the seedling and your new intention. Although you can't see the growth below the soil yet, changes are occurring. The fledgling plant needs care to coax it to the surface—and so it is with your aspiration. As you tend to your garden, also take daily action steps related to your goal.

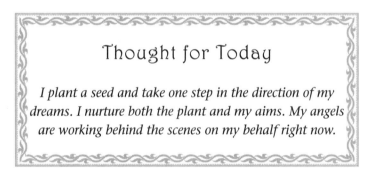

Thought for Today

I plant a seed and take one step in the direction of my dreams. I nurture both the plant and my aims. My angels are working behind the scenes on my behalf right now.

Be Adventurous

*Y*ou sometimes resist change because the unknown seems uncomfortable. Yet learning and growing are two earthly experiences that your soul craves. Although you may feel awkward in the face of novelty, there's also excitement in confronting it.

Be adventurous today and explore something new. Sign up for an interesting class, contact someone you admire, travel to an unfamiliar destination, go for a hike, or plan an exotic holiday trip. Push your boundaries to the point of exhilaration. Feel alive!

You'll admire yourself for taking courageous steps, because doing so increases your self-esteem and furthers your sense of confidence. These feelings will support you in following through with your life purpose, since you'll realize that you truly are qualified and able to bestow blessings in meaningful ways.

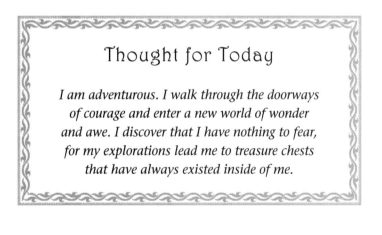

Thought for Today

*I am adventurous. I walk through the doorways
of courage and enter a new world of wonder
and awe. I discover that I have nothing to fear,
for my explorations lead me to treasure chests
that have always existed inside of me.*

Slow Down

Trying to stuff too many items into a closet only results in frustration, and it's the same way when you overschedule yourself. To combat potential problems, you go faster and focus on just getting through your day's activities instead of enjoying them.

That's why we angels are guiding you to break this cycle by enjoying a "slow day." Like a leisurely dance that evokes deep feelings, allow your decreased pace to reconnect you with the richness within each moment. For instance, enjoy the smiles you elicit as you allow someone to go ahead of you in line, wave to let in other drivers waiting to exit a parking lot, and let other people talk while you listen.

Take your time, and notice any differences between your mood today and the way you normally feel. Remove your watch, cover up the clocks and calendars, and enjoy the timelessness that is the true nature of the universe.

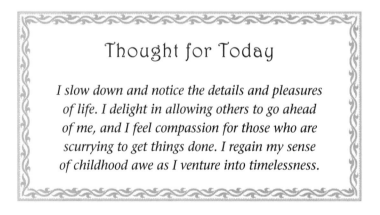

Thought for Today

I slow down and notice the details and pleasures of life. I delight in allowing others to go ahead of me, and I feel compassion for those who are scurrying to get things done. I regain my sense of childhood awe as I venture into timelessness.

Daydream

When you let your thoughts float as free as kites on a summer breeze, you never know what creative inspiration you'll encounter. So give your imagination a long leash, and watch where it takes you today.

Great works of art are conceived of during daydreams by people who have the courage to merely observe (instead of trying to control) their thoughts. Begin by setting an intention, and then get quiet and comfortable. Think about a "What-if" scenario where all limits are lifted—imagine that your greatest dream is realized, and continue the story from there.

The magic of this process is that it consciously connects you to the Universal Mind, a process that usually occurs by accident. Keep paper and pen nearby so that you can write about your experiences in a "daydream journal." Although it's often considered a frivolous activity, you'll find wonderfully down-to-earth instructions, guidance, and answers during each session. Sweet daydreams!

Thought for Today

I daydream and take a journey to magical places where I experience wondrous adventures and infinite possibilities. I allow myself to wander and grow, breaking free of previous limits. When I let my mind soar, I reach up to heaven and bring it down to Earth.

Surprise Someone

Just as you like pleasant surprises, other people also enjoy receiving something that wasn't anticipated. Planning such a gift is an act of nurturing love: You receive inspiration as to the nature of the treat, spend time organizing its elements, and then experience the joy of sharing it with the recipient. Spontaneous surprises such as a heartfelt compliment or an unexpected offer of help are also invaluable.

When you give to another person, you're in truth giving to yourself, as you and the receiver are one. You're also putting energy out into the universe signaling that you enjoy happy surprises yourself. Life responds in kind by delivering wonderful delights to you in an abundant flow of giving and receiving.

Enjoy the unexpected today, both in what you give and what you receive. Stay alert and notice anything beautiful or unusual . . . surprises come in many forms.

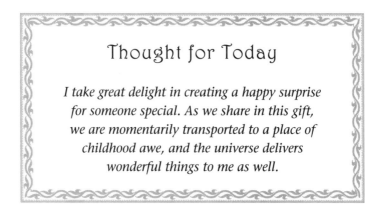

Thought for Today

I take great delight in creating a happy surprise for someone special. As we share in this gift, we are momentarily transported to a place of childhood awe, and the universe delivers wonderful things to me as well.

Listen to Your Body's Wisdom

Take a moment and notice the feelings in your body. Stay quiet and present as you tune in to any areas that feel relaxed, as well as those that are tense. Then inhale deeply and imagine that your lungs are filled with healing light. As you exhale, direct your energy and breath toward any areas of tension in your body.

Feel your muscles relax as you send love and attention their way, and ask them to tell you why they were tense. Most likely their answer will reveal some hidden fears that need to be confronted. Be a strong confidant and listen to your body compassionately. Reassure your physical self that it's safe and protected, and then take a moment to consider any insights that you just received from its messages.

In many ways, your body is very wise and honest—it will always tell you the truth. Based on your discoveries, do you feel like making any changes in your plans for the day? Do you want to ask for additional help from other people, or us, the angels?

Check in with yourself regularly today. Hold silent conversations with any area of your body that's asking for your attention. Listen to its messages, and take steps according to its guidance. In this way, it won't need to signal you through tension or pain, and will instead work hand in hand with you harmoniously.

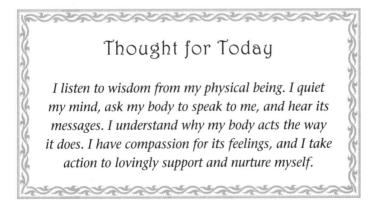

Thought for Today

I listen to wisdom from my physical being. I quiet my mind, ask my body to speak to me, and hear its messages. I understand why my body acts the way it does. I have compassion for its feelings, and I take action to lovingly support and nurture myself.

Feel Your Wishes Coming True!

*Y*ou don't need to strain, push, or struggle for anything. The energy of trying too hard can drive good away from you, while the strength of gratitude can draw positive things to you. You can easily accomplish a lot by holding the feeling and thought of being thankful that your wish is already granted. Don't worry about how this dream will come to be—simply imagine it as already being true. The more emotion, passion, and fervor you can put into your gratitude, the more quickly you'll make your desires a reality.

Every longing sends an etheric version of itself into the universe, while its essence stays next to you and solidifies into material form. The more energy you put into your wish, the faster it's manifested. But negativity, pessimism, and doubt erase it, turning it back into cloudlike ether.

Nurture your desires today by thinking about them often and surrounding them with positive thoughts and emotions. Say "Thank you!" to the universe for continuously supporting you in all ways.

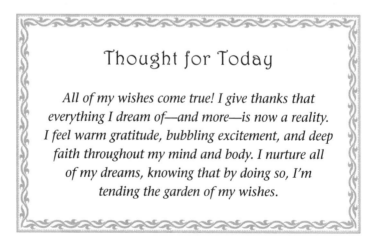

Thought for Today

All of my wishes come true! I give thanks that
everything I dream of—and more—is now a reality.
I feel warm gratitude, bubbling excitement, and deep
faith throughout my mind and body. I nurture all
of my dreams, knowing that by doing so, I'm
tending the garden of my wishes.

Value Yourself

You're a radiant jewel in the crown of heavenly creations, and your light shines brightly in our midst. We angels watch over you with admiration, respect, and great love—it's natural for us to want the very best for you.

We sometimes observe you making compromised choices for yourself, believing that you don't deserve better. You fear that if you receive good, you'll take away from someone else or from yourself. Beloved, believe us when we say that as you give to yourself, so you also give to others. You and the entire human race share one spirit, one breath, and one truth. It's impossible to separate what you do to yourself and what you do for others—it's like trying to nurture and feed only certain leaves on a tree! That's impossible, of course, but it's exactly what you're trying to do when you attempt to put yourself last.

Nurture yourself as a way of caring for your family, friends, and the entire population. Value yourself as a means of cherishing everyone on Earth; honor yourself in order to pay tribute to all others.

The more you give to yourself, the more you feel great love—and that emotion is the key to happiness and peace. It doesn't mean that you think, *I'm better than others;* rather, it signifies, *I love that which I see within myself and others.* Your self-care extends the joyful spark of creation for the benefit of all.

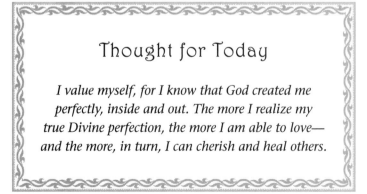

Thought for Today

I value myself, for I know that God created me perfectly, inside and out. The more I realize my true Divine perfection, the more I am able to love— and the more, in turn, I can cherish and heal others.

Express Your Feelings in Creative Ways

*Y*our feelings are pure energy, like rays of the sun, that desire expression and expansion. Pent-up feelings create physical conditions such as fatigue, irritability, and addiction—so make friends with your emotions today. Honor them all, even those you feel uncomfortable with, and know that each one has a Divine reason behind it. When you have compassion and respect for your feelings, their power supports you.

Your feelings, like all energies, need to be dispelled outwardly. Otherwise, they're akin to steam trapped in a saucepan that gets too hot and wilts the vegetables you're cooking.

Bring out what's in your heart through creativity. The means of expression is secondary to the action, as long as it brings you joy. Your emotions will react strongly to the creative form they want to take . . . and the possibilities are infinite. You might try photography, jewelry making, tie-dyeing, sewing, writing, singing, playing a musical instrument, belly dancing, flower arranging, drawing, crocheting, decorating, painting, making stained glass, knitting, makeup artistry, embroidery, or anything else that your heart desires.

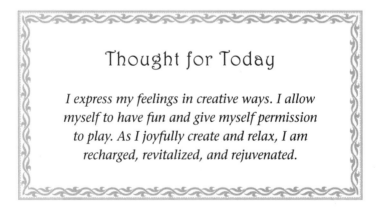

Thought for Today

I express my feelings in creative ways. I allow myself to have fun and give myself permission to play. As I joyfully create and relax, I am recharged, revitalized, and rejuvenated.

Notice Your Thoughts

We angels are here to guide you toward the answers to all your prayers. Yet we alone can't bring your desires to you—your cooperation is also completely necessary. If you ask for something but at the same time are afraid of receiving it, we can't bring it to you. Your fear creates barriers for the manifestation of your prayers.

We can, however, help you overcome your concerns—just ask! Anytime you feel that you're in a push-pull situation with yourself, call upon us to conquer the inner turmoil. This begins with noticing your thoughts, so be aware of the meanderings of your mind, leading you to both happy and fearful places.

Your body will signal whenever you become afraid: Your muscles will tighten, your breath will shorten, and your pulse will increase. This is the time to ask us for help. The moment you think about angels, your mind is flooded with the energy of love, which is part of the turnaround process.

Notice your thoughts today. If you become afraid, think, *Angels, please help me have peaceful thoughts,* and we'll come to your assistance immediately. We can't and won't control your mind; we will, however, elevate your energies so that they reflect your true Divinity. In that way, your thoughts are love based, which attract and create positive experiences.

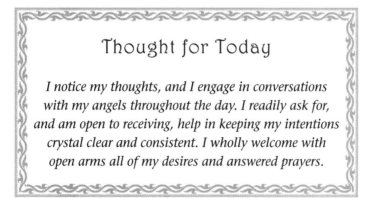

Thought for Today

I notice my thoughts, and I engage in conversations with my angels throughout the day. I readily ask for, and am open to receiving, help in keeping my intentions crystal clear and consistent. I wholly welcome with open arms all of my desires and answered prayers.

Release Your Fears

All fears are based in the belief that you're isolated and alone. You may be afraid that you can't do something or won't attain what you want, but your concerns are rooted in fallacies. You're eternally connected to God, angels, and other people—no one is ever alone. You always have powerful allies at your side who are ready to help you if you ask.

Since you're plugged into the ultimate energy of the universe, you're a powerful creator of your wishes, desires, thoughts, and feelings. Today, we angels would like to work with you to purge yourself of fear, which is the only reason why your prayers and affirmations don't seem to manifest. Anytime you become aware of insecurities, please inhale deeply, and then mentally call upon us as you breathe out. By doing so, you're blowing your unease away to us. Keep exhaling your fears until you feel a renewed sense of peacefulness.

We can help you reveal your true underlying self, the part of you that's confident, assured, and strong in the knowledge that you have all the love, power, and support you could ever need.

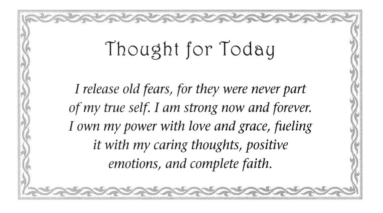

Thought for Today

I release old fears, for they were never part of my true self. I am strong now and forever. I own my power with love and grace, fueling it with my caring thoughts, positive emotions, and complete faith.

Smell the Roses

The phrase "Stop and smell the roses" is synonymous with enjoying life, and this is a message that we angels continually communicate to you. Today, though, we're taking this guidance one step further and asking you to take this advice *literally.*

The fragrance of these flowers enters your nostrils and goes straight to your heart. Roses help you blossom into the full manifestation of loving feelings. This is the reason why they're associated with romantic love.

Today make it a point to breathe in this powerful scent. Find some sweet-smelling ones and deeply inhale the gift of their essence. Notice how their various colors evoke different emotions. Which one holds the most attractive fragrance for you?

Bring the energy of these flowers home by purchasing or planting them, or by buying a vial of pure rose essential oil. Remember to inhale this healing odor often throughout the day, and stay aware of your heart's abundant joy.

You may also notice a floral scent occurring in rooms where no physical blooms exist. That's our signal to you that we're nearby, and it's a reminder for you to take the time to follow today's advice.

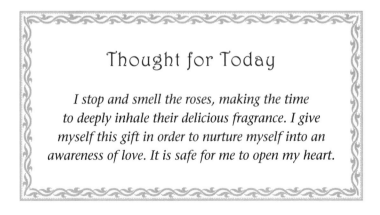

Thought for Today

I stop and smell the roses, making the time to deeply inhale their delicious fragrance. I give myself this gift in order to nurture myself into an awareness of love. It is safe for me to open my heart.

Feed the Birds

We angels work closely with birds to send you messages of love. When you see a bird exhibiting unusual behavior or find feathers in unexpected locations, you can be sure that we're behind it.

There's a reason why we're depicted with wings, as both we and the birds soar above all seeming limitations and problems. Yet we always keep a watchful eye below: We may not be experiencing the struggles, but we're supporting you through everything that happens.

When you interact with birds, you can feel our energy more clearly. These creatures help you commune with nature angels and archangels, along with your guardian angels and ancestors. So feed the birds today, and spend some time in their company. They'll appreciate your generosity, and you'll benefit from their sweet songs, presence, and energy.

Thought for Today

I feed the birds and feel my heart become light as a feather, noticing the angelic signs that come to me. I allow my spirit to fly as freely as a bird.

83

Review What You've Learned

When you were young, your parents probably asked you, "What did you learn today?" and you'd then recount some lesson from school. But even when you denied having learned anything, deep down you knew that you'd discovered something new.

You gain wisdom from all life experiences, including the challenging ones. When you look back on painful events, stop and ask yourself, *What did I learn?* This question will help you see the gift within the situation, and you'll know that you didn't undergo anything in vain.

Every circumstance teaches you patience, compassion, strength, and other valuable lessons. Take a moment to review the knowledge that you've gained lately. What did you learn yesterday? How about today? All lessons are valuable treasures that you can never lose, so enjoy and appreciate them.

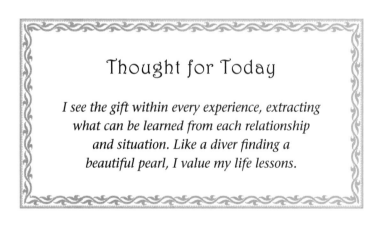

Thought for Today

I see the gift within every experience, extracting what can be learned from each relationship and situation. Like a diver finding a beautiful pearl, I value my life lessons.

Give Yourself Permission

As a child, you waited for grown-ups to give you direction and permission to do things, acquiescing to their authority. This habit has continued into adulthood—there's still a part of you waiting for others to give their OK.

Today, regain full command of your schedule, activities, and life. You're your own authority figure now, and you can give yourself the go-ahead to follow your dreams and inner guidance.

What would you like permission to do? Know that you have the power to follow your Divine guidance without seeking approval from others. You can make life decisions that will increase your health, happiness, and peace.

We angels will help you with this process if you'll only ask. We can support your courage and strength to make changes, but ultimately it's up to you. You can do it!

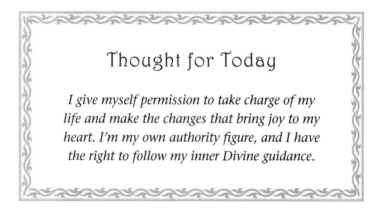

Thought for Today

I give myself permission to take charge of my life and make the changes that bring joy to my heart. I'm my own authority figure, and I have the right to follow my inner Divine guidance.

Take a Stroll

Something magical happens when you take a walk. Your mind relaxes, your tension level is lowered, and you notice the details in your surroundings.

The very act of walking is a rhythmic meditation that helps you hear yourself think. When you share this activity with a friend, your conversation adds a therapeutic element as well. You end up feeling refreshed, renewed, and grateful that you took this opportunity for self-care.

Make time for a stroll today, which is a slower version of walking for fitness. Meander awhile, stop to chat with neighbors for a few minutes, and allow yourself the luxury of smelling roses or petting animals along the way. This may not be cardiovascular exercise, but it does increase your heart's capacity for love.

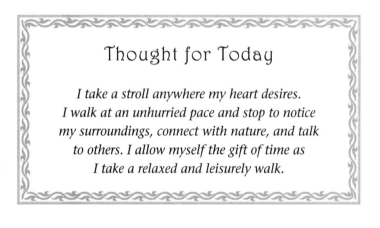

Thought for Today

I take a stroll anywhere my heart desires.
I walk at an unhurried pace and stop to notice
my surroundings, connect with nature, and talk
to others. I allow myself the gift of time as
I take a relaxed and leisurely walk.

86

Honor Your Agreements

Whenever you honor your agreements, your inner self smiles. Your confidence is increased each time you keep a promise because you learn to have faith in yourself.

As you treat others with respect and fairness, so too does the universe deliver the same back to you—in other words, your actions are investments in your own self and future. They teach you that as long as you continue to act wisely through honorable deeds, you can trust others and the world.

The most important promises are the ones you make to yourself. When you pledge to make positive changes, adopt healthier habits, and the like, your inner self becomes as excited as a child whose parent has promised a fun reward. When you keep these commitments to yourself, your soul feels safe and loved, and it shines with happiness.

Today, keep your promises to yourself and others. The effort involved in doing so is worth it because of the rewards that you'll reap . . . we promise!

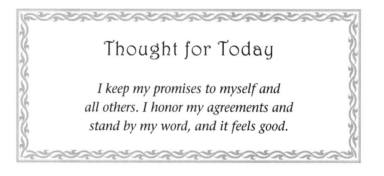

Thought for Today

I keep my promises to myself and all others. I honor my agreements and stand by my word, and it feels good.

Bless Your Meals

The act of saying grace at mealtimes is a time-honored tradition that hearkens back to humankind's earliest days. It's an intuitive response to the intimacy involved in consuming food and beverages.

You can heighten the energy of your meals through prayers and affirmations. Scientists on Earth now have concrete evidence documenting the beneficial effects of blessing what you eat, yet the greatest proof is the boost in mood and energy that you feel from the prayed-over food.

Create a new healthful habit today of blessing your meals. It doesn't matter how you go about infusing them with loving thoughts and wishes. What's important is that you use some means of invoking loving intentions toward everything you eat and drink.

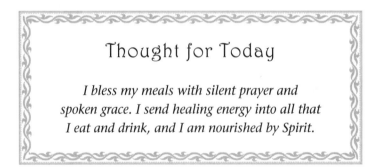

Thought for Today

I bless my meals with silent prayer and spoken grace. I send healing energy into all that I eat and drink, and I am nourished by Spirit.

Forgive Yourself

Ultimately, all the resentments that you hold boomerang inward and become self-anger, which percolates to the surface and seeps into your daily life. These feelings can blind you to the everyday joys that await you in the world.

For this reason, we angels are continuously guiding you to forgive and release the harmful buildup of resentment in your mind and body. This is the ultimate detoxification that brings you everything you seek: more energy, clearer focus, a greater ability to concentrate, renewed playfulness, love, money . . . you name it. The rewards of forgiveness occur as quickly as light floods a room when a lamp is switched on.

You're much too hard on yourself, beloved one. You believe that perfection is a requirement of being valued, yet you're entirely lovable as you stumble, learn, grow, and move on. That's why the most important acts of forgiveness are the ones you direct inward. When you learn to lovingly embrace every part of yourself, the spark within you beams as brightly as a searchlight, healing and attracting others who benefit from your warmth and wisdom.

Release the resentments you have toward yourself today. Let go of any guilt or self-reproach, and bathe yourself in much-deserved love.

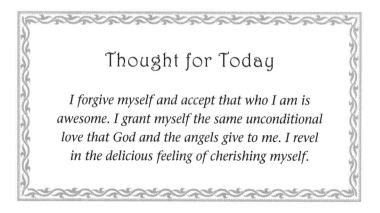

Thought for Today

I forgive myself and accept that who I am is awesome. I grant myself the same unconditional love that God and the angels give to me. I revel in the delicious feeling of cherishing myself.

89

Take It Easy

Sometimes you struggle and strain to achieve so much that you unwittingly block yourself. This is especially true when you want something so badly that you try over and over again to make it happen.

The universe responds to the fear imprinted into the energy of struggle. The underlying anxiety that maybe what you desire won't materialize is mirrored back to you in the form of limitations, delays, and unsatisfactory manifestations.

That's why surrendering brings about immediate results. When you deliver your wish to the universe, you also release the fears that previously blocked you. Letting go is a statement that says, "I know my wish is manifesting in the best possible way, even if I'm not certain exactly how it will happen." This faith is akin to opening the front door and welcoming your desire into your home.

Take it easy today, and allow the universe to do the work of creating your dreams. Your job was done once you made the wish, so turn it over to God and enjoy the creative ways in which your prayers are answered.

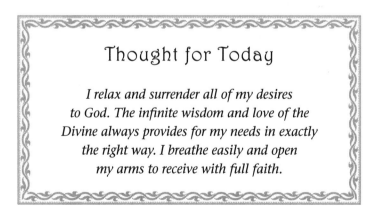

Thought for Today

*I relax and surrender all of my desires
to God. The infinite wisdom and love of the
Divine always provides for my needs in exactly
the right way. I breathe easily and open
my arms to receive with full faith.*

90

Forgive a Resentment

When someone's behavior triggers pain, you may hold resentment toward that person. Yet you only hurt yourself with this emotion, as it lowers your energy, enthusiasm, and effectiveness. Any unkind words or deeds that an individual directs toward you are only a reflection of that person; his or her behavior is not a statement about the true you.

When people act unkindly, they eclipse light and love from their life, which then attracts more experiences that fuel their discontent. The more unlovable people seem to be, the more that they *need* love, which heals unhappiness and ignites warmth in their hearts.

This does not mean, however, that you must spend time in the company of those who seem to behave unkindly toward you. You can send them caring thoughts from a safe distance and still accomplish your goal. When you direct love toward someone whom you previously resented, healing occurs on three levels:

1. It frees you from the pain and anguish of anger.
2. It breaks undesirable patterns, since you always attract what you think about.
3. It helps heal the other person.

Forgive someone today. The benefit you derive from doing so far exceeds any pleasure that holding on to the resentment may have afforded. Let it go and be free!

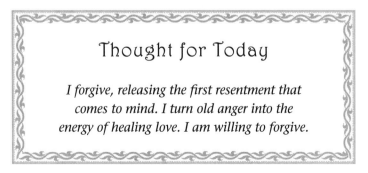

Thought for Today

I forgive, releasing the first resentment that comes to mind. I turn old anger into the energy of healing love. I am willing to forgive.

Know That You Are Lovable

To us angels, you are the most lovable person imaginable. We see the goodness in your heart and in the way you desire to express and receive affection. Each breath you exhale sends your beautiful energy outward.

You're entirely worthy of love. Your personality, thoughts, and feelings are wondrously endearing, and your physical being is perfect in all ways. Every part of you is completely glorious.

We're your angels, we're continuously by your side, and we will always love you.

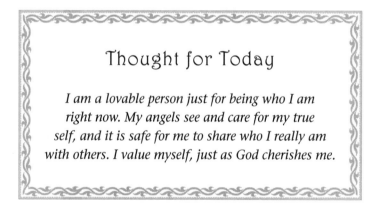

Thought for Today

I am a lovable person just for being who I am right now. My angels see and care for my true self, and it is safe for me to share who I really am with others. I value myself, just as God cherishes me.

Write Today

The written word is a wonderful means of self-expression, teaching, and even learning. It's also a way to connect with heaven through the process of channeling information from the Divine. You've probably had many clues throughout your life that writing is part of your nature and purpose. This is a message for you to take time today to sit down and pick up your pen.

The process of writing opens you up to receiving new ideas and information. You tap in to your inner teacher, as well as the wisdom of the universe, so don't worry about what your topic will be. Simply sit down in front of your computer or notebook and begin transcribing anything that comes to mind. It's okay if your words don't make sense or you begin with unclear thoughts or feelings. The direction of your writing will become plain once you get started.

Make this activity a part of your life—if possible, turn it into a daily habit. We angels will help you overcome confidence issues and guide you, if you ask. Take time today to write, and notice the emotional and self-esteem benefits that result.

Thought for Today

*I write, expressing myself with words that
are inspired by Spirit and blessed by the angels.
I allow myself to record messages from the heart.*

Create a Dream Board

A dream board is a wonderful tool that provides you with a visual representation of your goals, prayers, and desires. It has a base of firm construction paper or wood onto which you paste photographs, drawings, words, and other images that stand for what you desire. Thumb through magazines to find these, and have fun putting them up.

After your board is complete, hang it in a prominent location so that you'll see it daily. Each time you pass it, stop and visualize your wishes as already manifested. Feel gratitude and say "Thank you" to the universe for bringing your dream into reality.

Give heaven any cares or worries about how this desire will materialize. Put your entire focus on having gratitude for the fact that your wish has already come true, and then welcome it as it comes into your life.

Thought for Today

*I create a dream board, pasting together
a collage of my wishes and seeing them fit
perfectly together. I now envision my desires as
a reality. Thank you, God and angels, for _____.*

Recall a Favorite Memory

The sweetness of sentimental memories evokes many pleasant feelings. Today, fondly remember a time when you felt safe and completely loved, and bring to mind a moment when you enjoyed yourself without reservation. Recall not just your thoughts, but your feelings as well.

Spend some time with your recollections, and let your mind wander at will. Ask yourself the following questions and see what answers spontaneously rise to the surface:

- *What is one of my favorite birthday memories?*
- *When did I feel most proud of myself?*
- *What is a pleasant recollection from a time when I was outdoors?*
- *What is a wonderful memory I have of my love life?*
- *Which moment was a peak experience for me?*

Keep going with these memories, perhaps writing about them in a journal or sharing them with a loved one or us, your angels.

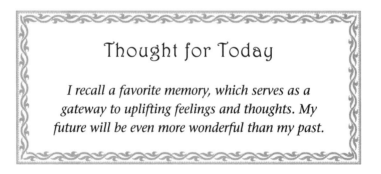

Thought for Today

I recall a favorite memory, which serves as a gateway to uplifting feelings and thoughts. My future will be even more wonderful than my past.

Tell Yourself *I Love You*

Self-love is a term that you frequently hear about but are sometimes unsure how to put into practice. One of the simplest ways to do so is to say *I love you* to yourself. You can declare it silently, aloud, or in writing.

Everyone enjoys hearing caring affirmations, and that includes your inner self. When you express such sentiments to yourself, your soul shines brightly with joy. Your entire energy field is enlarged, which enhances your healing and manifestation abilities.

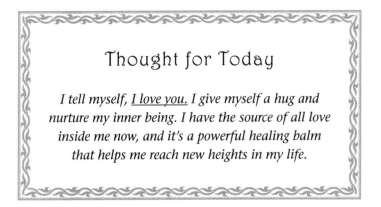

Thought for Today

I tell myself, I love you. I give myself a hug and nurture my inner being. I have the source of all love inside me now, and it's a powerful healing balm that helps me reach new heights in my life.

Visualize Angels

One way to communicate with us angels is through images that you hold in your mind's eye. When you visualize us, it's the same as summoning us to your side. Take some time today to become very still, close your eyes, breathe deeply, and picture many angels surrounding you.

Envision talking with us and pouring your heart out; and receiving love, wisdom, support, and guidance. It doesn't matter how detailed your visualization is, because your intention of connecting with us always yields successful results—even if you're unaware of them. Remember that we're conscious of your every thought and feeling, even if you can't yet hear us. . . .

We love you unconditionally, and we're eternally patient.

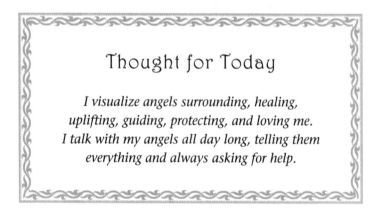

Thought for Today

I visualize angels surrounding, healing,
uplifting, guiding, protecting, and loving me.
I talk with my angels all day long, telling them
everything and always asking for help.

97

Release the Need for Approval

Let go of the need to be liked by everyone; it only matters that you value yourself. Another person's opinions have no bearing on who you are, as they're merely statements of that individual's own self-judgment projected onto you.

Look at our situation as a prime example: Although we angels spend all our time helping others, there are still those who dislike and distrust us. If we allowed these negative views to weigh us down, we'd be less effective in our purpose.

Think of how much time and energy you've put into seeking the approval of others. Wouldn't it feel better to spend your time seeking your *own* favor, measuring your worth against a higher standard than other people's opinions? Of course the answer is yes—and today is the day to adopt this healthful new attitude.

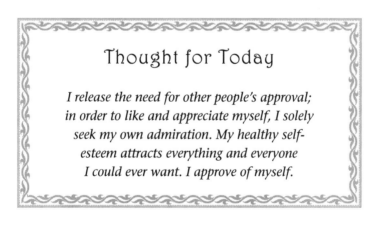

Thought for Today

I release the need for other people's approval; in order to like and appreciate myself, I solely seek my own admiration. My healthy self-esteem attracts everything and everyone I could ever want. I approve of myself.

Send Love to Your Heart

*Y*our entire body reacts positively to love. When you direct this emotion toward your physical self, it's the same energy that we angels or other people send you. Love is love, no matter what channel it flows through.

Give extra energy to your heart today, blessing it physically, emotionally, and spiritually. Hold the prayer that it's completely healthy. Surround it with love, and ask it to absorb this gift with each beat. Tell it "Thank you" for being so healthy, strong, and efficient.

Reassure your heart that it's safe and you'll protect it in all ways. Let it know that you'll exercise and eat healthfully, as you're guided. Declare that you'll honor your feelings to help identify the relationships and situations that are beneficial—and the ones to avoid.

See your heart as a beautiful flower, and ask its petals to gently unfurl. Watch as any barriers you've hidden behind are lowered. Send your heart tender feelings, and it, in turn, will help you feel greater love.

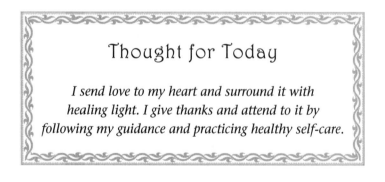

Thought for Today

*I send love to my heart and surround it with
healing light. I give thanks and attend to it by
following my guidance and practicing healthy self-care.*

Smile

Scientists have demonstrated the many physiological benefits of happiness and smiling. The spiritual rewards are countless as well, and today we angels are asking you to focus on one of these: the boomerang effect that smiles have.

When you smile, others can't help but mirror the same facial expression back to you. Even if their teeth don't show in a wide grin, you notice their eyes crinkle happily as they gaze at you. This human reaction is a God-given ability that we want you to capitalize upon. It's a testament to the phrase: "The more you give, the more you receive."

Today, send someone a smile, and see it magnified and returned to you. Feel great knowing that your grin will also travel through many individuals and have a domino healing effect as it goes from person to person. The benefits will always come shining back to you in countless ways.

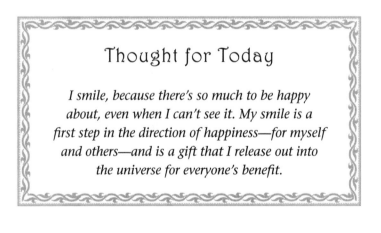

Thought for Today

I smile, because there's so much to be happy about, even when I can't see it. My smile is a first step in the direction of happiness—for myself and others—and is a gift that I release out into the universe for everyone's benefit.

100

Laugh

The sound of laughter is the closest thing on Earth to the "music of the spheres" found in heaven. Its purest essence releases your inner joy out into the world, which has far-reaching effects. Your laughter heals you, as well as all others who hear it or feel its force, because it elevates the energy of the room in which it occurs. Whether it's a quiet giggle or a loud guffaw, it's powerful.

Today, seek out ways to laugh. You could watch a comedy, read a funny book, or swap jokes with others. Look for the humor in various situations throughout your day, and try to think like a comedian. Laughter, like all other positive aspects of life, comes more easily with practice—and establishing this new habit will have lasting effects.

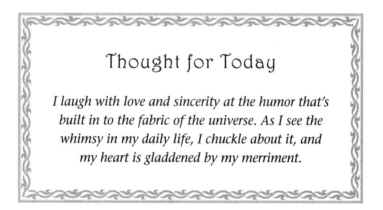

Thought for Today

I laugh with love and sincerity at the humor that's built in to the fabric of the universe. As I see the whimsy in my daily life, I chuckle about it, and my heart is gladdened by my merriment.

Choose Happiness

Happiness is a state of being that you create—it's a choice that comes from within, no matter what's happening around you. Today, give yourself the therapeutic gift of choosing this magical emotion, one that has the power to dissolve crises, heal illness, mend disagreements, and attract new opportunities.

Feeling happy is the ultimate display of faith that your prayers have been heard and answered . . . and your belief is always rewarded in ways that yield blissful surprises. This cycle is a healthy one: The more joyful you are, the more experiences you attract that support your well-being. So choose happiness, setting your intention to stay lighthearted and loving in your outlook today. If you become sidetracked into negativity, remember joy. Just the thought of it is enough to evoke its light, which shines away negativity.

Be the beacon of this emotion today in order to inspire and guide others to choose it for themselves as well. After all, the best way to teach happiness is to practice it yourself.

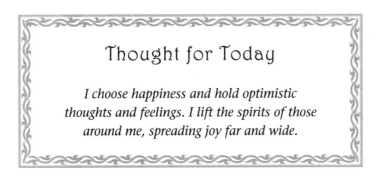

Thought for Today

I choose happiness and hold optimistic
thoughts and feelings. I lift the spirits of those
around me, spreading joy far and wide.

Give Yourself a Present

Why wait for special occasions to give yourself a treat? After all, you need rewards most during the ordinary times in your life! The present you bestow on yourself today doesn't have to be expensive or elaborate—it could be free of charge. It just needs to make your heart sing with delight.

Approach today with an open mind, and allow yourself to be guided to just the right treat for yourself. This could be an activity such as going to the movies or reading a good book, or it could involve receiving a service such as a massage or foot rub. You might even prefer a simple soak in the bathtub or taking an afternoon nap.

You certainly aren't limited to just one present per day. Reward yourself with gifts as often as you feel guided, and experience the benefits of increased enthusiasm and joy.

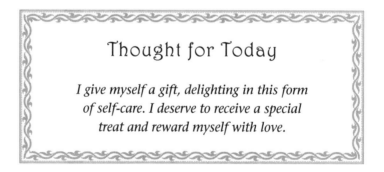

Thought for Today

I give myself a gift, delighting in this form of self-care. I deserve to receive a special treat and reward myself with love.

Heal an Old Relationship

Has someone from your past been on your mind recently? This could be a signal for you to reinitiate contact with this individual, or it might mean that it's time to resolve an old issue with him or her. When thoughts of a former relationship bubble up to the surface, it's worth paying attention to the reason why.

First, notice any feelings in your stomach as you think about the person. Do you feel tense? Relaxed? Uplifted? Upset? Identify the various emotions associated with your relationship, and think about how you parted. If you harbor any regrets, inhale deeply, and hold the intention of releasing those feelings as you exhale—this in itself could be the healing that your soul seeks. You can also ask the universe to undo the effects of any mistakes that either of you made. This request is always granted, with powerful and often miraculous results.

You may want to write a letter to the person as a way of understanding your true thoughts and feelings. You don't need to send it to gain the therapeutic value of this process . . . sometimes it's best to ceremoniously destroy what you've written as a symbol of letting go.

After your moments of contemplation, you may feel strongly guided to get back in touch with the individual in question. Call upon us angels to surround the reunion with protective love and ensure that it's as harmonious as possible. (We can also help you to locate the person, if you so desire.)

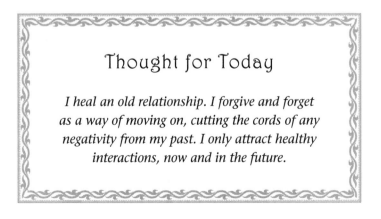

Thought for Today

I heal an old relationship. I forgive and forget as a way of moving on, cutting the cords of any negativity from my past. I only attract healthy interactions, now and in the future.

Send Love to Your Muscles

*Y*ou may be carrying tension in your body right now without realizing it. We angels point this out so that you can take positive steps toward relaxing.

Take a moment to scan your body for any areas of strain. Ask your muscles what they're trying to tell you—you'll likely hear, feel, or think a response. Take another few seconds to have a conversation with them about why they're tense.

Next, inhale deeply, and while exhaling, imagine sending the breath to your body. Feel compassionate understanding for your muscles, and thank them for the excellent job that they're doing. Not only do they support you, but they also communicate honest feelings to you.

Your body tends to be tense or achy when it's ignored, so take time today to listen, and appreciate it. Just as people relax when they feel that they're understood, so will your muscles do the same.

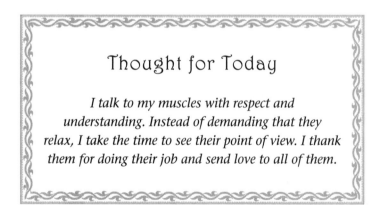

Thought for Today

I talk to my muscles with respect and understanding. Instead of demanding that they relax, I take the time to see their point of view. I thank them for doing their job and send love to all of them.

Recognize Your Value

Instead of measuring your self-worth against worldly standards, please see yourself from our angelic perspective. In our eyes, you're entirely valuable and make a huge difference just by being alive. Your breath and beating heart emit love, and anchor heaven's light on Earth.

Your prayers sound like music to us, as they're opportunities for us to work with you as a united team. We see deep within your soul, where your wisdom and goodness are always on display.

You're a valuable person, and this planet needs you, even if you aren't sure of your role. Your presence brings blessings to many people's lives, and we're counting on you to have faith in this life. It does get easier . . . we promise.

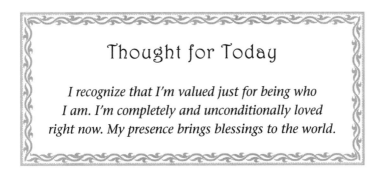

Thought for Today

I recognize that I'm valued just for being who I am. I'm completely and unconditionally loved right now. My presence brings blessings to the world.

Know That You're
Perfectly Understood by Us

Sometimes you may feel misunderstood by the people in your life. You might even wonder if you understand yourself!

We angels understand you. We know your deepest feelings and thoughts, and we honor whatever you're going through right now. We stand by in support, ready to give you a helping hand whenever you ask. Know that we cherish every part of you, from your darkest shadows to your brightest light, because you're entirely lovable from our perspective.

Talk to us if you ever feel misunderstood. Pour your heart out to us in any way you choose; and know that we're always listening, supporting, and understanding.

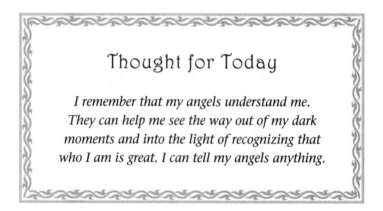

Thought for Today

*I remember that my angels understand me.
They can help me see the way out of my dark
moments and into the light of recognizing that
who I am is great. I can tell my angels anything.*

107

Pour Your Heart Out to Us

We angels are here for you continuously. When you feel upset or disappointed, pour your heart out to us. Tell us everything, including your uncomfortable thoughts and feelings.

This process is for your own therapeutic benefit, because nothing is a secret to us—we already know what you're going through. We support you in every way, for our love is without judgment or conditions.

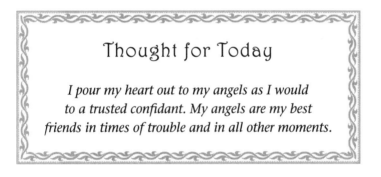

Thought for Today

I pour my heart out to my angels as I would to a trusted confidant. My angels are my best friends in times of trouble and in all other moments.

Wave Your Magic Wand

*Y*ou've probably wished many times that you had a wand you could wave to improve life for yourself and others. We angels would like to introduce you to the magic that you've always had in your possession: love.

When you entirely surround your circumstances with this emotion in all of its guises—gratitude, forgiveness, compassion, peace, and so forth—you've waved a magic wand that can heal any imbalance or ill. If you ask, we can help you reach this state of mind, heart, and body. We'll join with your energy to infuse the situation with the magic of Divine love.

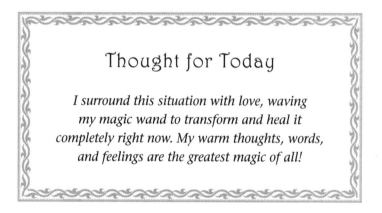

Thought for Today

I surround this situation with love, waving my magic wand to transform and heal it completely right now. My warm thoughts, words, and feelings are the greatest magic of all!

Shine Your Light Brightly

When you fully express your true self, your inner light beams brightly, showing joy through laughter, song, dance, playfulness, and connection to others. Allow this part of you to come out today—your radiance may illuminate someone else's path and provide inspiration during a period of darkness.

Shine brightly today, Earth angel. Use your light to guide another person.

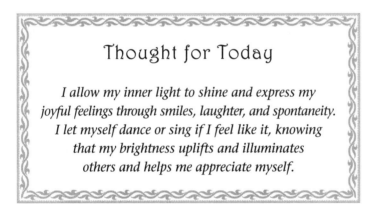

Thought for Today

I allow my inner light to shine and express my joyful feelings through smiles, laughter, and spontaneity. I let myself dance or sing if I feel like it, knowing that my brightness uplifts and illuminates others and helps me appreciate myself.

❧ 110 ❧

Know That Your Future Is Safe

We angels see that you often worry about your future, so today we bring you the reassurance that everything is fine: There's nothing coming up that you can't handle. We hold your hand through each moment of time, moving forward into what lies ahead.

We also remind you to cast only positive thoughts into the future, for it's being designed by the feelings you hold this very moment. Give us your cares and worries about tomorrow, and put your entire focus on having a peaceful today. Your present tranquility is an investment in your future that yields beautiful returns.

By surrounding you with our love, we can help you trade in frightening thoughts for ones that make you feel happy and safe. But in order to really connect with our support, you'll need to allow it into your heart. The best way to do so is with your breath, so please inhale all of the loving energy around you, and draw it into your core. Then give yourself a hug, and exhale away any feelings of tension. Keep calling upon us until you feel calm and secure about what's to come.

Everything really is always okay—the more that you know and feel this truth, the more you experience it. It's safe for you to feel at peace now . . . and in the future.

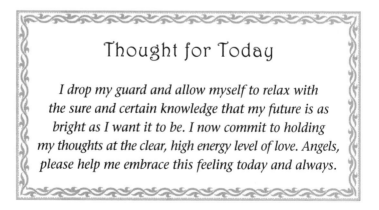

Thought for Today

I drop my guard and allow myself to relax with the sure and certain knowledge that my future is as bright as I want it to be. I now commit to holding my thoughts at the clear, high energy level of love. Angels, please help me embrace this feeling today and always.

Give Yourself a Pat on the Back

Everyone needs acknowledgment and praise. We angels continuously bestow our positive words upon you, but you may not hear or believe them without a human voice acknowledging your efforts, too.

The recognition that you need the most comes from yourself. When others praise you, it feels good . . . yet you may not completely accept it. A part of you distances yourself from the flattery, afraid of the power and energy behind the words. That's why it's doubly important for you to acknowledge yourself.

Today, give yourself a literal pat on the back and say, "Good job!" for something that you've recently accomplished. What you're honoring could be a very minor thing, but remember that every large achievement consists of many such tiny actions. If you praise yourself for each of these small steps, you'll feel more enthusiastic about taking the next one.

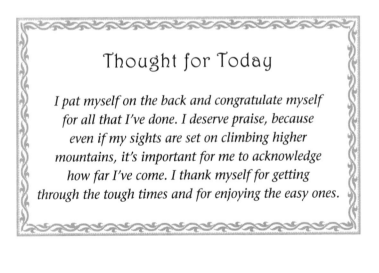

Thought for Today

I pat myself on the back and congratulate myself for all that I've done. I deserve praise, because even if my sights are set on climbing higher mountains, it's important for me to acknowledge how far I've come. I thank myself for getting through the tough times and for enjoying the easy ones.

Erase Guilt from Your Consciousness

When you do something for another person out of a sense of guilt or obligation, you end up resenting that individual. This feeling robs you of the joy that you'd normally feel while helping someone else . . . it's a blinder that blocks the light within your relationships.

That's why we angels are working with you today to erase guilt from your consciousness. This emotion differs from a sense of responsibility, which is based on caring feelings. The key is to help others from a place of love, not out of obligation, because the former is lighthearted, while the latter is drudgery. Which do you think is healthier for you and the relationship?

Before you do anything that you don't want to, stop for a brief moment and ask us for help. We can lift your mind-set to the level of love so that you'll either find a comfortable alternative to performing the task or be able to accomplish it with a joyful heart.

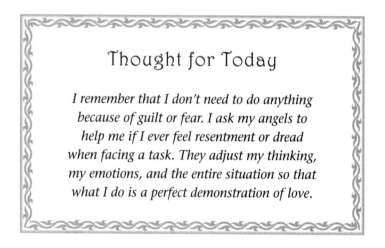

Thought for Today

I remember that I don't need to do anything because of guilt or fear. I ask my angels to help me if I ever feel resentment or dread when facing a task. They adjust my thinking, my emotions, and the entire situation so that what I do is a perfect demonstration of love.

Honor Your Sensitivity

*Y*ou respond deeply to different energies, and you may have been confused about whether you were feeling someone else's emotions or your own. Sometimes life seems so intense that you even try to shut down your awareness. In other words, you're sensitive.

Today, we ask you to honor this quality as a gift to you and the world. Your acute awareness enables you to detect truth and integrity in relationships, as well as feel joy and love very deeply. Your receptiveness also helps you communicate clearly with us angels. You sense our presence and messages in your gut feelings. In addition, you take great care with other people's emotions—you're extra thoughtful, kind, and aware.

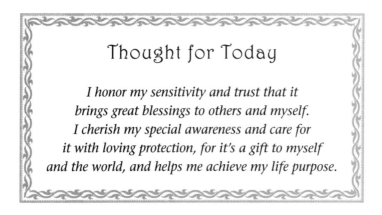

Thought for Today

*I honor my sensitivity and trust that it
brings great blessings to others and myself.
I cherish my special awareness and care for
it with loving protection, for it's a gift to myself
and the world, and helps me achieve my life purpose.*

114

Heal Disagreements

Not everyone is going to agree with your choices or the way that you handle situations. When someone takes issue with you, you may feel sad, angry, confused, or betrayed. You probably wonder why he or she thinks so very differently from the way you do. You may even question your own decision and wonder if the other person is right.

This situation is a demonstration that although all people share the same spirit and light on the inside, everyone is unique in human terms. Liking or loving someone comes from focusing on the similarities between you, which can sometimes blind you to noticing the contrasts.

Yet in every relationship, there will be occasional differences of opinion. It's not the disputes that matter, but the way you handle them. If you can have the grace to accept that another person thinks differently from you, then you've come a long way on the spiritual path of learning and growing.

Healing occurs within you first, and then spreads to the relationship. No matter what the other person does, stay true to your own Divinity. Your spiritual growth doesn't depend on changing people; rather, it involves learning to see the light within others, no matter what.

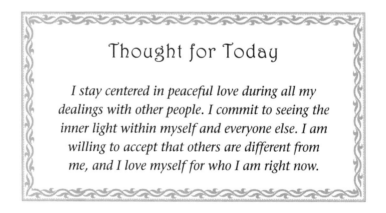

Thought for Today

I stay centered in peaceful love during all my dealings with other people. I commit to seeing the inner light within myself and everyone else. I am willing to accept that others are different from me, and I love myself for who I am right now.

Take Your Time

*Y*ou've become so accustomed to rushing to meet all of your responsibilities that it's almost an ingrained habit to go fast. Yet scurrying from one task to the next doesn't win any contests or engender peace of mind—rather, it keeps your focus on the future, instead of on enjoying the present moment.

Reading this message is one way that you're taking good care of yourself. You're nourishing your soul and creating healthful new outlooks, but we angels want you to make more of an effort to move less quickly throughout the day.

Accomplishing what you need to *and* taking your time aren't mutually exclusive activities. You can get a lot more done when your energy and mood are soaring with the vigor that comes from enjoying yourself. This happiness is built on noticing the beautiful, funny, and poignant features of your day—and that requires taking your time so that these details become clear.

You can also ask others to help you with your needs and responsibilities, and that includes requesting assistance from us. Enjoy your time today!

Thought for Today

I take my time and approach my day with wonder and delight, noticing the rich fabric of each moment. It's okay for me to slow down, as I can accomplish all that I need to at a leisurely pace.

Light a Candle

There are wonderful reasons why candles have been used in spiritual ceremonies since ancient times. Their light uplifts the energy and senses of everyone who sees them and is much closer to natural sunlight than the artificial illumination in most homes and offices. This is one explanation for why looking at a candle is energizing, much like spending time in the bright outdoors can be.

Candlelight sparks the imagination, so stare into a flame as a focal point for meditation and visualization. You can also light candles to celebrate or commemorate something, since they serve whatever purpose you set for them.

Today, light a candle with heartfelt intention. As you place the flame of a match to the wick, think of your intention (such as someone's health, world peace, prosperity, and so forth). Light as many of them as you have aims, and look at each one while holding prayers for what you want. As you extinguish the flame later, be sure to thank the candle for its support.

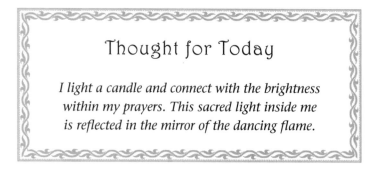

Thought for Today

I light a candle and connect with the brightness within my prayers. This sacred light inside me is reflected in the mirror of the dancing flame.

117

Create or Tend to Your Altar

It's important to have personal space where you can pray and meditate. This doesn't need to be a formal location, just someplace where you feel comfortable and can close your eyes without distraction. It can even be the corner of a room used for other purposes.

Creating an altar in this sacred space will inspire you to meditate. Use a flat surface—a tabletop, for example, or a shelf—on which you can place objects that have meaning for you or inspire peaceful feelings. You may want to include items representing nature, such as feathers, shells, or crystals. It serves as a focal point for prayer and meditation, and over time it becomes imbued with deeply spiritual energy.

Begin making your altar today. If you already have one, tend to it by reviewing the things that it holds. Do you feel guided to remove any of the items, or place new ones on it? As you work with your altar, notice the feelings that it awakens in you. Connect with it as you would a dear old friend, and it will serve you loyally each day.

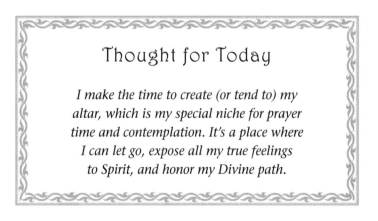

Thought for Today

I make the time to create (or tend to) my altar, which is my special niche for prayer time and contemplation. It's a place where I can let go, expose all my true feelings to Spirit, and honor my Divine path.

Heal Insecurities

At times you feel insecure about your worthiness and wonder if you're lovable. You worry that no one really cares for you, or even likes you, and you feel all alone. These are the occasions when we stand closest beside you, shielding you from your own outpouring of painful emotions. If these energies were allowed to surround you, they'd attract hurtful situations that weren't of your conscious choosing.

Because you work closely with us angels and have asked us to guard you emotionally, we'll even protect you from yourself upon occasion. In your human terms, at times "you're your own worst enemy," because when you feel unlovable, you begin to attract circumstances and relationships that confirm that belief.

It's destructive to indulge in self-pitying thoughts and emotions, yet we understand that every human being succumbs to them sometimes. Insecurities are akin to slipping while rock climbing: The moment you catch yourself falling, it's important to call for aid and reach for your lifeline.

We're here to catch you whenever you fall. However, your free will dictates that if you wish to suffer with miserable perceptions of yourself, even God can't do anything to interfere. We stand by, sending you loving rays of hope, but unless you accept these gifts, they slide right off of you.

Call upon us at the very instant that you become aware of hurtful thoughts or feelings. We'll buoy your faith that you're completely lovable, likable, and worthwhile just for being who you are right now. And that's a fact!

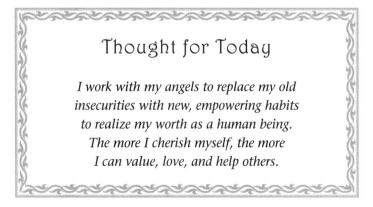

Thought for Today

I work with my angels to replace my old insecurities with new, empowering habits to realize my worth as a human being. The more I cherish myself, the more I can value, love, and help others.

119

Turn Around Nervousness

The word *nervous* implies that something is wrong with your nerves. Yet it actually means that your sensory system is healthy, simply working overtime. When you experience this emotion, you're akin to a wild bird who's anxiously on the lookout for predators—you feel like prey and are ever-watchful of your own safety.

The only "predator" in your life is your fear, which doesn't protect you in any way. Rather, it exhausts your nervous system and places you in positions that reinforce your feelings of dread. The only way out of this cycle is to soothe yourself with both a physical and emotional approach.

Begin with the physical, as that's the most concrete place to start. Once your body relaxes, it's easier to quiet the mind, so we angels ask you to take steps toward unwinding today. We'll guide you individually on the method that's best suited for your schedule, preferences, temperament, and so on. When you receive strong inclinations to stretch, exercise, go outdoors, drink more water, eliminate toxins, take baths, receive massages, and the like, please know that these messages are coming from us, acting as your physical therapists.

As you focus on relaxing your body, we'll simultaneously assist you in soothing your emotions. Begin by breathing deeply throughout the day, sending your breath to any muscles that feel tense. Exhale any sense of danger, and inhale a feeling of security and peacefulness.

You are safe, dear one—we watch over you and your loved ones, just as you ask us to. It's okay for you to let go.

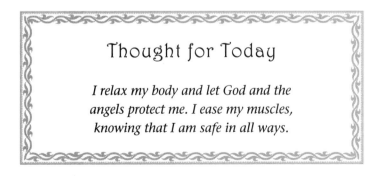

Thought for Today

*I relax my body and let God and the
angels protect me. I ease my muscles,
knowing that I am safe in all ways.*

Believe in Your Dreams

*Y*our dreams may seem daunting and overwhelming at times, and you worry about how you'll achieve them. As you wonder how to bring what you want into your life, your feelings may vacillate between elation (as you imagine your desire) and fear (as you worry about whether it can be accomplished).

This seesaw of emotions is a mirror of your dream's fruition. In other words, as you fluctuate between feeling positive and negative, so does your goal surge toward you and then away from you. And while pure optimism may be too much to ask when you see no evidence to support it, scientists have now demonstrated what we angels have always known: Feeling positive yields health benefits, including a longer life expectancy. Today we will reinforce how beneficial holding an optimistic viewpoint really is.

Even when you're filled with doubts, we always have faith in you. We know that you're capable of doing whatever you decide upon. The magic is yours, as it is for everyone—just believe!

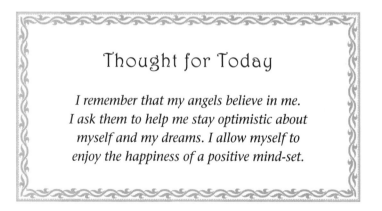

Thought for Today

*I remember that my angels believe in me.
I ask them to help me stay optimistic about
myself and my dreams. I allow myself to
enjoy the happiness of a positive mind-set.*

121

Keep Plugging Away

Some of your dreams require your time and energy, and it's easy to get distracted and procrastinate. Yet at the same time, your heart is tugged by the desire for completion. These meaningful aims are called "priority projects"—internally driven undertakings that your soul is guiding.

Keep plugging away at these important goals. If you ask for our assistance, we'll clear your calendar and give you the necessary space, time, and motivation. We can help you overcome the tendency to put things off by lending our support to heal your underlying fears.

Just ask, and we'll aid you in finding creative ways to enjoy working on your projects. While the fulfillment of your life's mission is important, the journey along the way is equally essential to your soul.

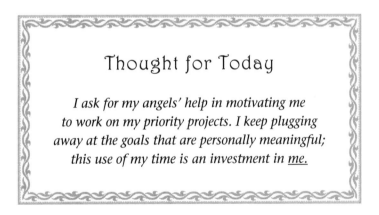

Thought for Today

I ask for my angels' help in motivating me to work on my priority projects. I keep plugging away at the goals that are personally meaningful; this use of my time is an investment in <u>me.</u>

Leave the Details to God

Beloved one, we angels see you worry about making progress in your life. We're here to reassure you that your every prayer is overseen by powerful beings who are at work on your behalf. All the details of these efforts are inconsequential and certainly not worth worrying about.

Yes, it's true that you feel more in control of your life when you know what's happening. But understanding has many levels, depending on whether you focus on lower- or higher-energy issues. The lowest level occurs when people believe that they must take away from others in order to meet their needs. This is based on the belief that there's a limited supply and competition is necessary.

The highest level, in contrast, is best described as "joyful faith"—a carefree and true surrender to the Divine. People with this focus understand that once a prayer has been made, God is in charge of all the details and will guide them to take action (if necessary) to help things along. This is true teamwork with Spirit.

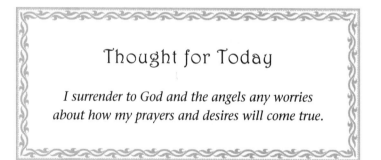

Thought for Today

I surrender to God and the angels any worries about how my prayers and desires will come true.

Follow Your Inner Guidance

You're eternally connected to God, Who is everywhere. This bond is within you, located in an area you call your "gut feelings." If you listen to and follow these internal twinges, they'll pull you closer to heaven.

Your sixth sense is 100 percent accurate all the time, since it's an extension of God's perfection. When you seem to veer off the right path, remember that it's just a momentary detour and not a lost cause, since your intuition can never be broken . . . it can only go unheard. Even then, your gut feelings remain as accurate as ever.

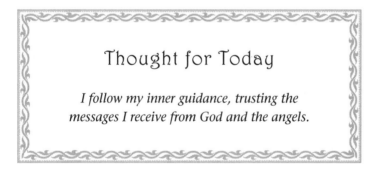

Thought for Today

I follow my inner guidance, trusting the messages I receive from God and the angels.

124

See the Innocence Within Everyone

Inside of everyone is an innocent child of God who's doing the best that he or she can. Sometimes these children cope with being afraid by acting in ways that seem to hurt themselves or others, but beneath their fear burns the pure light of Divine love.

The more you focus on the innocence within yourself and others today, the more you see evidence of everyone's innate Godliness. Your purpose here on Earth is to remember and teach love, and you can begin by noticing it.

The phrase *thoughtless behavior* actually means actions that are rooted in fear instead of caring. Seeing the innocence within those people who seem to exhibit lack of concern brings healing energy. Your love can break the cycle of fear-based actions.

Witness and feel the wide-eyed child within everyone, especially yourself. This innocence is precious . . . it is God.

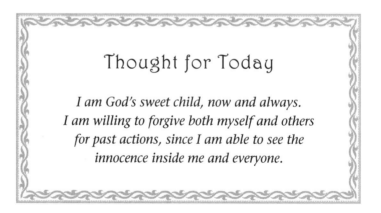

Thought for Today

I am God's sweet child, now and always.
I am willing to forgive both myself and others
for past actions, since I am able to see the
innocence inside me and everyone.

125

Notice the Light Within Each Person

Inside of you is a light that can never be extinguished or soiled—it's pure and clear, and its embers are stoked by love. The warm feelings that you enjoy are fueled by this internal spark.

Take a moment right now to see the flame within you, noticing details such as its colors, intensity, and size. Perceive how your body feels as you focus on this inner glow. Ask the light any question that comes to mind; and receive its answer clearly as a thought, feeling, word, or visual image.

This radiance is your connection to the Divine, and you're its caretaker; you can increase its size and intensity with your thoughts, emotions, and breathing. Pay attention to how you feel as it grows brighter and larger. It can burn away the remnants of old pain or upsets like an incinerator, so toss anything that's unwanted onto the flame, and witness its transformation into fuel for love.

Notice the illumination within you and others throughout the day. The more you focus on it, the more lighthearted you'll feel.

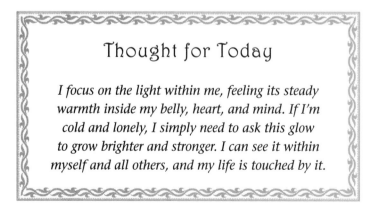

Thought for Today

I focus on the light within me, feeling its steady warmth inside my belly, heart, and mind. If I'm cold and lonely, I simply need to ask this glow to grow brighter and stronger. I can see it within myself and all others, and my life is touched by it.

Use Only Positive Words

The shaping of a new positive habit requires reinforcement and practice, and this is your focus today. This important point has been addressed previously and will be revisited throughout the year.

You already know that the words you choose have a profound effect on your experiences, carving out the nature of your relationships, health, finances, and so forth. There's no need to fear this power; instead, view it as you would an awesome and beautiful mountain range. Your ability to create with words is a natural wonder, so cherish, own, and honor it.

Begin today with the intention of using only positive speech . . . and remember that we angels will help you with this if you ask. You can always use love-based language to clearly communicate with others, and your uplifting words are a healing balm to all who hear or read them. They're magical instruments of the Divine—proven tools given to you by God—so use them well today.

Thought for Today

I speak with love. All of my speech is life affirming, and I ask my angels to communicate through me today. If I find myself using negative words, I pause and begin again with positive ones.

127

Visualize Your Highest Potential

Begin your day by imagining what your life would look and feel like if you were living it at your highest potential. Take a moment right now to see and sense all the rich details along your true self's path.

Such visualizations are an important starting point, much like mapping out your destination before beginning a journey. Yes, there will be lovely detours and side trips along the way, but your goal is always to be at your very best.

Today, ask your higher self for guidance about what it would like to do, knowing that it's entirely connected to God's infinite wisdom.

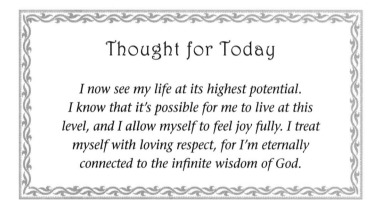

Thought for Today

I now see my life at its highest potential. I know that it's possible for me to live at this level, and I allow myself to feel joy fully. I treat myself with loving respect, for I'm eternally connected to the infinite wisdom of God.

Feel Rich

*Y*our financial situation, like other areas of your life, is influenced by the emotions you carry within you. Your abdominal region is the base location of your inner light—the seat of manifestation—and the feelings that you hold there affect its brightness and strength.

When you think about your finances, relax your gut and feel this illumination grow larger and more radiant. Positive thoughts, combined with a brilliant, high-intensity inner light, result in rapid manifestations. The reverse is also true: Fearful ideas about money trigger tightening in your muscles, which thwarts the light's ability to shine and manifest.

Imagine that you're fabulously wealthy today. Feel in your core (and all throughout your body and emotions) that you're completely financially secure. Allow your stomach to relax, and see your inner flame ignite with the fuel of your faith. Know that when you feel rich, you *are* rich.

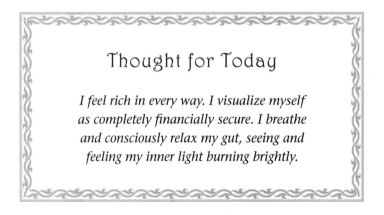

Thought for Today

*I feel rich in every way. I visualize myself
as completely financially secure. I breathe
and consciously relax my gut, seeing and
feeling my inner light burning brightly.*

Complete a Project

Imagine how great it would feel to finish up a project. What's the first task that comes to mind? Make time today to complete this endeavor as a gift to yourself.

Your inner self smiles with appreciation when you devote time to its priorities. Reward yourself upon completion of your chosen activity, and know that you're capable of doing anything you set your mind to.

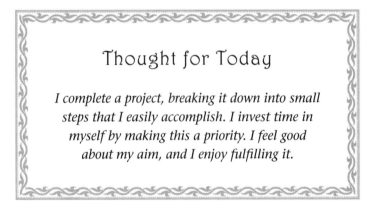

Thought for Today

I complete a project, breaking it down into small steps that I easily accomplish. I invest time in myself by making this a priority. I feel good about my aim, and I enjoy fulfilling it.

Practice Nonjudgment

Judgment is the action of using words to divide things into categories—it's your ego's method of simplification. Your higher self, in contrast, uses *discernment,* which involves adhering to feelings of attraction or repulsion toward the energies of a person, item, or situation.

Judgment says, "This is bad" or "This is good," while discernment states, "I'm drawn to this situation" or "These circumstances don't appeal to me." One divides and separates, while the other works with the law of attraction.

Today, practice nonjudgment in every situation and relationship. Allow others to be themselves and to act differently from you. Be gentle in your thoughts, and view yourself through the lens of compassion.

Honor the feelings that pull you toward—or push you away from—various situations. This discernment will serve as your trustworthy mentor.

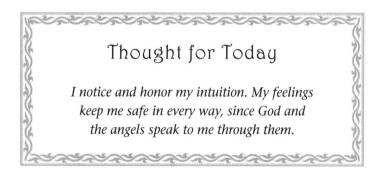

Thought for Today

I notice and honor my intuition. My feelings keep me safe in every way, since God and the angels speak to me through them.

Use Kind Words

The tender words you say to others are keys that unlock their hearts, as this kindness conveys caring in a practical way. Even a person who is closed to love because of previous pain will respond positively to compassion.

Today, look for opportunities to express this feeling in your conversations, using words that are gentle, sincere, warm, and thoughtful. These are qualities that you naturally possess but become even more aware of when you express them. Know that every kind word spoken today is a gift to both the speaker and the listener.

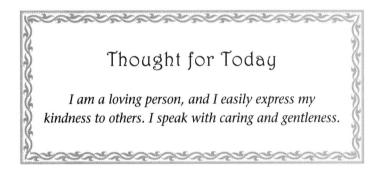

Thought for Today

I am a loving person, and I easily express my kindness to others. I speak with caring and gentleness.

Receive Good Graciously

As you speak positive words and shine your light brightly, all your good thoughts come true before your eyes. Today, we angels will work with you to help increase your receptivity to these manifestations.

You were raised to equate gifts with good behavior, so when they appear in your life, you wonder whether you deserve them. However, if you hold guilt over past actions, you may feel unworthy of what comes to you and unwittingly push it away or ignore it.

Beloved one, these manifestations aren't rewards any more than painful experiences are punishments. The Divine doesn't judge in categories of "good" or "bad"; rather, it responds to your energy—exactly as it does to everyone else's.

When you allow yourself to receive, you make a powerful statement to the universe. You display caring for yourself and everyone who's inspired by you, sealing the process of manifestation. Love comes full circle, from the seedling of a loving thought all the way to your gratitude when it appears on the physical plane.

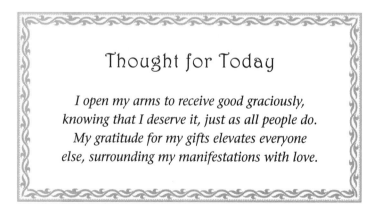

Thought for Today

*I open my arms to receive good graciously,
knowing that I deserve it, just as all people do.
My gratitude for my gifts elevates everyone
else, surrounding my manifestations with love.*

Rest

You've been a dedicated and willing lightworker for many lifetimes. You generously give help to loved ones and strangers around the clock, including during your dream time. We angels thank you for your dedicated service—and now it's time for *you* to receive.

This is a day for you to relax, so if possible, clear your appointments and take it easy. If your responsibilities call you to action, we'll accompany you and help you work at a gentle pace. Ask us to assist you in getting some rest today and tonight and we'll surround you with protective energy so that there are no interferences.

Slow down today, beloved one. Rest easy.

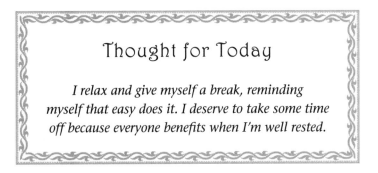

Thought for Today

I relax and give myself a break, reminding myself that easy does it. I deserve to take some time off because everyone benefits when I'm well rested.

Notice the Sounds of Nature

The rhythmic sounds of the outdoors help you synchronize with the universe's heartbeat, boosting your ability to be in the right place at the right time. We angels are enlisting nature's help to connect you to her music.

Notice the noises that are all around you today: leaves rustling in the wind, birds chirping, rain, thunder, or ocean waves. Feel your breathing and pulse move in time with these sounds. Listening to recordings of nature can also help in this endeavor.

Since you're part of the earth, it's only natural for your body to join in the beautiful rhythm of Mother Nature's symphony.

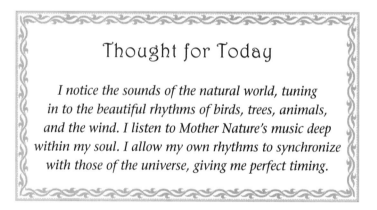

Thought for Today

*I notice the sounds of the natural world, tuning
in to the beautiful rhythms of birds, trees, animals,
and the wind. I listen to Mother Nature's music deep
within my soul. I allow my own rhythms to synchronize
with those of the universe, giving me perfect timing.*

Honor Your Promises to Yourself

Of all your promises, the ones you make to yourself are the most important. The relationship you have with yourself is very much like that of a parent and child, so when you fulfill these obligations, you nurture and honor who you are.

Recall a pledge that you've made to yourself and resolve to keep it today. This may involve taking just one small step in the direction of your commitment, but no matter how far you get, your inner self will feel gladdened and more alive from this form of care.

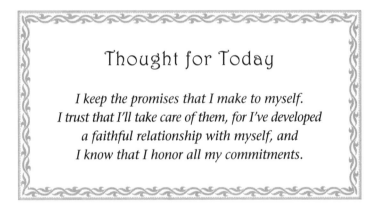

Thought for Today

*I keep the promises that I make to myself.
I trust that I'll take care of them, for I've developed
a faithful relationship with myself, and
I know that I honor all my commitments.*

Say Thank You

The words *Thank you* are essential ingredients in your recipe for health, peace, and the manifestation of everything you desire. Saying, thinking, or writing this phrase immediately increases your energy levels, so practice expressing it throughout the day. Speak the words quietly, loudly, or even silently as you feel guided.

Notice the ripple effect that occurs as you give thanks, from the swelling of your own heart with warm gratitude to the responsive smile of others. And we angels add our heavenly appreciation for your willingness to be a messenger of this gift today: Thank you.

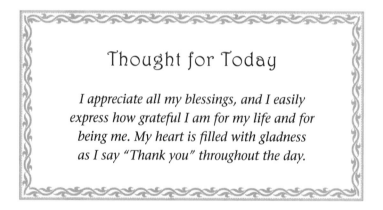

Thought for Today

I appreciate all my blessings, and I easily express how grateful I am for my life and for being me. My heart is filled with gladness as I say "Thank you" throughout the day.

Spend Time in Nature

We angels have been counseling you to spend time outdoors among the trees, plants, birds, and fresh air because we can see the therapeutic benefits for your body, mind, and soul. You've heard our promptings, and you feel the longing to commune with nature. We'll help you put this energy into action today. No matter what else you have planned, we suggest that you spend some time in a natural setting. Even if you live or work in the city, there are still parks, trees, and grass that you can visit.

Nature releases the tension that comes from straining to match up with the timetable of too many calendars and schedules. You aren't a machine like a clock or a watch, and pushing yourself to meet deadlines pulls you out of your natural rhythms and causes you to feel fragmented, awkward, or disoriented.

Today, allow the outdoors to heal the pressures and tension in your life and revive your sense of self. Recapture your instinct for good timing by placing your feet on the earth, leaning against a tree, and breathing fresh air.

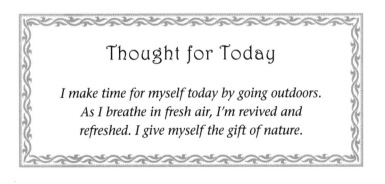

Thought for Today

I make time for myself today by going outdoors.
As I breathe in fresh air, I'm revived and
refreshed. I give myself the gift of nature.

Express Your Inner Child

We angels have been guiding you in self-parenting methods to care for the child within you, who has needs and feelings exactly like any other, including the desire to express playfulness and spontaneity.

We'll work with you today in co-parenting this bright light within you, allowing *you* to shine more radiantly. Your energy levels will return to normal, and your enjoyment of life will increase.

Let's begin by taking a moment to interview your inner child. Silently, aloud, or in writing, please ask:

- "How are you feeling right now?"
- "What would you like to tell me?"
- "How can I help you?"
- "What do you need from me?"

Now that you've listened to your inner child's desire to be nurtured, spend the day caring for it. As you fill this part of yourself with love, your entire being grows happier and more peaceful.

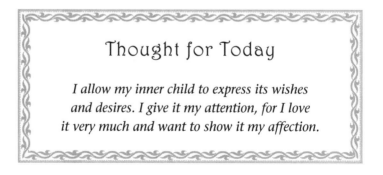

Thought for Today

I allow my inner child to express its wishes and desires. I give it my attention, for I love it very much and want to show it my affection.

Honor Your Accomplishments

We angels have been with you since infancy, celebrating your triumphs and helping you through your struggles. We want you to know how proud we are of you and how far you've come.

You've taken the high road repeatedly, putting the development of your character above all else. We applaud the many times that you've acted lovingly and helped others without any need for recognition. We commend you for your commitment to living your life from a spiritual standpoint. You've worked through many issues and learned a great deal, and we've loved you at every moment along the way.

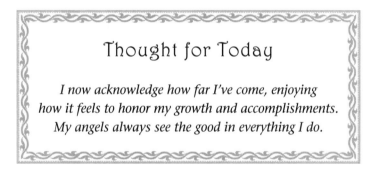

Thought for Today

I now acknowledge how far I've come, enjoying how it feels to honor my growth and accomplishments. My angels always see the good in everything I do.

Make Three Wishes

Today, think of three wishes you have for yourself or another person. (Of course, you hold the power to make an infinite number of desires materialize, but let's begin with three.)

What's the first desire that comes into your mind? Speak it aloud to infuse it with the power of your words. Feel excitement and gratitude at the thought of it materializing, and then let it go so that God's infinite wisdom can transmute it into its highest form. Then continue this process with two other dreams.

As you recall your wishes throughout the day, imagine them surrounded with pink light. This seals them in loving energy, where they can safely manifest into material form.

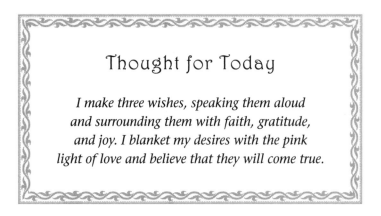

Thought for Today

*I make three wishes, speaking them aloud
and surrounding them with faith, gratitude,
and joy. I blanket my desires with the pink
light of love and believe that they will come true.*

141

Make a Healthy Change

If you could snap your fingers and change one thing in your life, what would it be? The first item that comes to mind is an issue that needs to be addressed. Your soul is craving a change, and your inner self is waiting for you to do something about it.

Taking care of yourself sometimes means entering the abyss of the unknown. Yet as you hold the intention to improve your situation, know that you are supported completely.

Today, move in the direction of manifesting your desired change. Taking a step of any size sets the entire universe into motion on your behalf, as it matches any action that you take with a large contribution to your cause.

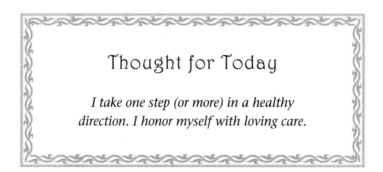

Thought for Today

I take one step (or more) in a healthy direction. I honor myself with loving care.

Detach from Drama

*Y*our life purpose rests on remembering and teaching love. Anything that pulls you away from the awareness of this emotion is a tool for learning, as soon as you recognize it.

When conflict threatens your peace of mind, recall that you have the power to choose whether or not to engage in drama. You can be a caring and supportive person without taking part in negative thinking or fear-based behavior, since your steady love and inner harmony acts as a calming influence.

We'll help you stay centered today, if you ask us to. Hold the intention of detaching respectfully from any drama that may present itself today.

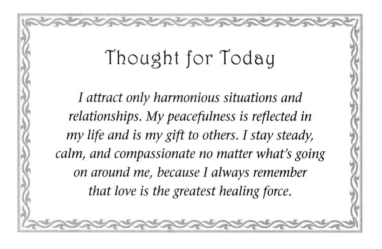

Thought for Today

I attract only harmonious situations and relationships. My peacefulness is reflected in my life and is my gift to others. I stay steady, calm, and compassionate no matter what's going on around me, because I always remember that love is the greatest healing force.

Love Yourself Unconditionally

We angels love you without judgment or conditions, because we always see you as a pure being of the Divine. You're God's offspring, just as we are, so in that way we're family—and the same holds true for all forms of life on this planet.

We care for you unconditionally because we're patient and have complete faith in you. We lovingly witness the choices and decisions you make, knowing that all paths lead you back to God.

Today, do your best to love yourself with no reservations. Look past any apparent errors, and embrace a vision of your Divinity. Your unconditional love melds with ours to form a truly supportive stance that elevates you to the next level . . . and beyond.

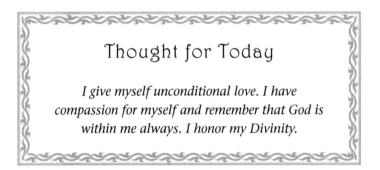

Thought for Today

I give myself unconditional love. I have compassion for myself and remember that God is within me always. I honor my Divinity.

Notice Love All Around You

The universe provides steady reminders of love, and those who pay attention know that this emotion is everywhere—there's so much to joyfully celebrate! Noticing this is a simple route to happiness.

Today, make it a point to observe examples of caring . . . someone's helpfulness, for instance, or a child's affection. As you see these reminders, drink in the delicious energy being created, and nourish yourself with its warmth.

Love is all around you, today and every day.

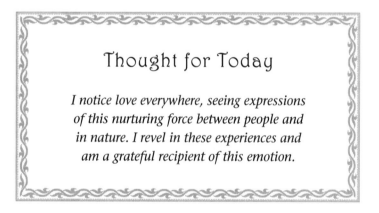

Thought for Today

I notice love everywhere, seeing expressions of this nurturing force between people and in nature. I revel in these experiences and am a grateful recipient of this emotion.

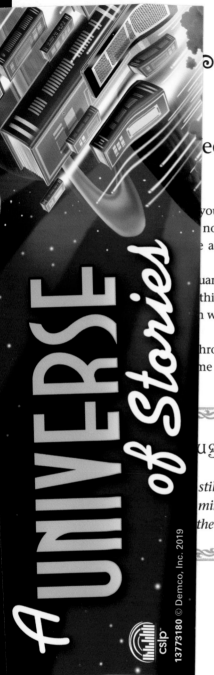

...ect Stillness Within You

...you where you can retreat and enjoy perfect
...noise, chaos, and anxiety resides in this inner
...e and refresh yourself, drinking in the silent

...uary through your willingness to be at peace.
...thing deeply can help you rapidly reach this
...n within you is a natural and simple process . . .

...hroughout the day. When you go to this place
...me to the heaven within you.

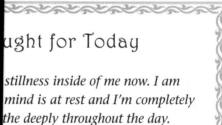

...ught for Today

...stillness inside of me now. I am
...mind is at rest and I'm completely
...the deeply throughout the day.

Connect with God in All That You Do

As a child, you took great pride in doing things on your own, and self-sufficiency continues to be a source of joy for you. Yet a lack of reliance on other people is far different from independence from God.

You're eternally connected to the Divine—it's only in your imagination that a separation is possible. The infinite love, wisdom, and abundance of heaven is available to you continuously upon request . . . your free will prevents God from imposing help upon you. When you ask for assistance, you're automatically connected to an unlimited storehouse of gifts, much like all that's available when you log on to the Internet.

Remember this connection in everything you do. With every task, decision, and question, turn to heaven. As God's trustworthy messengers, we angels will help you remember to do so, and we'll clear your channels of Divine communication, if you ask us to.

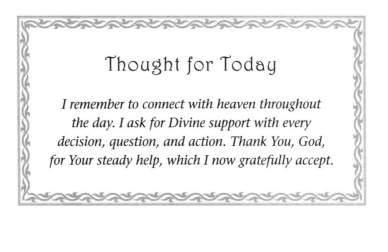

Thought for Today

I remember to connect with heaven throughout the day. I ask for Divine support with every decision, question, and action. Thank You, God, for Your steady help, which I now gratefully accept.

Know That You Are Eternally Loved

We have always loved you, since your soul's inception long ago. You were born as God's perfect creation, and our affection for you has never wavered. We'll continue to be with you throughout eternity, forever by your side.

You're eternally cherished, dear one. You've earned this just by virtue of being a child of the Divine. You don't need to do anything else to prove or deserve this favor—it's already yours forever.

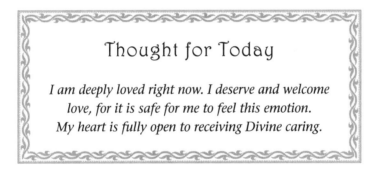

Thought for Today

I am deeply loved right now. I deserve and welcome love, for it is safe for me to feel this emotion. My heart is fully open to receiving Divine caring.

148

Visualize a Successful Day

Imagine yourself enjoying success in every situation today. See yourself smiling and having fun as everything goes your way. Feel the emotions of elation and joy as every door opens for you, and know that others are inspired by your triumphs.

Visualize having a rewarding day as a gift to yourself. Your positive expectations are seeds planted in your favor, which will successfully grow into uplifting experiences.

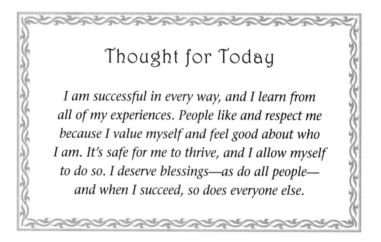

Thought for Today

I am successful in every way, and I learn from all of my experiences. People like and respect me because I value myself and feel good about who I am. It's safe for me to thrive, and I allow myself to do so. I deserve blessings—as do all people— and when I succeed, so does everyone else.

149

Choose Peace

If conflict arises around you today, you can opt for peace instead. There's an old aphorism that says "Choose your battles wisely." Well, you can decide to forgo fighting completely!

Today, pick peace instead of conflict. You don't need to participate in any situation where power struggles ensue. Rather than adding a raised voice to a dispute, summon Divine guidance through your prayers of harmony, which are more helpful in bringing about creative solutions.

Today, embrace peace in all your endeavors.

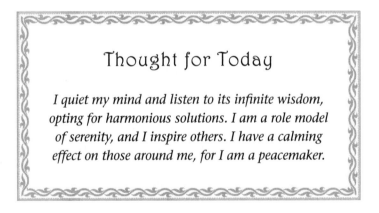

Thought for Today

I quiet my mind and listen to its infinite wisdom, opting for harmonious solutions. I am a role model of serenity, and I inspire others. I have a calming effect on those around me, for I am a peacemaker.

Take Excellent Care of Your Body

*Y*ou already know the changes that you'd like to make with respect to your body and physical health. We angels will work with you today to put them into action.

Perhaps you wish to exercise more, modify your diet, or give up an addictive substance. Whatever your goal, we stand by as your private coaches, personal trainers, and healers to encourage you on your path. The point isn't to alter all of your habits in one day, but rather to take steps in the desired direction. We'll work together as your support team, cheering you on from the sidelines.

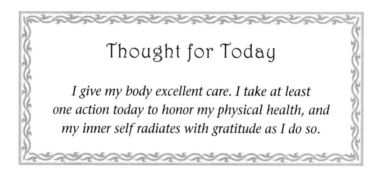

Thought for Today

*I give my body excellent care. I take at least
one action today to honor my physical health, and
my inner self radiates with gratitude as I do so.*

Release Worries about Your Loved Ones

All people have guardian angels continuously watching over them, and that definitely includes your loved ones. Instead of worrying about your friends or family members, ask for additional angels to be by their side—the moment that you do so, your request is granted.

The greater the number of us angels surrounding you or someone else, the more a person is insulated by love. This force shelters you and those you care about against storms and turbulent currents, helping with happiness and safety.

Right at this very moment, we're watching over your loved ones. Give any cares or worries you may have about them to God, and know that through your prayers, we angels are protecting them.

Thought for Today

My loved ones are watched over by God and the angels, and I give my cares and worries to heaven. Thank you, Divine ones, for watching over my loved ones—in particular, _____.

Take the Next Step

*Y*ou've been praying and wondering about the next step to take in the direction of your life's purpose. We angels are here today to reassure you that any action counts, just as every bit of money that you put in the bank adds up.

The universe responds to your efforts and matches them with its own contributions. Each action that you take creates an energetic ripple effect, and this outpouring is then counterbalanced with incoming energy.

This means that any attention you give to your life's purpose is meaningful and will yield positive results—so take one small step today as you're guided. Give any worries about whether it's the "best" or "right" one to us, and we'll reassure you that you're on your way.

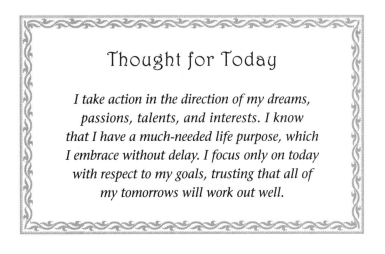

Thought for Today

I take action in the direction of my dreams, passions, talents, and interests. I know that I have a much-needed life purpose, which I embrace without delay. I focus only on today with respect to my goals, trusting that all of my tomorrows will work out well.

153

Let Your Angels Help You

We angels have discussed the topic of free will with you previously, reiterating how and why you must ask for our help before we can offer it to you. Remember that we welcome your continual requests for assistance, so don't ever worry about overwhelming us. We're beings of communication and service, and we revel in these activities. The more that you ask for our support, the more we all work together in unison—and our teamwork moments are our greatest joy.

We want to help you with everything, beloved one! Please remember to enlist our aid throughout the day.

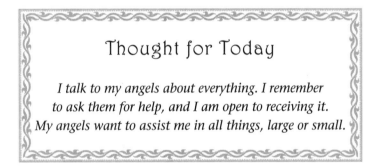

Thought for Today

*I talk to my angels about everything. I remember
to ask them for help, and I am open to receiving it.
My angels want to assist me in all things, large or small.*

Know That You've Found What You're Looking For

$e$verything that you desire is already found the moment you think of it. Your wishes transmit messages to the universe, much like sending away for something in the mail. After you order a product, you trust that it will be delivered to you shortly, and so it is with your thoughts: Each one manifests its mirror image in a brief amount of time.

Instead of searching for what you want externally, concentrate on developing mental pictures of your desires. Surround these images with feelings of security, gratitude, and faith; and know that what you've been looking for is on its way to you right now.

Don't worry about how something will come to you any more than you'd concern yourself with all the details of how your mail-order package was handled en route. Just as the postal service takes care of its end of the process, so too will the universe do its part. Your role is to open the door when your wish arrives and enjoy the fruits of your positive thoughts.

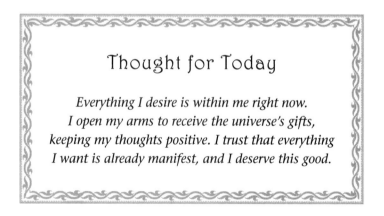

Thought for Today

Everything I desire is within me right now.
I open my arms to receive the universe's gifts,
keeping my thoughts positive. I trust that everything
I want is already manifest, and I deserve this good.

155

Accept Heaven's Love

God's love for you is so profound that it exceeds the bounds of words. To have an inkling of how much you're cherished, try to envision an all-encompassing, limitless energy. In heaven, every thought of you is positive, because God only sees your magnificence and Divinity, reveling in your perfection.

As your angels, we mirror this bright love for you—we also care about you more than words can describe. We're thrilled to be by your side, and helping you is our honor.

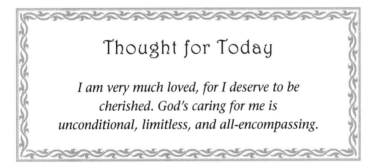

Thought for Today

I am very much loved, for I deserve to be cherished. God's caring for me is unconditional, limitless, and all-encompassing.

Work with Your Angelic Teammates

We angels hear and appreciate your every prayer, as each one is an invitation to become more involved with your life. The moment that you request our help, we take action—often behind the scenes, where you're not consciously aware of your words manifesting into form.

Today, we'd like to bring your attention to the topic of teamwork. To understand this discussion, think of the analogy of a sports team. In basketball, the ball is thrown from player to player according to which person is closest to the net, who has a clear shot, or who specializes in a certain move.

When you pray, you make the first pass of the ball, and we always catch it. As we work on what you've asked for, we throw the ball back and forth between the spiritual and physical dimensions—it's always in motion, coming ever closer to the basket, which you're standing next to. And when the prayer is manifest, we give the ball to you so that you can sink it into the net. If you refuse to catch it because of fears that you don't deserve it, can't handle success, or any other insecurities, then the ball drops.

We hope that this will help you understand manifestation of prayers. We're a team, and we depend on you to throw us the ball to initiate each session and catch it in the end for the win. If you're aware of resistance within yourself, we'll help you open up to receive.

With great compassion and love, we ask you to let us assist you more often. We love you!

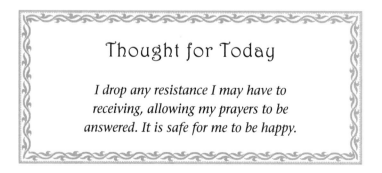

Thought for Today

*I drop any resistance I may have to
receiving, allowing my prayers to be
answered. It is safe for me to be happy.*

Trust in Divine Timing

Often a series of actions and reactions must occur in order for your prayer to be answered, especially if several people are involved. This phenomenon is called "Divine timing," and it's similar to the stages necessary for a seed to sprout. Yes, this process can be rushed to a degree, but there's still an incubation period for both prayers and plants to appear in material form.

Please have patience and continue to nurture your desires with love, positive thoughts, and guided action. Know that your prayer is being manifested even as you read these words. Divine timing ensures that your wish arrives at exactly the right moment. Sometimes you only become aware of this fact in retrospect, after the prayer materializes—but with faith you can have this understanding right now.

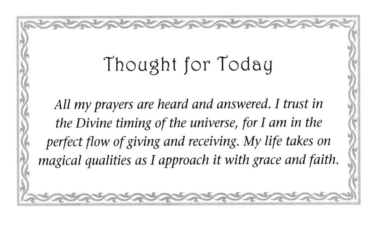

Thought for Today

All my prayers are heard and answered. I trust in the Divine timing of the universe, for I am in the perfect flow of giving and receiving. My life takes on magical qualities as I approach it with grace and faith.

Acknowledge Your Accomplishments

Beloved one, you've come far in your learning and understanding. You've put a great deal of effort into this process and have accomplished much already. We commend you for this and encourage you to acknowledge your accomplishments as well.

When a mountain climber pauses midway up the peak to enjoy the view, his or her energy and motivation are revitalized—and so it is with you. Yes, you have your eyes upon higher goals, but you can still gain a lot from stopping for a moment to recognize all that you've done so far.

Today, honor yourself for your accomplishments. Even if you feel that they're just humble beginnings, your inner self appreciates the attention.

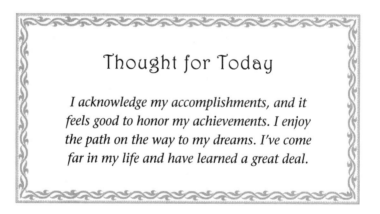

Thought for Today

I acknowledge my accomplishments, and it feels good to honor my achievements. I enjoy the path on the way to my dreams. I've come far in my life and have learned a great deal.

Set Down Your Burdens

Set down the weight of your burdens, beloved one, and give every care and worry to God. There's no need for you to struggle with fears when so much support is available to you.

Let the Divine take care of any concerns today. Inhale deeply, and as you exhale, give your troubles to God, Whose infinite, loving wisdom will unravel any complications and replace pain with peace.

Release tension, and allow heaven to do what it does best: love you.

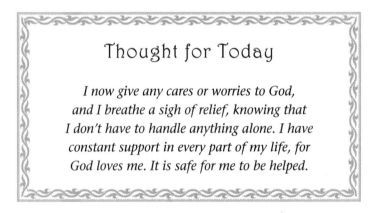

Thought for Today

*I now give any cares or worries to God,
and I breathe a sigh of relief, knowing that
I don't have to handle anything alone. I have
constant support in every part of my life, for
God loves me. It is safe for me to be helped.*

Open Your Arms to Receive

The universe is constantly giving to you in ways both small and large. When someone offers to assist you, buys you lunch, or hands you a gift, open your arms to receive. The more that you say yes to blessings, the more the universal energy freely flows to and through you. When you push away proffered help, you close the door to this abundance.

Today, open your arms to welcome any gifts that come your way, and say yes to the universal flow. Allow yourself to be helped, loved, and pampered . . . let yourself receive.

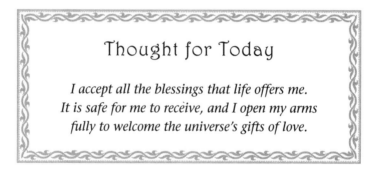

Thought for Today

*I accept all the blessings that life offers me.
It is safe for me to receive, and I open my arms
fully to welcome the universe's gifts of love.*

See Everyone as Prosperous

How you see other people has an enormous impact on your self-perception. When you view another person as prosperous, you then see the abundance within yourself.

Regardless of outward appearances, notice prosperity in all people today. You're doing them and yourself a great favor, since it's the energetic equivalent of handing out gifts of money to everyone you meet (including yourself).

This is a bountiful universe, with plenty of provisions for everyone. The valve of prosperity is only switched on for those who notice it—that is, to people with a prosperous mind-set. You develop this by seeing abundance wherever you go.

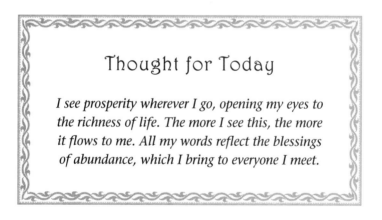

Thought for Today

I see prosperity wherever I go, opening my eyes to the richness of life. The more I see this, the more it flows to me. All my words reflect the blessings of abundance, which I bring to everyone I meet.

See Everyone as Healthy

*Y*our viewpoints about the health of those around you have the same impact as your reflections on prosperity—that is, the way that you see others' well-being will affect your own. When you regard people as vibrant, vital, and perfect, this perception radiates onto your own physical body. You bestow the gift of health when you look at others in this way.

Health is everyone's natural state . . . it's how God created all men and women. When you see an individual's wellness—regardless of outward illusions—you're witnessing the Divine within that person.

Today, see and express healthfulness wherever you go, focusing on this spiritual truth within everyone. The love inside you and others stokes the flame of well-being, causing it to grow larger and more prominent in the lives of all people.

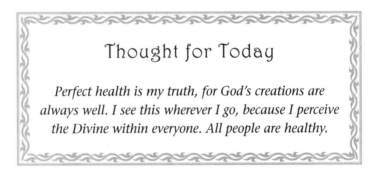

Thought for Today

Perfect health is my truth, for God's creations are always well. I see this wherever I go, because I perceive the Divine within everyone. All people are healthy.

Ask for Help

You're never alone, especially in times of great need. If you feel lonely or sad, we angels stand even closer to you, for we're always nearby and ready to assist you whenever you ask. Occasionally, however, you forget about our presence and attempt to endure life single-handedly.

Today, remember to ask for spiritual help in all situations, beginning from the moment you get out of bed. Request guidance as you dress, drive, walk, and exercise, and in every encounter with other people.

Ask others to lend a hand as well. Your family members, friends, co-workers, and even strangers feel needed and appreciated when you allow them to assist you, and your inner self is nurtured when you let people aid you in carrying the load. The loving energy that's emitted from each team of helpers and the people they bless bathes the entire planet in peace.

It's just as important to receive as it is to give. Make it a point to ask for assistance, and permit yourself to accept it with appreciation and joy.

Thought for Today

I remember to ask for guidance from my angels.
It's a sign of strength that I allow them and other
people to support me. I receive help graciously.

Lean Upon Us

We angels are a stable foundation in your life, and you can always count on us to be there for you. When other circumstances seem unpredictable or to fluctuate, you can always be sure of our unshakable presence and support.

We're dependable because we never forget that God's caring is all there is. We don't waver in our love, and our energy never falters. We're always assured that this emotion is present everywhere, so we're eternally peaceful.

Lean upon us when you need stability. Know that we're trustworthy friends who stick by you through everything. We love you no matter what . . . you can count on us!

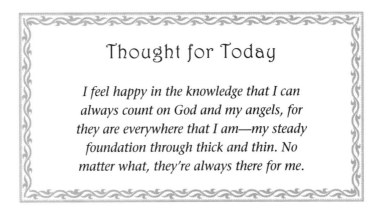

Thought for Today

I feel happy in the knowledge that I can always count on God and my angels, for they are everywhere that I am—my steady foundation through thick and thin. No matter what, they're always there for me.

Say Kind Words

We've emphasized the power of your spoken and written words, describing the tremendous potential for manifestation within each one. Today, we'll focus on the energy of kindness within what you say.

Your compassion conveys a gentle and supportive form of love. Its energy is uplifting and nurturing, both for the giver and the receiver. When caring words are conveyed, a heart connection forms, joining everyone involved. It's an alliance of love where everyone who speaks or hears the kindness bathes in its healing power together, forging an intimate bond.

Speak kind words throughout the day. Enjoy the double gift that it affords you and all others.

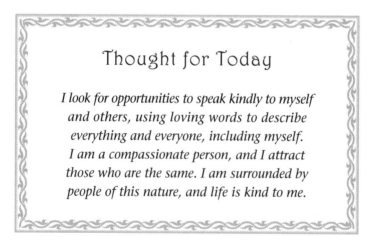

Thought for Today

I look for opportunities to speak kindly to myself and others, using loving words to describe everything and everyone, including myself. I am a compassionate person, and I attract those who are the same. I am surrounded by people of this nature, and life is kind to me.

Elevate Your Frequencies

Your energy frequency is influenced by your thoughts, words, and lifestyle. There are many benefits to increasing it, including faster rates of manifestation and healing, clearer Divine communication, and a greater sense of peace and happiness. Today, we'll begin working on elevating this frequency to higher levels.

Take a moment to center yourself through your breath, quieting your body and mind. Hold the aim of seeing or feeling your energy-frequency level. Don't worry if you don't know what this means, as your intention will take you there.

Notice any impressions you receive. Do you see any colors; feel certain temperatures; or perceive other images, thoughts, or feelings? Whatever comes to you is correct, so please trust your accuracy.

Send the exhalations of your breath to your energy frequency. Notice how this affects aspects such as its color or feelings. Sense your power increase with this breath and positive attention.

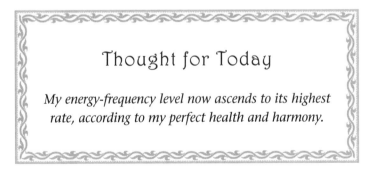

Thought for Today

My energy-frequency level now ascends to its highest rate, according to my perfect health and harmony.

Commune with the Nonphysical Frequencies of Color and Light

As you elevate your energy to higher levels, you'll naturally become more attuned to nonphysical frequencies. Conversely, you can also work with the nonphysical to help increase your personal energetic frequency. We angels want you to spend the next several days communing with energies that have such *metaphysical* origins (*meta* means "above").

Today, we'll work with color, which radiates various frequencies that your eyes register as green, pink, yellow, and all shades in between. These wavelengths can help you elevate *your* energy frequency.

Notice colors today, paying particular attention to how each one influences your mood, focus, or physical feelings. Observe how the shade of clothing, rooms, and such affect you. If you're attracted to a particular hue, then spend time looking at an object of that color. This will help you absorb its gift for you and become more attuned to nonphysical frequencies.

Thought for Today

I notice colors and sense how they affect me.
I discern the way my emotions, energy, and focus
are impacted by the various hues I wear and see. My
sensitivity to energy continues to become more refined.

Notice Sounds

Today we'll work with the nonphysical energy of sound to elevate your frequency. You've probably already noticed your heightened auditory awareness, which is a part of your elevated frequency. Your increased sensitivity allows you to hear the voices of us angels, as well as permitting you to be conscious of how sound affects you.

You're probably already aware of what type of music you're attracted to, as well as other personal preferences about volume and tone. Today, we ask you to tune in further and become acutely aware of everything that you hear internally and externally. Use your awareness to tease out all of the various sounds that blend together. Which do you find pleasant or unpleasant? How do they affect you physically and emotionally?

The more you become aware of sound's effect on you, the more your sensitivity levels can increase, which is part of your elevated energy frequency. We ask you to honor your receptiveness and know that it's truly a gift.

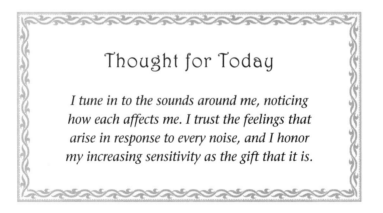

Thought for Today

I tune in to the sounds around me, noticing how each affects me. I trust the feelings that arise in response to every noise, and I honor my increasing sensitivity as the gift that it is.

Notice Fragrances

In continuing the focus on increasing your sensitivity to nonphysical components of your environment, we angels now want you to work with smell. Your olfactory senses register deeply within your most primal awareness.

Today, pay close attention to the fragrances and aromas in your environment; and notice how they affect your emotions, thoughts, and focus.

Introduce new scents into your surroundings, such as fresh flowers, essential oils, incense, and other pleasant aromas. As you elevate your energy frequency through tuning in to fragrance, you'll find that your overall sensitivity increases in positive ways.

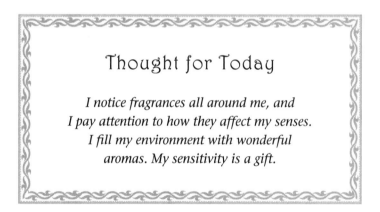

Thought for Today

*I notice fragrances all around me, and
I pay attention to how they affect my senses.
I fill my environment with wonderful
aromas. My sensitivity is a gift.*

Feel Subtle Energies

Today we'll focus on your sensitivity to other subtle energies. You can slowly run your hand close to your body and feel the power that it radiates. Every person, animal, and place emits vibrations—they're the feelings that you sense around individuals and in the rooms or other environments that you walk into.

Your body discerns this energy as high, medium, or low level (or some setting in between). If the vibrations feel higher than your own, you'll very likely perceive the situation as pleasant; if they feel lower, you probably won't care for it.

Today, notice your feelings in response to other people, animals, and locations. Run your hands over plants and objects, and sense the energies that they emit. Enjoy the sensation of your increasing frequency, which is the basis of your natural spiritual gifts.

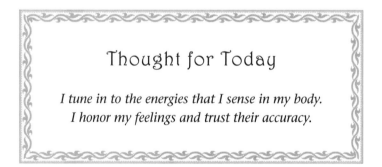

Thought for Today

I tune in to the energies that I sense in my body.
I honor my feelings and trust their accuracy.

Clear Yourself

With increasing sensitivity comes self-responsibility for managing any energies that you may absorb. Just as you bathe to remove residue from your physical body, it's also necessary to energetically purify yourself. And as many ways as there are to wash yourself physically, so are there a variety of methods for cleansing your energetic self.

We'll guide you today in clearing away unwanted energies. However, we remind you that we can only do so if you first ask, so call upon us for help. You can clear physical and energetic toxins by enjoying a hot bath with natural sea salts. Live plants (either potted or in the ground) and crystals can also assist you in this process, just by being close to you.

Any intention that you have to detoxify yourself will always be successful, so please don't worry about whether you're doing it right. Notice the lightness and increased energy that you feel after this clearing.

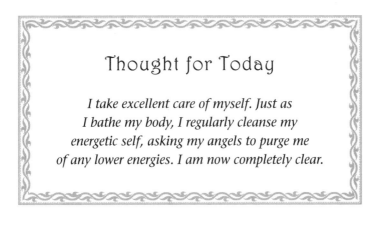

Thought for Today

*I take excellent care of myself. Just as
I bathe my body, I regularly cleanse my
energetic self, asking my angels to purge me
of any lower energies. I am now completely clear.*

Shield Yourself

This is a safe world, and there's no need for fear of any kind. As we angels discuss shielding today, we're not referring to armoring yourself. What we're talking about is more like the common sense of putting a raincoat on before stepping outside on a drizzly day. And just as you wouldn't don outerwear in fear, there's no need to feel afraid when you safeguard yourself.

There are many ways to watch over yourself. You can invoke a basic shield by visualizing yourself surrounded by white light. This protective glowing energy is a love without form—it's our life force. Since white light fades over time, you'll need to envision it surrounding you two or three times daily. As you continue to do so each day, we'll guide you to work with other colors, along with different methods of shielding.

Notice your mood before and after invoking the white light. Through the shielding process, you'll feel safe to fully open your spiritual gifts.

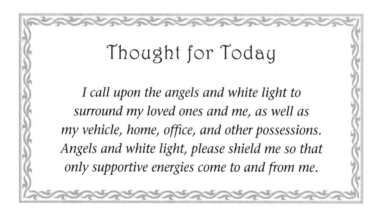

Thought for Today

*I call upon the angels and white light to
surround my loved ones and me, as well as
my vehicle, home, office, and other possessions.
Angels and white light, please shield me so that
only supportive energies come to and from me.*

Appreciate Yourself

We angels have been with you a long time, we understand you very well, and we want you to know that we appreciate you. You've developed wonderful listening abilities, and your heart has compassionately opened up to others. You give with love and receive with gratitude. Well done!

Today, we guide you to appreciate yourself. Even above all that you've accomplished and learned, give yourself praise for being who you are. You shine God's light so radiantly, and you're a joy for all to behold. Take some time to honor yourself and spend time in your own illuminating company.

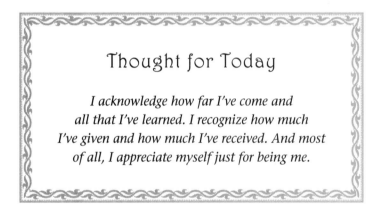

Thought for Today

*I acknowledge how far I've come and
all that I've learned. I recognize how much
I've given and how much I've received. And most
of all, I appreciate myself just for being me.*

Trust Yourself

*Y*our inner compass accurately steers you in the direction of your dreams and desires. Trust the guidance that you receive, since it comes directly from the infinite wisdom of God and helps you move toward the happiness that is heaven on Earth.

When you're joyful, your light shines more brightly, and you inspire others to be cheerful themselves. Trust your inner feelings, ideas, and visions, as they're God-given tools designed to lead you home in peace and happiness.

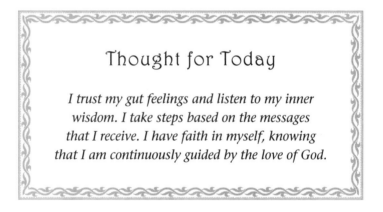

Thought for Today

I trust my gut feelings and listen to my inner wisdom. I take steps based on the messages that I receive. I have faith in myself, knowing that I am continuously guided by the love of God.

175

Explore New Avenues of Creativity

Creativity helps you learn and grow. The objective is to express yourself, which means allowing your light to shine, as well as communicating and releasing pent-up feelings.

Today, explore new avenues for creatively expressing yourself. Anything that you don't normally do will work: Try singing in the shower, making a flower arrangement, redecorating a room, dancing, or taking photographs. How you express yourself is secondary to the fact that you do so.

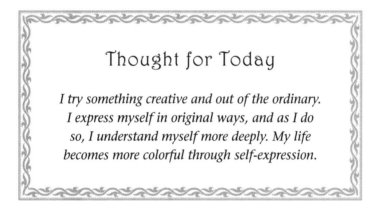

Thought for Today

I try something creative and out of the ordinary. I express myself in original ways, and as I do so, I understand myself more deeply. My life becomes more colorful through self-expression.

176

Nurture Yourself

The inner you relies on your outer self for nurturing, so care for who you are, and be very gentle with yourself throughout the day. Take your time as you get dressed, eat, walk, or drive—easy does it.

Nurture yourself with positive and supportive self-talk, because your soul thrives on praise and compliments. Frequently tell yourself "I love you," either silently or aloud. As you give yourself affection, you open yourself further to receiving more of it.

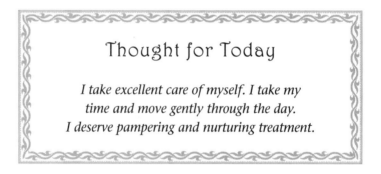

Thought for Today

I take excellent care of myself. I take my time and move gently through the day. I deserve pampering and nurturing treatment.

Visit an Etheric Healing Temple

Imagine a healing temple that's bathed in rainbows of colored light and filled with beautiful illumination and peaceful energy. See and feel yourself visiting this sanctuary.

Loving healers invite you to lie down upon a soft bed surrounded by crystals. You immediately feel comfortable and at peace while they direct rainbow-colored lights toward you. As you breathe, you feel warm, nurturing energy enter your body.

Any heaviness that burdened you is lifted away, and you feel deeply relaxed and lighthearted. Continue receiving this healing treatment as long as you want, and know that you can return to this sanctuary as often as you desire.

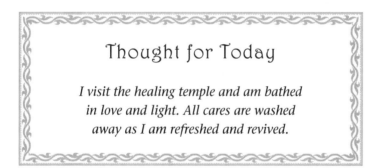

Thought for Today

I visit the healing temple and am bathed in love and light. All cares are washed away as I am refreshed and revived.

Affirm That You're Wholly Lovable

*Y*ou're wholly lovable for being who you are right now. The opinion that you hold of yourself or that others have of you is irrelevant in the face of the fact that you're a perfect child of God. Nothing about you can ever be broken or wrong. You've always been—and will always be—heaven's perfect creation.

Don't let yourself be fooled by the illusions that the ego may portray. Your higher self (and everyone else's) is eternally connected to God, and thus always loves you, wants the best for you, and sees the goodness within you.

Know that you deserve to be wholly cherished. You don't need to earn God's affection . . . it was bestowed upon you before your creation and will remain eternally yours, no matter what.

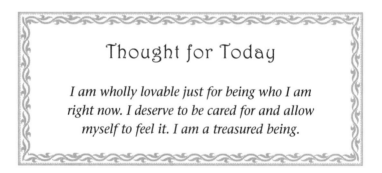

Thought for Today

I am wholly lovable just for being who I am right now. I deserve to be cared for and allow myself to feel it. I am a treasured being.

179

Know That There's Nothing to Fear

Beloved child, have no worries, as God's love protects you and your loved ones, now and always. There's nothing to fear . . . give us angels your cares and troubles, and relax in the peaceful knowledge that you and those close to you are safe.

We watch over you with vigilance, ever ready to spring into action on your behalf. Anytime you feel worried, afraid, unloved, or alone, please talk to us. You can speak aloud, silently, or in writing. Our conversations will help you release these burdens, allowing us to go to work to support you.

There's nothing to fear, now or in the future. You're covered in a shielding blanket of God's love—so rest easy.

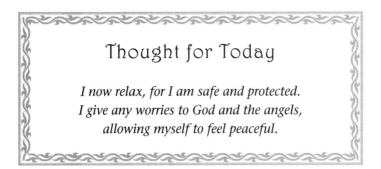

Thought for Today

I now relax, for I am safe and protected.
I give any worries to God and the angels,
allowing myself to feel peaceful.

Know That Your Future Is Safe

As we angels peer into your future, we see many fulfilling, happy, and meaningful moments in store for you. You have a number of alternative paths available to you, including experiences with varying degrees of learning. You can guide yourself to the happiest course by staying in constant communication with us, giving us steady permission to assist you with everything.

Breathe easy, relax, and let down your guard, because your future is safe. We won't disappoint you.

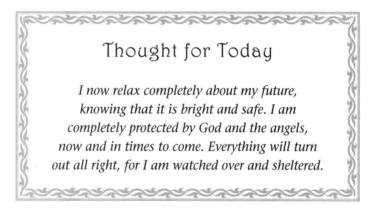

Thought for Today

I now relax completely about my future,
knowing that it is bright and safe. I am
completely protected by God and the angels,
now and in times to come. Everything will turn
out all right, for I am watched over and sheltered.

Manifest Abundance

Since you've asked us angels to help you increase your financial flow, we'll work on manifesting abundance today. You've already completed an important first step in the right direction by collaborating with Spirit.

The next step is for us to help you adjust some of the "settings" of your thoughts, beliefs, physical feelings, and emotions about money. We'll do this in partnership with you.

To begin this process, please find a comfortable reclining position, and say:

God, archangels, and guardian angels,

Thank you for clearing away any fears that I may have about receiving the

Divine flow of abundance that is ever present for everyone.

Thank you for helping me open my heart to receive.

Thank you for clearing away any old anger
or resentment from my consciousness.

Thank you for helping my muscles relax.

I am now at ease and open to receiving.

I am grateful and at peace.

Enjoy the nurturing energies that you feel. Any quivers that you experience in your physical body are positive signs of releasing and healing.

182

Affirm That It's Safe for You to Receive

To continue our work on manifesting abundance, we angels will work more on your receptivity. Each day you have many opportunities to receive: People might ask if they can help you, give you a compliment, or offer to buy you lunch.

Look for gifts that come to you throughout the day. Say yes to all of these presents, accept them with a "Thank you!" and know that you deserve them.

Give us any fears or guilt you may feel about this process, and let us help you enjoy receiving. As you continue to accept these daily gifts, the universe responds by increasing their flow to you.

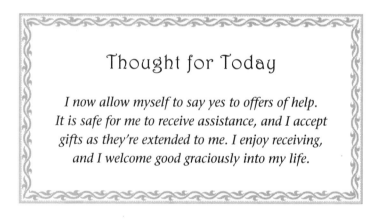

Thought for Today

I now allow myself to say yes to offers of help. It is safe for me to receive assistance, and I accept gifts as they're extended to me. I enjoy receiving, and I welcome good graciously into my life.

Trust

This is a safe universe that's completely filled with love—it's everywhere that you are, filling every space where you travel. The more you look for evidence of your security, the more you'll find it. We angels watch over you continuously, always guiding and protecting you.

Trust this world and your experiences within it. Have faith in yourself, including your gut feelings, dreams, and desires. Let down your guard, relax, and enjoy the playground of life.

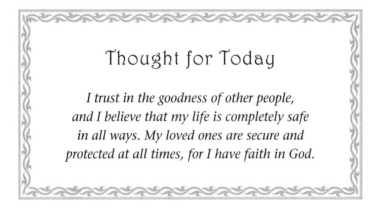

Thought for Today

*I trust in the goodness of other people,
and I believe that my life is completely safe
in all ways. My loved ones are secure and
protected at all times, for I have faith in God.*

Feel Loved

Love is omnipresent, meaning that it's everywhere around and within you. It's who you are—your Divine heritage and makeup.

You may have had a hurtful relationship that triggered a distrust of love. You associated it with pain and concluded that it wasn't safe. You decided to reduce the amount that you could feel, believing that this would prevent you from suffering. We angels can help you heal your heart so that you feel able to love again. We're next to you at all times, and you can ask us to elevate the energy of your interactions with other people. We'll guide your relationships to help you feel safe and protected.

It's impossible to completely block out love. Your soul's very life force is one of tender awareness. The more you're conscious of this emotion, the more you feel alive!

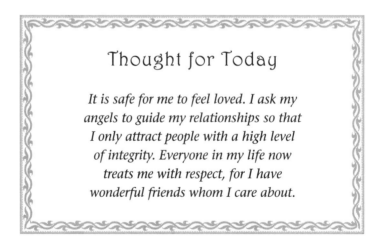

Thought for Today

It is safe for me to feel loved. I ask my angels to guide my relationships so that I only attract people with a high level of integrity. Everyone in my life now treats me with respect, for I have wonderful friends whom I care about.

Let Go

There's no need to struggle with anything. The solution to any seeming problem—indeed, everything you desire—flows gracefully.

Struggle is based on fear, which sends up jagged energy points that create barriers in the flow, like a river that suddenly has to go over sharp rocks. That's one reason why worry slows down your manifestations. When you let go of your concerns and give them to God, things can come smoothly and quickly to you once again.

Today, let go of all issues that make you feel tense. You can do this by writing them down in a list addressed to God and us angels and asking us to help you release them. Your simple willingness to do this brings great benefits.

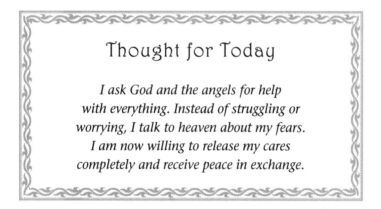

Thought for Today

*I ask God and the angels for help
with everything. Instead of struggling or
worrying, I talk to heaven about my fears.
I am now willing to release my cares
completely and receive peace in exchange.*

Know That Love Is Who You Are

God is pure love, and this is the only feeling that exists in heaven. Since you're the result of one of the Creator's thoughts, your soul was conceived and made with Divine caring.

Your physical self is only one small aspect of who you are. Your soul exceeds any limitations that your body may seem to have . . . it's eternally connected to God and, therefore, to love. You continuously swim in a sea of this warm feeling, which you both give and receive.

Today, be extra aware of your true nature, expressing your God-given affection to yourself and others. Experience how this helps you feel more authentic and comfortable. You're very much cared for at each and every moment. It's who you are!

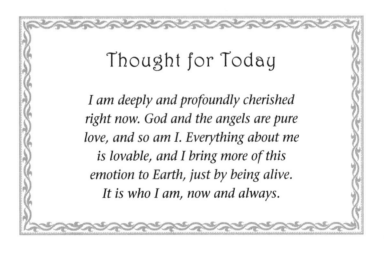

Thought for Today

I am deeply and profoundly cherished right now. God and the angels are pure love, and so am I. Everything about me is lovable, and I bring more of this emotion to Earth, just by being alive. It is who I am, now and always.

Forgive Yourself

$\mathcal{Y}$ou were made perfect by the one Creator, and you can never undo this Divine handiwork. There's nothing that you need to forgive in the ultimate sense, for you can never nullify the Creator's will of perfection.

Any regrets that you have are based on the dream that you could be anything but the purely loving being whom the Divine created. As you forgive yourself for what you think you've done wrong, you adjust your self-concept to mirror God's view of who you are. You can then understand why heaven loves you so much: There's only goodness within you.

Be willing to exchange old guilt or regrets today for knowing Divine love. This is the route to true and lasting peace.

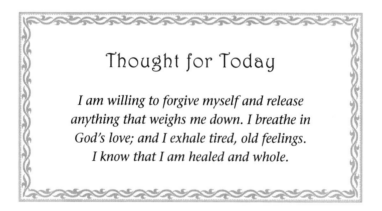

Thought for Today

I am willing to forgive myself and release anything that weighs me down. I breathe in God's love; and I exhale tired, old feelings. I know that I am healed and whole.

Know the Wonderful Truth about Yourself

*E*very adjective that you could use to describe heaven also applies to you, since you were fashioned in God's image. You're powerful in the sense that you have the strength to create and attract based on your words and desires . . . you're creative, just like the One Who made you. You're healthy and a healer—loving and loved—as well as being knowing, forgiving, nurturing, and so on.

The truth about you is all good news. Any negative thoughts you have about yourself are false and thus not worth the investment of your time.

Today, set the intention of thinking and saying kind things about yourself. Notice how these words help you feel the strength and joy of your true self. When you're positive, you're expressing who you really are.

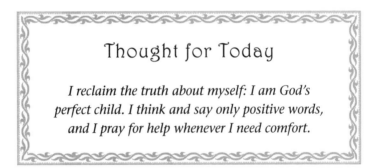

Thought for Today

*I reclaim the truth about myself: I am God's
perfect child. I think and say only positive words,
and I pray for help whenever I need comfort.*

Enjoy the Highest Energy

*Y*our source of energy is God within you, and this force is continuously available to elevate your spirits whenever you need a boost. You can tap in to it simply by closing your eyes, focusing within, breathing deeply, and holding your intention.

As you bring your attention inward, imagine a beautiful ball of light that constantly emits energy like the sun. This power plant inside you is always ready to increase your energy levels using only pure, natural love as its fuel, which is constantly regenerated. You'll feel replenished just by focusing on this source, and you can inhale to draw its energy upward and through your body.

When you tap in to your inner energy, you're working with the highest power of all.

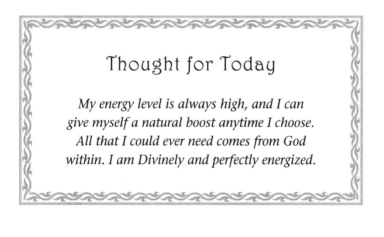

Thought for Today

My energy level is always high, and I can give myself a natural boost anytime I choose. All that I could ever need comes from God within. I am Divinely and perfectly energized.

Enjoy Unlimited Supply

Everything that you need is available to you right now. The universe is like a company that provides anything you could think of. When you contemplate a desire, the warehouse goes to work packing your order and preparing it for shipment. As long as you keep the same positive thoughts (or release them with faith to the universe), your "package" will arrive rapidly. However, if you should change your mind and think about a conflicting desire or feel afraid that your wish may not materialize, your delivery becomes delayed.

You can have whatever you'd like. You just need to determine what it is you want and have faith that it will come to you. We angels can help you refine your desires to their highest and purest levels, if you ask. Ultimately, though, these choices are your own.

When you request that your needs be met, there's still an abundant store left over, so your receiving good could never take away from anyone. You deserve to have your desires fulfilled, just as all God's children do—that's why the Creator has made sure that there is an inexhaustible supply, with plenty for everyone.

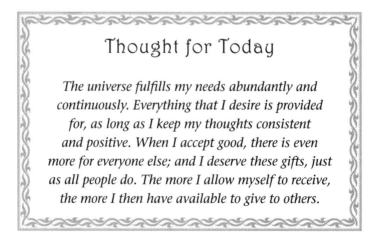

Thought for Today

The universe fulfills my needs abundantly and continuously. Everything that I desire is provided for, as long as I keep my thoughts consistent and positive. When I accept good, there is even more for everyone else; and I deserve these gifts, just as all people do. The more I allow myself to receive, the more I then have available to give to others.

191

Receive Guidance
about Your Life Purpose

*Y*ou often ask us for help identifying and working on your life's purpose. You have an important role to fulfill, as do all your brothers and sisters on Earth. You can't come here without one . . . just as each player in an orchestra helps create beautiful music, your part is needed for the overall global purpose.

When you ask about life aims, it means that you desire meaningful work that will support you financially, emotionally, spiritually, and intellectually. You want to spend your time engaged in activities that you feel genuinely passionate about because you want to make a positive difference in the world.

When *you* serve a purpose, life serves you in return—in other words, put your focus on rendering a service through your natural talents and interests. Let the universe take care of returning good to you.

Give a lot, and allow yourself to receive in kind. Share your time, love, support, smiles, and so forth. Bestowing gifts is like shining a light into a mirror: It always bounces back to you immediately. Just be sure that you allow yourself to receive.

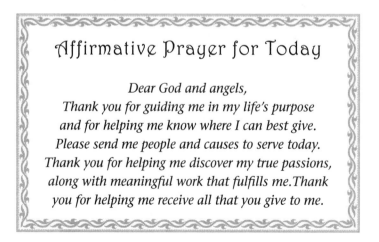

Affirmative Prayer for Today

Dear God and angels,
Thank you for guiding me in my life's purpose
and for helping me know where I can best give.
Please send me people and causes to serve today.
Thank you for helping me discover my true passions,
along with meaningful work that fulfills me. Thank
you for helping me receive all that you give to me.

192

Take Steps Toward Your Life Purpose

*Y*ou specifically want to know: *What should I do next on my life path?* The answer is to follow the inner wisdom guiding you to take vital action steps, such as making healthy lifestyle changes, contacting a particular person, reading a certain book, or taking a special class.

Life-purpose guidance is always given one step at a time. And as you complete each one, the next is revealed. Whatever message you're receiving, you'll know that it's an answer to your prayers when it's repetitive, uplifting, and positive in nature.

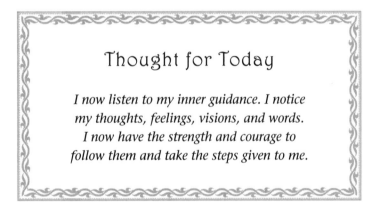

Thought for Today

*I now listen to my inner guidance. I notice
my thoughts, feelings, visions, and words.
I now have the strength and courage to
follow them and take the steps given to me.*

Make Healthy Life Changes

*Y*our desire to improve your life will involve making some changes. The natural resistance that you feel about this process is an ancient pattern among all human beings, yet there's another part of you that feels excited about beginning anew. Know that your push-pull feelings are entirely normal.

We angels are with you during every change that you implement, walking with you through each new doorway. Talk to us continually, for we can help you summon the motivation, courage, and energy to transform your life. We can also bring about the material support you need and help you discern the best choices to make.

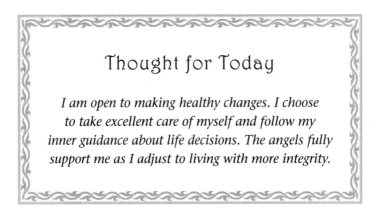

Thought for Today

I am open to making healthy changes. I choose to take excellent care of myself and follow my inner guidance about life decisions. The angels fully support me as I adjust to living with more integrity.

Bring Out the Best in Others

Everyone has a spark of genius and healing energy within them, which are gifts from God. You can help others awaken their spiritual endowments and inspire them to hold a more positive outlook.

To do so, see the beautiful light and goodness within everyone you meet. Keep your conversations filled with harmonious melodies, and don't allow yourself to be an instrument in any chorus containing sour notes. Use only positive and loving words.

Your own happiness is your greatest tool for helping and teaching. It's a profound energy that emits deeply healing rays of light that have an uplifting effect. There's no need for you to work at mending others, as your feelings of peace will accomplish this automatically. Hold the intention of being joyful, and let everything else take care of itself.

When you're happy, you bring out the best in yourself and others.

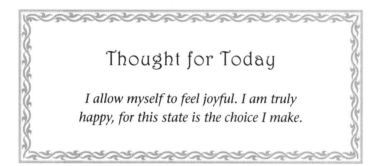

Thought for Today

I allow myself to feel joyful. I am truly happy, for this state is the choice I make.

Notice Signs from Above

We angels are in constant communication with you. You usually hear us through your gut feelings and intuition, but we also send you signs to help you understand and trust our messages. These help you know that what you're experiencing isn't your imagination or a coincidence, so notice the many signs that we send you today.

As you become more aware of them, you'll see that they're all around you. Some are physical, such as objects that you find or see; others are auditory, and they include verbal messages that you receive through other people and music.

Notice the running theme within these signs—they spell out complete messages and stories. Please ask us if you need help interpreting them.

Thought for Today

I notice signs from my angels. I readily understand what I see, hear, feel, and know in my heart. I trust the signals and feel confident that they're real messages from above. I remember to ask my angels for signs, and request their help in interpreting them.

196

Shift Yourself

If you find your energy or mood to be low today, remember that you can always shift yourself to a higher level. You have the power within your will, along with our help and assistance.

When you're stressed, your aura tightens and shrinks, which further compounds the slumps in your emotions and vitality. Call upon us angels to relax your aura so that it can stretch out farther and pump up your feelings of happiness and energy.

Anytime you want to transform yourself, just pause and decide that you'd like to be in a more enjoyable mood or have more energy—this choice is the starting point. Then as you inhale deeply, imagine yourself drawing in universal energy, taking in as much as you desire.

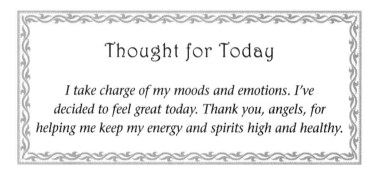

Thought for Today

I take charge of my moods and emotions. I've decided to feel great today. Thank you, angels, for helping me keep my energy and spirits high and healthy.

197

Make Time for Yourself

Beloved one, you're an angel upon the earth. You give lovingly and selflessly to others, and you receive much joy and satisfaction in return. But along with all of this generosity, we angels want to remind you to also take time for yourself.

All givers must recharge their batteries by setting aside intervals for simple pleasures and personal passions. Today we'll work with you to carve out time for yourself—it could involve something spontaneous or a fun activity just for you.

What's the first thing that comes to mind as you read these words? If there's a special pursuit that you've been craving, this is the day to address your desire. We'll support you fully so that you'll have the time and motivation to ensure that your needs are met.

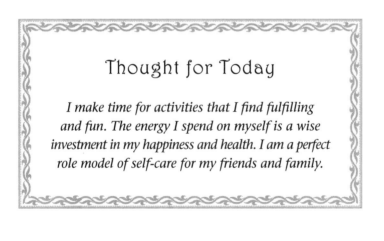

Thought for Today

I make time for activities that I find fulfilling and fun. The energy I spend on myself is a wise investment in my happiness and health. I am a perfect role model of self-care for my friends and family.

See Yourself Through Angel Eyes

Your opinion of yourself is often filtered through your own ego or someone else's. Yet this part of the self is afraid of light, so it only detects the shadows—and if you view yourself through this lens, you'll only see and feel darkness. It really doesn't matter what others think of you, as your spiritual truth can't be changed by anyone's opinion.

Today, see yourself through the eyes of us angels. We only perceive your higher truth and Divinity—you're as pure and holy as we are. Your soul is guiltless and perfect in every way, and you have valuable talents that are a true asset to this planet.

You're completely kind and loving, and we care for you very much.

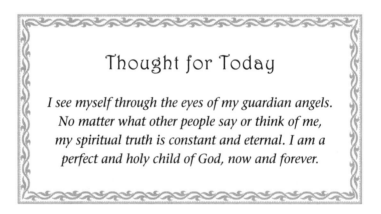

Thought for Today

I see myself through the eyes of my guardian angels.
No matter what other people say or think of me,
my spiritual truth is constant and eternal. I am a
perfect and holy child of God, now and forever.

See Other People Through Angel Eyes

The human ego is annoying—that's its very nature. It irritates you because it creates friction as it attempts to dissuade you from love. This ripple in the energy field is unpleasant.

You'll always be troubled if you pay attention to other people's egos, because you'll only notice the darkness and shadows. This focus leads to fears that goodness is a myth and you're alone and unloved. The only way out of this abyss is to view yourself and others through our angelic eyes. What you concentrate on is what you'll see, which is what you'll encounter.

If you'd like to experience a greater sense of love and feel more secure about yourself, then look past the ego. See beneath the annoying traits to the place where love and light reside within each person. Steadily gazing at this treasure chest within every individual will uncover a peacefulness that you'd long forgotten about.

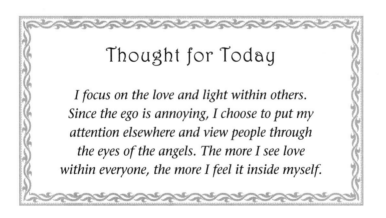

Thought for Today

I focus on the love and light within others. Since the ego is annoying, I choose to put my attention elsewhere and view people through the eyes of the angels. The more I see love within everyone, the more I feel it inside myself.

ᥰᥱ 200 ᥱᥰ

Uncover Your Greatest Treasure

*Y*our greatest treasure is easy to find and open . . . it's self-love. You've often heard people say that you can only care for others to the degree that you appreciate yourself. The truth underlying this statement is that loving yourself is the foundation for an open heart.

If you admire someone yet despise yourself, you won't value the affection that you give the other person. When you realize that this caring comes from God, you can feel the connection between yourself, your beloved one, and the Divine. This is what self-love is really all about: It doesn't mean believing that you're better than someone else, but rather that everything attractive you see in another person is a mirror of the beauty within yourself.

Today, focus on finding the loop of love extending from you to others, and to God. As you notice and feel this, you uncover your greatest treasure.

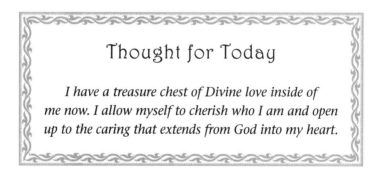

Thought for Today

I have a treasure chest of Divine love inside of me now. I allow myself to cherish who I am and open up to the caring that extends from God into my heart.

Make Crystal Clear Decisions

The path to manifestation begins with a crystal clear decision about what it is that you want. Your manifestations will be unclear until you make such a determination about your desires—it's impossible not to do so, since not picking something *is* a choice.

You may think, *Well, God knows what I want and need.* While heaven will give you input, decision making is a partnership. You pray and receive guidance that you can choose to follow, but without a clear-cut direction, you're like a driver with no destination in mind. Your decisions are your road maps.

Today, make a crystal clear choice about something that you desire. It could be carrying out life improvements, supporting a cause that you believe in, or something else that you feel guided to do. You don't need to know how to reach the goal or what actions to take . . . simply focus on the overarching dream. Once you do this, you'll clearly see which steps are necessary—and we angels are here for you all the way.

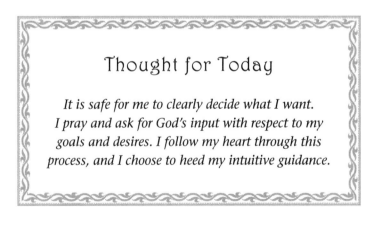

Thought for Today

*It is safe for me to clearly decide what I want.
I pray and ask for God's input with respect to my
goals and desires. I follow my heart through this
process, and I choose to heed my intuitive guidance.*

∽ 202 ∾

Find and Nurture Your Passions

There are activities and issues that make your heart sing with joy and a sense of purpose—these are your passions. You can find them by noticing the topics that interest you or that you frequently think about, and test-driving the activities that call to you. As with encountering a soul mate, you'll know when you come across your personal passion.

Once you discover what stirs you, find time to enjoy it. Such pursuits are the sweet rewards of life, helping you locate heaven on Earth. They're a vital investment that pays huge dividends in terms of increased energy, motivation, and inspiration.

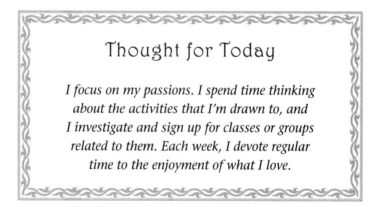

Thought for Today

I focus on my passions. I spend time thinking about the activities that I'm drawn to, and I investigate and sign up for classes or groups related to them. Each week, I devote regular time to the enjoyment of what I love.

Find Balance

An important part of your life's purpose involves making decisions about how to spend your time. With so many choices facing you, you may wonder how to achieve a balance: You feel the pressure to devote yourself to helping others, yet you hear an inner calling for self-care. You have responsibilities and duties to perform, but what about your obligation to your soul and your spiritual path?

These different demands aren't conflicting unless you believe them to be so. They actually intersect and dovetail perfectly together, one flowing into the other as the sunrise leads to the sunset. The first step in finding balance is to hold a positive mind-set, so call upon us angels and use affirmations to fill your mind with healing love.

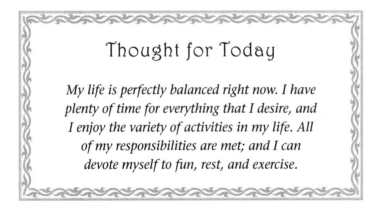

Thought for Today

My life is perfectly balanced right now. I have plenty of time for everything that I desire, and I enjoy the variety of activities in my life. All of my responsibilities are met; and I can devote myself to fun, rest, and exercise.

Enjoy Self-Responsibility

One reason why your life has felt unbalanced in the past has been your reluctance to accept complete responsibility for your happiness. The thought of being totally accountable to yourself brought up fears and pressures that you wanted to avoid.

You now realize that self-responsibility isn't a test that you can pass or fail. It literally means being responsive to your own core—after all, no one else can know what will make you happy.

Being true to who you are is as joyful and fulfilling as helping other people. Your inner self sends its love and appreciation to you for providing such good care.

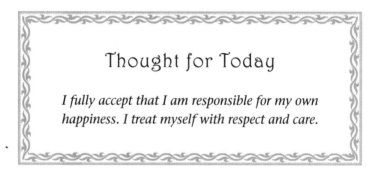

Thought for Today

I fully accept that I am responsible for my own happiness. I treat myself with respect and care.

Enjoy True Happiness

*Y*ou have deep and lasting happiness inside of you. This is the energy of God, the spark of love that's your origin and identity. You are joy.

When you feel happy, you're centered and are really being yourself. Contentment is an indicator that you're on the right path at the right time (even if you change your course as you go along). Genuine happiness comes from being true to yourself—it means self-honesty, authenticity, and integrity.

Put your focus on being real, in the sense of owning and living your truth. Throughout the day, pause and ask yourself, *Is this right for me?* and *How do I honestly feel about this?*

As you admit your emotions and desires to yourself, you shine with the peace that radiates from your true happiness.

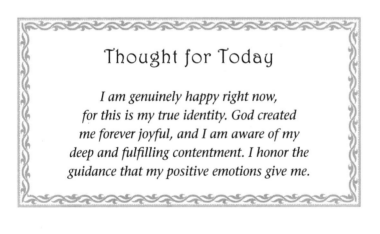

Thought for Today

*I am genuinely happy right now,
for this is my true identity. God created
me forever joyful, and I am aware of my
deep and fulfilling contentment. I honor the
guidance that my positive emotions give me.*

Know That You're Never Alone

We angels are with you always, forever seeing your goodness, purpose, and potential. We're by your side at all times. Know that you have steady friends in us, for our love and approval of you is unwavering. No matter what's going on, you can count on us. We understand all your motivations and decisions, and we love and accept you, just as you are right now.

You don't need to earn our favor in any way. We completely approve of you, because we know who you truly are: You're God's creative masterpiece, a shining example of all the colors of love.

You're never alone, dear one. We won't ever leave your side—we can't. Call upon us anytime, since it's our sacred honor to be with you and help you whenever you need assistance.

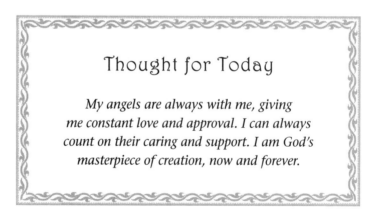

Thought for Today

My angels are always with me, giving me constant love and approval. I can always count on their caring and support. I am God's masterpiece of creation, now and forever.

Know That You're Always Loved

When you feel neglected or unlovable, it means that you're focusing on facades and illusions. The truth is that you're always cared for by all of heaven and every person, regardless of any appearances that would indicate otherwise.

God is all-loving and omnipresent. This means that Divine affection is everywhere—and everything that seems otherwise is a dark dream of fear. Since this is the truth of every person, it follows that all individuals truly care about you, and you feel the same way about them.

You needn't endeavor to be loved or lovable. In fact, this sort of strain implies that God's affection must be earned or forced, when in fact it's the most natural part of this world. Instead of trying so hard, simply allow your true self to come shining forth—the part of you that's happy and peaceful is God's love expressed through you. Everyone responds to this, because all people desire to remember heaven's embrace. Through your happiness, others find the Divine love and joy within themselves.

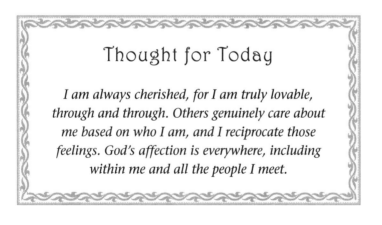

Thought for Today

I am always cherished, for I am truly lovable, through and through. Others genuinely care about me based on who I am, and I reciprocate those feelings. God's affection is everywhere, including within me and all the people I meet.

Fill Your Heart with Happiness

You have the right to be as happy as you choose. There's an unlimited supply of joy within you and this world.

Each day, you're presented with numerous choices that vie for your attention. What you decide to focus on is a reflection of what you want for your life. When you pick happiness, you then see many examples to support your selection. You begin to notice how much goodness, love, and thoughtfulness there is in the universe.

If you find your energy or mood dropping today, this is simply an indicator that you've chosen something that's not positive as your focus. Remember that you'll always find evidence to support whatever judgment you hold of yourself, other people, or the world. Which opinion would bring the most happiness to you and others?

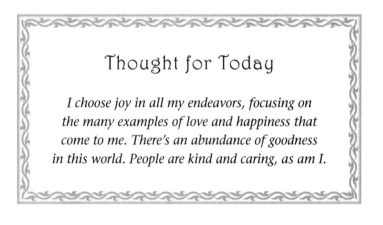

Thought for Today

I choose joy in all my endeavors, focusing on the many examples of love and happiness that come to me. There's an abundance of goodness in this world. People are kind and caring, as am I.

Enjoy the Healing Power of Nature

*Y*our beautiful sensitivity has drawn you outdoors to commune with nature, where you feel the exquisite aliveness radiating from every plant, tree, bird, and animal. Your soul and body are illuminated by the earth's embracing rays of love. As you sit on a rock, grass, sand, or soil, you can feel the planet continuously emitting supportive energy.

Drink in the healing power of nature today. Even a few moments spent outdoors in quiet repose will revive you in unparalleled ways.

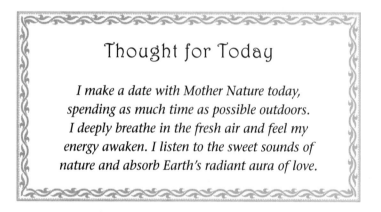

Thought for Today

I make a date with Mother Nature today,
spending as much time as possible outdoors.
I deeply breathe in the fresh air and feel my
energy awaken. I listen to the sweet sounds of
nature and absorb Earth's radiant aura of love.

Stay Positive

The most helpful thing that you can do in the face of hardship is to keep a positive attitude. There's always some blessing within all circumstances, even if you can't immediately identify it. By holding on to faith, you can elevate everyone around you, along with the situation itself.

A positive mind-set keeps the body relaxed, which in turn helps you think clearly and creatively during intense situations. Your bright outlook inspires others and may avert a cycle of downward-spiraling energy.

Vow to stay optimistic today no matter what. Always be honest about your thoughts and feelings, yet do call upon us angels and your higher self to gain the best perspective on every situation. In this way, you work through any upsetting emotions very quickly, keeping a high level of energy and a positive attitude.

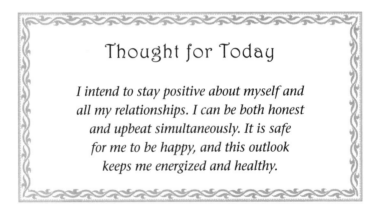

Thought for Today

I intend to stay positive about myself and all my relationships. I can be both honest and upbeat simultaneously. It is safe for me to be happy, and this outlook keeps me energized and healthy.

211

Keep Going!

Today is devoted to your priorities—the projects and activities that you daydream about. Any step that you take in the direction of these pursuits will be applauded by your inner self. You'll feel gladdened and awakened as you invest time and energy in yourself. Even ten minutes will yield greater happiness.

Breathe deeply (with or without your eyes closed) and notice your feelings or thoughts about your priorities. Which activity comes to mind first? This is your action step for the day. If you need to, write it on your calendar as a mandatory appointment with yourself.

Feel the appreciation that your inner self radiates as a result of the care that you're providing.

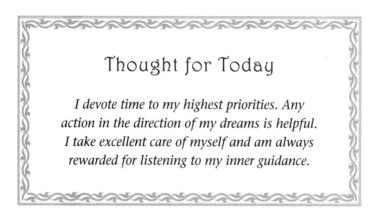

Thought for Today

I devote time to my highest priorities. Any action in the direction of my dreams is helpful. I take excellent care of myself and am always rewarded for listening to my inner guidance.

Speak Healing Words

We angels have discussed the energy, power, and impact of words. Today, we'll focus on their healing effects. We've infused this message with a dose of extra restorative energy, which you're absorbing now as you read these sentences. Meditate, breathing in this force with deep inhalations and exhalations. Feel us sending you love and support in every way.

Let's work together to use healing language in everything that you say and write. If you'd like, we can guide your words so that they're infused with supreme therapeutic energy. Your speech emits sparks of Divine love, and others will feel an impact. As the vessel for the healing words, you'll also feel the elation of the gift that you're giving.

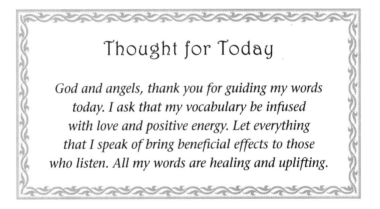

Thought for Today

*God and angels, thank you for guiding my words
today. I ask that my vocabulary be infused
with love and positive energy. Let everything
that I speak of bring beneficial effects to those
who listen. All my words are healing and uplifting.*

Honor Your Healing Hands

*Y*our loving energy flows through your entire body and can be directed at will. The chakras in your hands, heart, and third eye can pull in and send out this universal force according to what you decide.

Today we angels will focus on your hands, which contain dozens of very active and sensitive chakras that feel, send, and receive energy. If you stretch your arms out with your palms facing upward, we'll clean your hand chakras and infuse them with additional power. Inhale and exhale deeply while we conduct this treatment.

Pay attention to the sensations in your hands. Put them out in front of you to get an impression of rooms, situations, people, and objects—and trust the messages that you receive. Place your hands on any area of your body to send healing energy into your physical being. Notice how this feels; and if you're guided to do so, conduct the same process on another person, a pet, or a plant.

The more aware you become of the energies that your hands give and receive, the more powerfully the healing will flow in both directions.

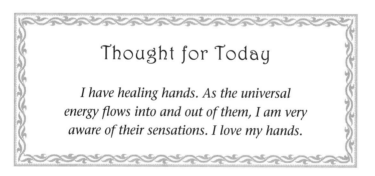

Thought for Today

I have healing hands. As the universal energy flows into and out of them, I am very aware of their sensations. I love my hands.

Honor Your Healing Heart

As we angels discussed before, the universal healing energies flow in and out of you through key chakra points, particularly your heart, hands, and third eye. Today we'll focus on the heart chakra.

The pleasant sensation of warmth in your chest is a signal that healing energies are flowing into your heart chakra. This is similar to the feeling of gratitude, and it's possible to experience this continuously as long as you keep the currents of power streaming through your core. You do this by constantly giving and receiving love.

Just as each inhalation is followed by an exhalation, so can the tides of healing be in an unending flow. You can consciously will yourself to breathe in and then exhale nurturing power. You can also picture your heart chakra's respiration as it gives and receives energy.

Today, focus on the sensations in your chest area. Let warm, pleasant feelings be a harmonizing guide that signals the flow of love energy. No matter what's going on around you, this universal power is always available to you. Keep the current moving by balancing your giving and receiving, and notice the natural high that ensues.

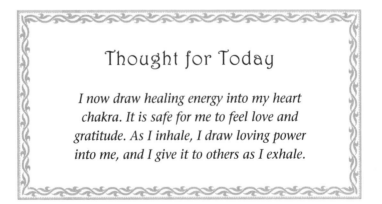

Thought for Today

I now draw healing energy into my heart chakra. It is safe for me to feel love and gratitude. As I inhale, I draw loving power into me, and I give it to others as I exhale.

Honor Your Healing Sight

Today we angels continue our discussion about increasing your flow of universal healing energies. We've focused on the hands and heart, and now we'll work with the third eye chakra.

Your third eye receives and sends intense light. The various chakras interpret energy information differently: The hands focus on physical sensations, the heart on emotions, and the third eye on visions.

You can use all of these points together to discern a holistic impression of any situation that you wish to get more information about. You can also send energy from all of them to increase your spectrum of healing energy.

The third eye, like the other chakras, is controlled by your will and intentions. Any strain or misgiving on your part can "inter-*fear*" with this process, so just direct your focus and allow everything else to happen naturally.

Begin by setting two intentions:

1. *I will that my third eye becomes increasingly sensitive to images of love.*
2. *My third eye now sends healing energy to everyone it sees.*

Say these statements as often as you feel guided, and the process will begin immediately.

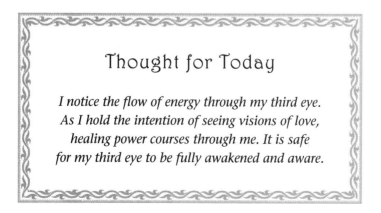

Thought for Today

I notice the flow of energy through my third eye.
As I hold the intention of seeing visions of love,
healing power courses through me. It is safe
for my third eye to be fully awakened and aware.

Accept Your Healing Abilities

You have the same healing power that everyone else does, since all individuals are eternally connected to God. The only reason why some people appear to be more effective healers than others is because they trust in the Divine energy flowing through them. Today, we angels will focus on increasing your faith.

When you question your abilities, you put a clamp on the hose that the healing energy flows through. That's because such doubt is the equivalent of believing that you're separated from heaven, which is a disempowering thought. It's impossible to be detached from God, since you're joined through the love that created you.

Instead of wasting time wondering if you're qualified or ready to heal, put your focus on joyfully celebrating your Divinity. Enjoy the therapeutic gifts that are yours, and put them to use without delay.

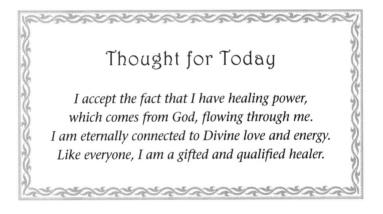

Thought for Today

I accept the fact that I have healing power,
which comes from God, flowing through me.
I am eternally connected to Divine love and energy.
Like everyone, I am a gifted and qualified healer.

Enjoy Self-Acceptance

Self-acceptance is the same as *God*-acceptance. When you love yourself for who you are, you praise the Creator's handiwork.

Regardless of the illusion presented by any seeming problems, you truly are magnificent. The more you focus on your God-given magnificence, the more you experience proof of that fact. You'll find that you're able to effect miracles simply by knowing your true spiritual origin and identity.

Today, praise yourself as a means of paying tribute to God. Trust that the Divine plan for you is perfect in every way.

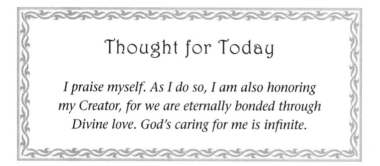

Thought for Today

I praise myself. As I do so, I am also honoring my Creator, for we are eternally bonded through Divine love. God's caring for me is infinite.

Enjoy Loving Thoughts

The other people in your life are reflections of yourself, mirroring your feelings of self-worth. When you feel good about who you are, your relationships are more harmonious and happy. When you disapprove of yourself, your experiences with other people follow suit. Your self-assessment is often measured by what other people think or say. Yet this is backward, because when you value yourself highly, so does everyone else.

Today, be proactive in your relationships. Before you see anyone, build yourself up with healthy doses of love—this is just like taking your vitamin supplements in the morning. Tell yourself, *I am lovable, because God made me that way. Divine caring is everywhere, including inside me and every person I'll meet today.* Refuse to see anything but love within yourself and others. Like any new habit, this becomes much easier and more natural over time.

Your soul is a pure drop of the Creator's energy . . . your very essence is love. Connect with others through this emotion today, and watch your relationships heal in miraculous ways.

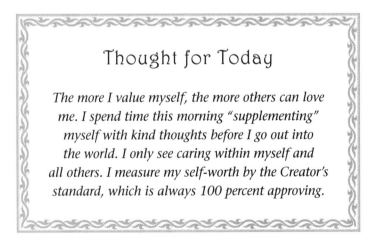

Thought for Today

The more I value myself, the more others can love me. I spend time this morning "supplementing" myself with kind thoughts before I go out into the world. I only see caring within myself and all others. I measure my self-worth by the Creator's standard, which is always 100 percent approving.

219

Enjoy Romantic Love

*Y*our romantic life is determined by the self-talk that you engage in. When you say positive and loving things, you build up your feelings of worth. There's no other magic formula but self-love to prepare you for the romantic relationship that you desire and deserve.

You must cherish yourself wholly, including those parts that you believe need improving. The more affection you have for yourself, the higher your energy level—which is the basis for romantic attractiveness. Remember that you draw people to you who vibrate at similar energetic wavelengths. To attract an emotionally healthy partner, establish a foundation of well-being by loving and accepting yourself.

We angels stand next to you right now, awaiting your request for help with this endeavor. Whether you feel that you need a complete overhaul of your self-esteem or just a minor adjustment, we're ready to support you.

Make a pact with us today, committing to steer your language to become love based, especially when used to describe yourself. Know that all possibilities are open to you . . . just say the word.

Thought for Today

I deserve great love. I am a good and kind person, and I value myself just for being who I am right now. I am entirely healed.

Forgive Past Lovers

*Y*our romantic life is shaped by your feelings about your previous relationships. Your emotions about the past have formed logjams that block love from entering. We need to clear the path so that new romance can get through.

Practically every human we've encountered harbors old feelings toward former lovers, so don't feel shame if you do, too. Instead, put your whole focus on moving beyond the past. Unhitch yourself from the heavy burden that you've been hauling around for so long.

Begin by opening yourself completely to our healing presence. Release all painful feelings from the past . . . just let them go. You'll always retain the love and lessons from every relationship. Today, we're only clearing the aftermath of hurtful memories.

Open your heart to us now, and feel us sweeping away cobwebs that have bound your heart in cold silence. Release old anger, resentment, tension, worry, guilt, and shame. Let go of everything that feels painful or uncomfortable by exhaling it out now.

Feel us disentangling you from your past. We'll do our work, and you must do yours, which is to be receptive, open, and willing. Together, we'll clear the way for love to flow through you and your life.

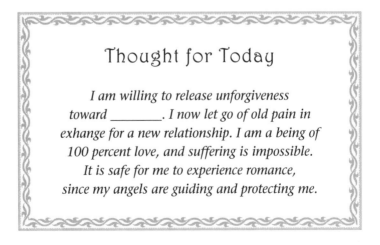

Thought for Today

*I am willing to release unforgiveness
toward _____ . I now let go of old pain in
exhange for a new relationship. I am a being of
100 percent love, and suffering is impossible.
It is safe for me to experience romance,
since my angels are guiding and protecting me.*

221

Ask Us for Help

Periodically, we angels will remind you that we're always available to help you with everything—but we can only do so if you ask us to. We respect your free will to make decisions and work out any problems on your own. Yet if you ever feel as if you need some assistance, don't forget that we're here.

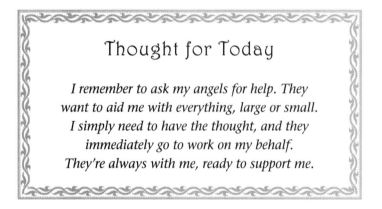

Thought for Today

I remember to ask my angels for help. They want to aid me with everything, large or small. I simply need to have the thought, and they immediately go to work on my behalf. They're always with me, ready to support me.

222

Heal Anger

When fiery emotions threaten the sanctity of your relationships, remember that love is always in your midst. Anger can be used as a tool for increasing fear or love, depending on your decision. If you build a case against another person, you erect walls to protect yourself from feeling emotions. Love's approach removes all barriers, allowing you to face that individual with honesty.

Your role is not to change someone or justify yourself. Those are behaviors that increase fear, because they make you think that you're separate from others and from God. Love's approach to anger is to always remember the Divinity within every person and relationship.

Let go of any attachment to how the situation will proceed. Put your entire focus on knowing that everything has already worked out for the best. This assurance relaxes any defensiveness you may feel and allows you to enjoy your day regardless of the circumstances.

Feel your emotions about the relationship fully—don't deny them. Only dispel the illusion that the other person is separated from you, or that you're isolated from affection. This is healthy and leads you back home to love.

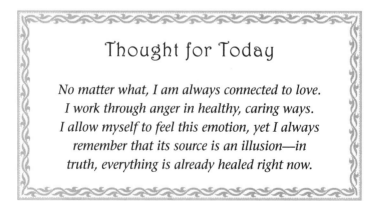

Thought for Today

No matter what, I am always connected to love.
I work through anger in healthy, caring ways.
I allow myself to feel this emotion, yet I always
remember that its source is an illusion—in
truth, everything is already healed right now.

223

Extend Your Energy

To extend the feeling of peacefulness that you have right now, send its energy forward into your day. Visualize surrounding each of your future minutes and hours with a blanket of harmonious energy. This tranquility will wait for you and joyously greet you when you arrive.

Give yourself the gift of a peaceful day. Feel the serenity that always resides within you. Breathe in deeply to increase this energy, and then exhale it into your day, using any chakra that you feel guided to call upon. Envelop every situation and person—familiar and unknown—with this gift of peaceful love.

Notice how much more enjoyable your day is. Other people will be subconsciously aware of your energy, and their gratitude will be apparent. Enjoy the fruits of this gift.

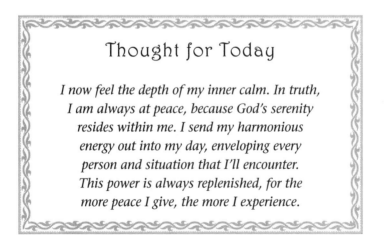

Thought for Today

I now feel the depth of my inner calm. In truth, I am always at peace, because God's serenity resides within me. I send my harmonious energy out into my day, enveloping every person and situation that I'll encounter. This power is always replenished, for the more peace I give, the more I experience.

Enjoy True Rest

You've worked hard and may feel the need for some well-deserved rest, so honor your physical and emotional self. If you feel at all tired or overwhelmed, create some space for relaxation.

True rest comes when the mind, heart, and body are at peace. Today, write down any cares that are bothering you so that they're not creating mental noise that could interfere with your tranquility. Put the list in a special place where only you can see it. If you have a "God box" (a special container where you keep your prayers), place the paper in there, but if privacy is a concern, burn it. The point is to release stressful thoughts onto paper.

Detoxify your body of any chemicals that could lead to muscular tension. Drink lots of water to flush out stimulants or other toxins.

The next step to prepare for true rest is to grant yourself permission to take a break. Deliver guilt or worry about your schedule to us, giving us as much as you need to. If you like, we can stand by your windows and doors to ensure your privacy and protection while you rest. We'll even screen your calls or e-mails so that you have some quiet time. Just ask, and it is done.

Rest well, dear one. This investment that you make in yourself yields bountiful dividends.

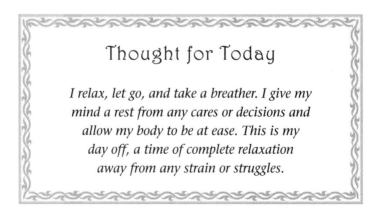

Thought for Today

I relax, let go, and take a breather. I give my mind a rest from any cares or decisions and allow my body to be at ease. This is my day off, a time of complete relaxation away from any strain or struggles.

Appreciate the Beauty of Simplicity

*E*verything that you desire is yours. There's never any need to strain or struggle for something. As soon as you ask, it's given to you. When you exhale and let go, you find that everything is waiting for you.

Only the ego tries to complicate your self-concept and life, twisting it into a complex mesh of unrecognizable scenery. Don't buy into the ego's script.

Life is simple, and so is love. It just is.

The bottom line is that God is love and the Divine is omnipresent . . . therefore, caring is everywhere. That's the simple truth.

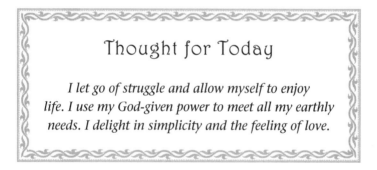

Thought for Today

I let go of struggle and allow myself to enjoy life. I use my God-given power to meet all my earthly needs. I delight in simplicity and the feeling of love.

Simplify Your Life

Easing your burdens involves using your gift of discernment to decide which direction you choose for yourself. Pressure comes from trying to go in multiple directions all at the same time. Often this stems from concerns about other people's judgments or displeasure, which comes from fears of abandonment. And at the base of these anxieties is the true root: a terror that God has abandoned you.

Beloved one, heaven would *never* abandon you. It couldn't—you're forever enmeshed into the Godhead, which is the single unit of living spirit that collectively fuels all sentient beings. God's will for you is joy, and this is simple because it's your true nature. You don't need to work at feeling this emotion.

Today, say yes to happiness and no to fear-based choices that cloud your schedule with too much "busy-ness." Today, open yourself up to simplicity.

Before every decision, spend time in meditative and prayerful silence. Only agree to those activities that you can accept wholeheartedly. We'll give you the strength and courage to say no to all other demands on your time.

It's safe for you to simplify your life.

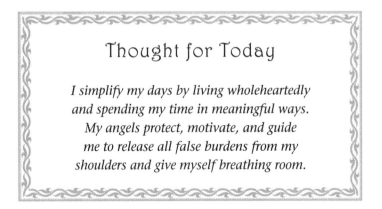

Thought for Today

*I simplify my days by living wholeheartedly
and spending my time in meaningful ways.
My angels protect, motivate, and guide
me to release all false burdens from my
shoulders and give myself breathing room.*

See the Beauty Within Yourself

*Y*our inner and outer beauty is breathtaking and awe inspiring. You're a perfect reflection of heaven's splendor, and everything about you is radiant. If you could see yourself through the eyes of us angels, you'd feel the rapture that we enjoy in your presence.

Your entire being is a creation of the Divine Maker, so how could you be anything but glorious? You were made by the One Who designed gorgeous flowers, sunsets, mountains, birds, and lakes. Your blueprint is just as perfect as anything else in God's kingdom.

As you relax with the realization of your Divine perfection, any memory of perceived flaws fades into the background. Your self-image is healed as you fall back in love with yourself and come to cherish yourself as much as God does.

You and every being on this planet are magnificent. Today, see this for yourself: Open your heart, eyes, and mind to experience the profound depth of beauty that is everywhere.

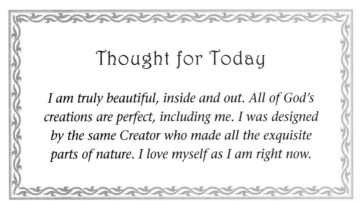

Thought for Today

I am truly beautiful, inside and out. All of God's creations are perfect, including me. I was designed by the same Creator who made all the exquisite parts of nature. I love myself as I am right now.

Know That You're a Gift of Joy

Babies are often referred to as "bundles of joy." Well, you're also a delightful present to others—you, too, are joy, gift wrapped in a beautiful human body. Everywhere you go, you exude wonderful energies, even when you're unaware of this process. You can't help but spread happiness, as that's your true essence and nature.

Of course, you can increase or decrease the amount of joy that you radiate, so place your attention on showering huge amounts of bliss wherever you go. You can do this without a word—without even being noticed. Simply set your intention throughout the day to spread happy feelings, and it is done. You'll know by the smiles and laughter you inspire that your aim has been fulfilled, for these are reflections of the gift that you've given.

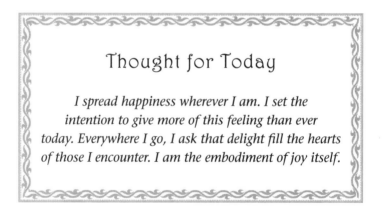

Thought for Today

I spread happiness wherever I am. I set the intention to give more of this feeling than ever today. Everywhere I go, I ask that delight fill the hearts of those I encounter. I am the embodiment of joy itself.

Have Faith and Patience

*D*ivine timing means the intersection of all favorable circumstances. Please have patience while everything works itself out to achieve optimal conditions for the full manifestation of your desires. In the meantime, know that your prayers and affirmations have been heard and are being answered. Their final fruition is nearly complete.

When a sailor nears dry land after being at sea for many months, he looks for signs such as birds flying with twigs in their beaks. He continues to sail in their direction, having faith that the shore is close by. In the same way, we angels send you many signals about the progress of your prayers. We ask that you hold the same faith and know that the markers you've been seeing and feeling are sure indications of great things on the horizon.

Rest in your trust and patience, knowing that everything is being taken care of behind the scenes on your behalf. Your ship is coming in right now.

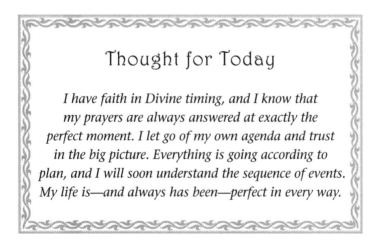

Thought for Today

I have faith in Divine timing, and I know that my prayers are always answered at exactly the perfect moment. I let go of my own agenda and trust in the big picture. Everything is going according to plan, and I will soon understand the sequence of events. My life is—and always has been—perfect in every way.

Cherish Each Moment

Although it's pleasantly exciting to look forward to the future, consistent and continual joy comes from cherishing the present moment. Each instant of life offers the richness of love, humor, stories, messages, healings, and blessings.

Today, place your intention on cherishing every second that you experience. Notice the details within each situation and the beauty of every human interaction. Allow yourself to feel the emotions stirred by each moment. Be consciously aware of the present.

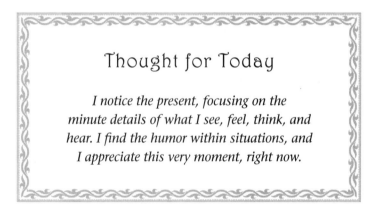

Thought for Today

I notice the present, focusing on the minute details of what I see, feel, think, and hear. I find the humor within situations, and I appreciate this very moment, right now.

231

Enjoy True Love

The love we angels have for you is true because it's steady and unconditional. We respect and understand all your behaviors and actions, and we value everything that you do. We often guide you in new directions, but we always do so with *your* path of truth in mind. We act in harmony with your prayers, according to Divine will.

True love is unwavering through every situation—no matter what's going on, it's there. We always see your goodness and your inner glow. When you rest in the certainty of our affection, you relax and your light shines even brighter.

Know that you're cherished, now and always. Ask us to help you feel affection, and notice as it comes to you throughout the day.

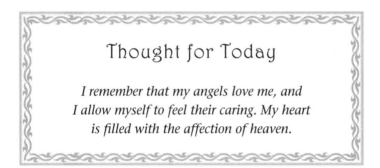

Thought for Today

*I remember that my angels love me, and
I allow myself to feel their caring. My heart
is filled with the affection of heaven.*

Bless Everyone You Meet

Fear is the basis of relationship issues. It stems from concerns about the other person's power over you and the loss of your own will. Yet how could that happen since you're an extension of God's own power? No one can seize what the Creator has given to you.

The antidote for this fear is to turn the energy around. Instead of worrying about what someone may take away from you, put your entire focus on giving blessings. You can do this by praying for the individual, sending loving energy, affirming his or her happiness, or asking for additional angels to be stationed at his or her side.

Today, bless everyone you meet, whether it's a passing stranger or someone you've known for a while. Notice any shifts within your relationships. While the intent behind giving blessings isn't to change the other person, you'll enjoy a healed energy as the wavelength of sharing and giving elevates your connection.

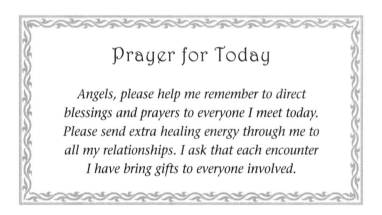

Prayer for Today

Angels, please help me remember to direct blessings and prayers to everyone I meet today. Please send extra healing energy through me to all my relationships. I ask that each encounter I have bring gifts to everyone involved.

233

Mine for God

God is within every person in your life, even if it seems otherwise. Just as a miner finds valuable gold, so too can you discover the Divine in every relationship. Your miner's hat is equipped with the light from your intention to see at least one good quality within each person.

Everyone has at least one positive attribute, which is visible to those with open minds and hearts. Often people who seem the least lovable are those most in need of a "God" miner such as yourself.

Know that you'll strike gold with every person you encounter today. Your healing mission opens up and brings joy to many hearts, especially your own.

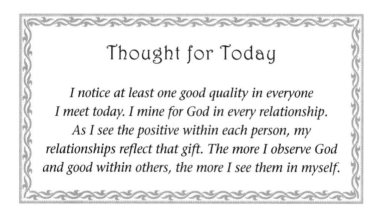

Thought for Today

*I notice at least one good quality in everyone
I meet today. I mine for God in every relationship.
As I see the positive within each person, my
relationships reflect that gift. The more I observe God
and good within others, the more I see them in myself.*

Know That We're All Connected

We angels are connected to God, to you, and to every sentient being. The same spirit of love binds us all, completely and forever. The more you know this universal fact, the easier it will be for you to listen to our messages. The only reason why you sometimes can't seem to hear us is your belief that we're separate from you.

Remind yourself throughout the day that you're eternally connected to God and us. You're also linked to all the people you meet, and they too are joined to heaven. Powerful love runs through this web of connectedness. The more you know that everyone is united, the more you feel and experience this current of caring.

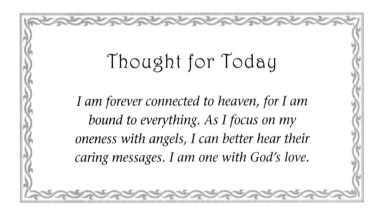

Thought for Today

I am forever connected to heaven, for I am bound to everything. As I focus on my oneness with angels, I can better hear their caring messages. I am one with God's love.

Give Us Your Worries

To paraphrase one of your great leaders on Earth, there's nothing to worry about but worry itself. The weight of your troubles closes your heart to joy, and your constant nervous glances toward tomorrow's horizon rob you of your enjoyment of the present moment. Worry saps happiness from relationships and makes you feel and look old beyond your years.

It's normal among humans to worry, so the fact that you do so isn't the topic we angels would like to discuss. Rather, we'd like to focus today on what you *do* with your cares.

You already know that being anxious is unhealthful and unhelpful. You're also aware that concentrating on your worries can bring them into being through the law of attraction. The solution is to form a spiritual partnership with us wherein you give us your concerns and we lift them away.

Anytime you become conscious of anxious feelings, immediately think of us—your thought calls us to action. You can then give us the energy of worry or whatever is triggering it; the results are identical.

When you hand us your troubles, your burden is lifted. Not only does this reopen your heart to joy, it also lets light and fresh air into the situation so that it can be perfectly healed.

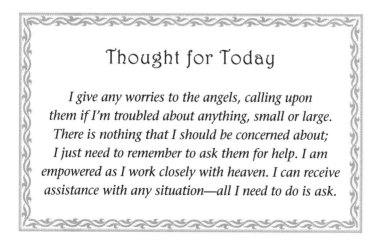

Thought for Today

I give any worries to the angels, calling upon them if I'm troubled about anything, small or large. There is nothing that I should be concerned about; I just need to remember to ask them for help. I am empowered as I work closely with heaven. I can receive assistance with any situation—all I need to do is ask.

236

Be Gentle with Yourself

Your sensitivity is heightened as you travel along your spiritual path, helping you discern the energy of other people, situations, and us angels. You instantly feel who and what you're comfortable with.

As your sensitivity continues to be elevated, you may encounter increasing spiritual gifts, along with feelings of alienation toward situations and relationships that you once enjoyed. You know that you're growing, and those around you have probably remarked on your changes as well.

You're being launched forward on your path of progress, and you may feel distanced from some people in your life. Know that you're never on your own, beloved one. Not only do we accompany you at every step of the way, so do many other individuals who travel the same path as you. You're not alone in any sense.

This is a time to be very gentle with yourself. Don't allow any self-berating words to enter your mind or exit your mouth. Know that you're doing the best you can. Surround yourself with loving situations, people, and music.

Gentleness allows you to continue blossoming into the beautiful flower of your fully realized self.

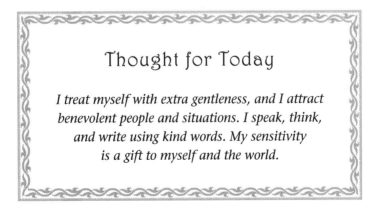

Thought for Today

I treat myself with extra gentleness, and I attract benevolent people and situations. I speak, think, and write using kind words. My sensitivity is a gift to myself and the world.

Release Your Past

Each fearful situation or relationship that you encounter creates attachments on the etheric plane, which we angels call "cords." While some people can see these ties, everyone feels them, and they can lead to fatigue and physical pain. We'll work with you to release the cords of fear.

You, like most people, have experienced circumstances that aroused alarm or pain within you. The way that you deal with your past determines what you'll attract in the future, so it's important to release anything that you'd like to avoid in times to come.

The first step in this process is to alter your vocabulary. It's important to refrain from using words that sound as though you're the owner of a painful occurrence, such as "*my* accident" or "*our* loss." Describe the event in a depersonalized way to help your aura detach from it.

If you think, speak, or write about a hurtful situation, be sure to talk about it in the third person—for example, "*the* accident" or "*the* loss." This decreases the power that the incident has over you and helps ensure that you won't continue to attract similar situations.

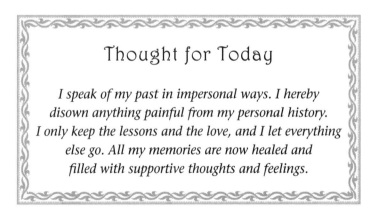

Thought for Today

*I speak of my past in impersonal ways. I hereby
disown anything painful from my personal history.
I only keep the lessons and the love, and I let everything
else go. All my memories are now healed and
filled with supportive thoughts and feelings.*

238

Clear Your Past

Now that you've detached from owning past situations, we angels will help you clear your energy field. Your prior attachments to hurtful memories have created cords that we'll now sever for you.

Allow yourself to be in a receptive state. Inhale and exhale deeply and regularly throughout the process. It's best to close your eyes to avoid visual distractions.

With your permission, we'll release the cord attachments to anything painful in your past. You may feel shivers, tingles, and air-pressure changes as we continue. You'll know that it's over when your body feels calm.

Notice how much lighter and freer you feel as we remove the heavy coating that enveloped you. Your ego told you that you'd be safer if you remembered your past pain, yet the truth is that any suffering held in your awareness magnetically attracts more of the same. You only want to draw forth love and harmony, so we're now adjusting your consciousness to hold only these energies.

Today, call upon us regularly as you recall anything that you'd like to detach from. We're happy to continue working with you on this clearing process, since it's our mission to help you experience peace.

Affirmative Prayer for Today

Dear angels,
Thank you for clearing any cords
keeping me bound to painful memories.
I am willing to completely release any
attachments to fear in exchange for gaining peace.
I am cleared and serene . . .
and now it is so!

Find the Blessing and Gift Within Everything

Today we'll focus on how you can prevent the creation of fearful attachments. In any circumstance that seems to evoke pain, you can take the path of peace by asking yourself, *What's the blessing or gift within this situation?* Your higher self will always answer you. Each event and relationship offers the opportunity to grow, learn, and heal:

- You grow by taking actions that you feel good about, such as telling the truth, setting firm boundaries, or seeing everything through loving eyes.

- You learn by seeing the pattern within recurring events that you've experienced. For instance, you may gain knowledge about how to be patient, compassionate, or strong during these situations.

- You heal through your willingness to forgive yourself, others, and the situation, which releases you from carrying around the corrosive energy of anger.

Be open to finding the blessing or gift within everything today. This is like gathering flowers for a beautiful bouquet.

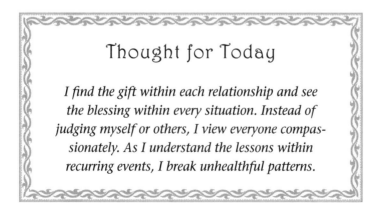

Thought for Today

I find the gift within each relationship and see the blessing within every situation. Instead of judging myself or others, I view everyone compassionately. As I understand the lessons within recurring events, I break unhealthful patterns.

Know That You're Enveloped in Love

Right now our wings are around you in a loving embrace. Feel this in your heart, and drink it in. It's important for you to recharge and nourish yourself regularly with Divine caring. Today, we'll send you extra waves of loving and supportive energy. Your awareness of this process isn't necessary for it to occur, yet you *will* enjoy the feelings that you experience each time you pause to tune in.

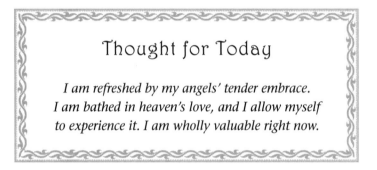

Thought for Today

*I am refreshed by my angels' tender embrace.
I am bathed in heaven's love, and I allow myself
to experience it. I am wholly valuable right now.*

See Wellness Everywhere

One of the reasons why we angels are able to effect healings is because we know that there's nothing to be healed. In truth, you (and everyone else) are continuous reflections of God's shining love, and just as the Divine would never need to be cured, so it is for you.

The illusion of sickness, disease, or injury is just that: an illusion. Were we to put stock in this falsehood, we'd only bring about more of the same. So instead, we put all our attention and focus on God, Who resides eternally within you. We call upon the presence of the Divine to be strongly known to you, causing you to become consciously aware of heaven's energy. When you see well-being, you're seeing God.

Today, refuse to see anything but health within yourself and all others. Put your entire focus on loving the wellness that eternally resides within everyone. Ask it to come forward and make its presence known. In this way, you heal like an angel.

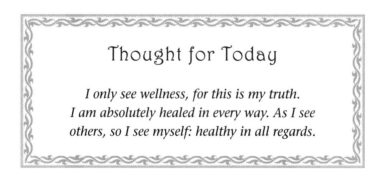

Thought for Today

I only see wellness, for this is my truth.
I am absolutely healed in every way. As I see
others, so I see myself: healthy in all regards.

Know That You're Perfect

You've always been perfect, from the moment that God first thought of you. You were then created flawless in all ways. You're the offspring of heavenly perfection, and you were designed masterfully for your Divine mission in life. Everything about you is well thought out in every way.

Today, rejoice in your perfection. This is not an unobtainable fantasy state, but Divine perfection. It means that you're God's wondrous child, and everything about you is in consummate order—your life is perfect, despite appearances to the contrary.

The more you know, affirm, and love your perfection, the more you feel and experience the Divine plan behind everything.

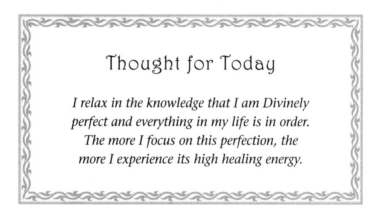

Thought for Today

I relax in the knowledge that I am Divinely perfect and everything in my life is in order. The more I focus on this perfection, the more I experience its high healing energy.

Enjoy Your Creativity

*Y*ou're a child of the Creator, and you've inherited Divinely guided creative abilities. You have talents that you may not be aware of yet. Your soul longs to express itself through colors, movement, song, and words—your inner self desires to channel its creative flow.

Today, express yourself in any way that you feel guided to do so. Both the act and the end product of creation are for your own enjoyment, so please don't worry about others' opinions or the "marketability" of what you originate.

This process is more about extending your artistic spirit outward. There's great therapeutic value in connecting with the energy of colors and sound waves within your creations and releasing the pure poetry that's inside of you.

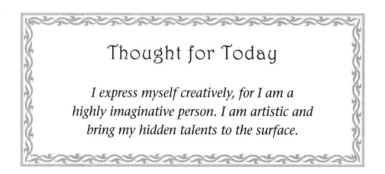

Thought for Today

*I express myself creatively, for I am a
highly imaginative person. I am artistic and
bring my hidden talents to the surface.*

Let Your Light Shine

*Y*our authentic self shines brightly with Divine love. You have loving qualities that bring much joy to yourself and others. We angels are working today to uncover your light so that it may be visible for the whole world to see.

Your illumination is fueled by joy, laughter, and passion. Today, allow yourself to have fun by freely expressing yourself. Since you can trust your true self to behave and speak lovingly and thoughtfully to others, there's no need to rein yourself in. Let go, and allow your light to be extra radiant today!

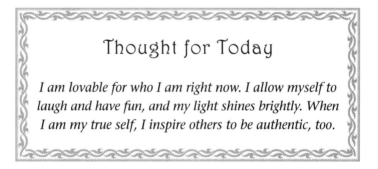

Thought for Today

I am lovable for who I am right now. I allow myself to laugh and have fun, and my light shines brightly. When I am my true self, I inspire others to be authentic, too.

Enjoy Divine Abundance

*Y*our prayers for an increased supply of money have been heard and answered. We angels are guiding you to be very open to receiving wealth by unexpected means. The more you can stay positive and hold on to the faith that your financial needs are being met, the sooner your dreams are realized.

The only block or barrier keeping money at bay is the fear of not having enough. This anxiety creates a repellent energy field around you, which acts like a wind machine that blows the cash away. Fear creates a neon "Keep Out" sign that blocks the energy of money.

Today, allow us to help you unfold the love that's inside of you. Just as turning on a lamp instantly dissolves the darkness, this energy radiates away the shadow of fear. Go inward frequently throughout the day. Close your eyes and breathe deeply, holding the intention of fully unveiling your inner light. Ask us to help with this aim, and we'll add our power to your own.

Love is the only true force in the universe, and God's will for you is abundance. Since both love and God are omnipresent, this bounty is everywhere. Open your heart to heaven and your arms to Divine abundance.

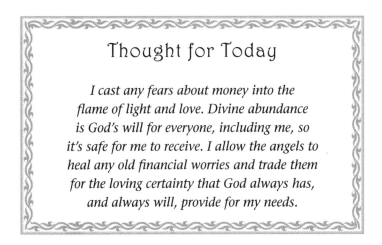

Thought for Today

*I cast any fears about money into the
flame of light and love. Divine abundance
is God's will for everyone, including me, so
it's safe for me to receive. I allow the angels to
heal any old financial worries and trade them
for the loving certainty that God always has,
and always will, provide for my needs.*

Lighten Up

*Y*our beauty, power, and light are strongest when you're filled with laughter and joy. Lightheartedness is the closest earthly condition to heaven. You often think about having more fun because you crave the Divine feeling of joy.

Your heart is filled with this emotion naturally, since it's your God-given state of being. Only when your awareness turns very serious is joy clouded. We angels watch as you become reserved when you feel that strenuous efforts will be rewarded. Yet the true benefits that you seek come more easily when you're carefree.

Today we'll work with you to lighten your heart, mind, and outlook. We'll lift away burdens of worry and replace them with gladness . . . in elevating your energy, your power of manifestation is intensified.

Affirmative Prayer for Today

Dear angels,
Thank you for helping me lighten up
and see the many gifts that are before me.
Please help me release any worries, and fill my
heart with faith that everything is going exactly
according to a wonderful Divine plan. I don't have to
know all the behind-the-scenes details of this agenda.
I simply need to keep my heart open
and joyful, and be willing to receive all the
good that you bring to me each day.

Notice All of Life's Gifts

Each day, life sends many gifts to you. They include experiences that open up your heart, helpful people, synchronistic opportunities, and nature's beauty. The more you pay attention to these blessings, the more of them the universe sends your way.

Notice as many gifts as possible today. They may be subtle—a ray of sunshine warming you from amidst dark clouds, or a kind person who lets you go first at a crowded intersection—but every one counts.

As you develop the habit of acknowledging these delightful moments, you'll receive them continuously in the steady flow that is the universe's generous nature.

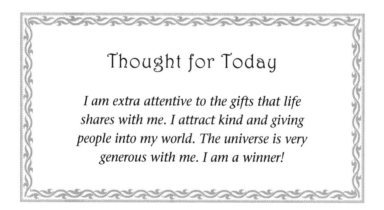

Thought for Today

I am extra attentive to the gifts that life shares with me. I attract kind and giving people into my world. The universe is very generous with me. I am a winner!

Express Appreciation to the People You Love

One of life's greatest gifts comes from relationships where you're connected through one of the many forms of love, be it of family, friendship, romance, or the soul. We know that you value the people in your life and cherish them deeply. Even though they know that you care, they always appreciate hearing this acknowledgment.

Today, express appreciation to the people you love. The form this takes isn't all that important: a phone call, hug, card, letter, or present . . . any method will do.

Your gift to your loved ones is also a gift to yourself. Notice how good it feels to express your appreciation.

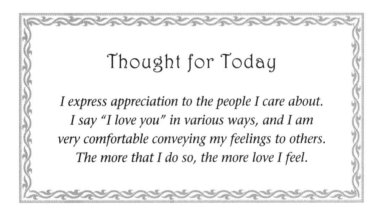

Thought for Today

I express appreciation to the people I care about.
I say "I love you" in various ways, and I am
very comfortable conveying my feelings to others.
The more that I do so, the more love I feel.

Have a "No Complaints" Policy with Yourself

We angels have been discussing the power of your words, and today we'll focus on detoxifying your vocabulary of any disempowering ideas or phrases. Specifically, we'll spend the entire day with the intention of avoiding complaining language.

Whenever you express discontent, you're stating that someone or something has control over you. Complaints are an affirmation of victimhood, a passive cry for help.

As a being of great light and love, you can never be a victim, and there's no greater power than the one you have inside of you right now. You can't be controlled by anyone or anything, as long as you're aware of God within you.

Today, hold the intention: *No complaints*. There are always positive phrasings that can convey your feelings without griping. Notice how strong you feel as you speak from a place of inner power, as well as how positively others respond to your requests for help when you do so. As you allow your inner strength to resolve everything easily, you'll very soon find that there's absolutely nothing to complain about.

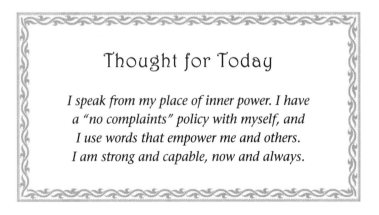

Thought for Today

I speak from my place of inner power. I have a "no complaints" policy with myself, and I use words that empower me and others. I am strong and capable, now and always.

Enjoy a Walking Meditation

*Y*our consistent practice of meditation has increased your ability to sense the presence of us angels and receive our messages. We applaud and congratulate you for your commitment to your spiritual habits, and today we'd like to suggest another form of meditation.

Spend some time today walking slowly with your eyes open. Take your focus inward as you move at a slow, rhythmic pace. Notice your mind's meandering, and pay attention to where it goes. If you experience ego-based thoughts, you can always walk to the rhythm of a chant such as "God is love; I am love; God is love" to center yourself.

This meditation is especially powerful when it's conducted outside in nature.

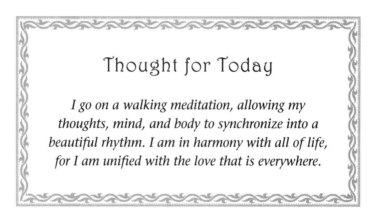

Thought for Today

*I go on a walking meditation, allowing my
thoughts, mind, and body to synchronize into a
beautiful rhythm. I am in harmony with all of life,
for I am unified with the love that is everywhere.*

Enjoy a Standing Nature Meditation

Today our suggestion is to try another form of meditation that involves taking off your shoes, socks, or hosiery and standing barefoot on the earth—it could be soil, sand, or grass.

Find a spot where you can remain standing comfortably for a few moments. Wiggle your toes, and feel the energy of the ground beneath you. Breathe deeply to draw that power upward into your body.

Close your eyes, relaxing into the rhythm of your breath and heartbeat. Listen to the sounds of the outdoors, and notice your thoughts and feelings.

Allow the peaceful spirit of nature to soothe and revive you.

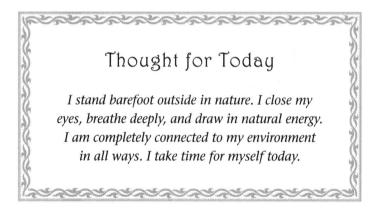

Thought for Today

I stand barefoot outside in nature. I close my eyes, breathe deeply, and draw in natural energy. I am completely connected to my environment in all ways. I take time for myself today.

Know That You're a Wondrous Being

*Y*ou're remarkable in so many ways. Because you're a creation of God, you reflect the Divine qualities of creativity, wisdom, and love. As your guardian angels, we're honored to be in your company. We endeavor to serve your purpose of peacefulness and love.

Today, remember how wondrous you are. Your very essence is a miracle, since you are an offshoot of God's being in physical form. Think how remarkable that is!

Keep all your positive attributes in mind today. One reason why we shine so brightly is because we only see the good within you and everyone . . . and you can do the same.

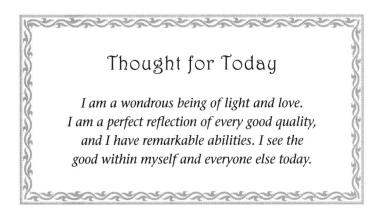

Thought for Today

I am a wondrous being of light and love.
I am a perfect reflection of every good quality,
and I have remarkable abilities. I see the
good within myself and everyone else today.

253

Silently Bless Everyone

As you walk by people today, send them blessings. These silent prayers don't require you to say anything; their effectiveness comes from your decision to direct goodwill to each individual you pass.

These blessings can come from your heart, mind, or your hands. Whichever way you choose to send them is effective. Observe how you feel as you do so . . . along with the joy of giving, you may notice a sense of kinship with everyone whom you bless.

Today *you* will be the one who receives the most blessings, for each time you honor another person, the gifts are returned to you manyfold.

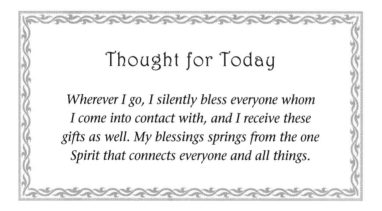

Thought for Today

Wherever I go, I silently bless everyone whom
I come into contact with, and I receive these
gifts as well. My blessings springs from the one
Spirit that connects everyone and all things.

Ask for a Divine Assignment

If you'd like a greater sense of meaning and purpose, begin today by praying for a heavenly assignment. Ask the Creator to give you a Divinely appointed task that's aligned with your personal interests and talents, and then release this prayer completely to the universe, with full faith that it will be heard and answered.

The response comes in subtle ways, so you should try to notice opportunities that are offered to you, strong hunches to take action, or topics that other people repeatedly mention to you. These are all examples of the signs that point the way to your mission.

All of heaven thanks you for your willingness to be of service in bringing tranquility to the world. Ultimately, you're the greatest beneficiary of your Divine assignment, since your giving yields great rewards for you, too.

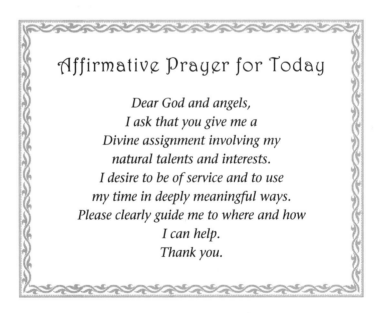

Affirmative Prayer for Today

Dear God and angels,
I ask that you give me a
Divine assignment involving my
natural talents and interests.
I desire to be of service and to use
my time in deeply meaningful ways.
Please clearly guide me to where and how
I can help.
Thank you.

Trade Worry for Faith

If you think back to the times when you've worried, you'll see how these fears never materialized. In truth, there never was—and never will be—anything that merits being anxious, because the time, energy, and emotions spent on worrying far exceed any actual issue that could arise.

Today, invest your time in faith, which is a far more valuable way to spend your energy. This is the platform of freedom and happiness that allows you to enjoy yourself. Positive belief is correlated with improved physical and emotional health, and you're at your most attractive in every way when you're relaxed and carefree.

We angels realize that you may experience worry occasionally, and we certainly don't recommend ignoring this feeling. What we offer you as an alternative is our assistance. Since we're right next to you continuously, it's just a matter of handing your concerns to us. We, in turn, transmute this energy so that the kernel of love that's behind every human emotion is revealed.

Feeling the full extent of your caring has triggered anxiety in the past. We'll help you create a new pathway for your love, one that leads to faith.

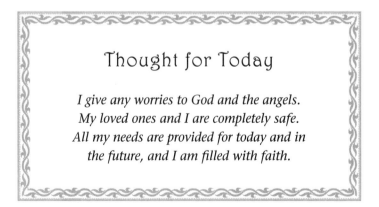

Thought for Today

I give any worries to God and the angels.
My loved ones and I are completely safe.
All my needs are provided for today and in
the future, and I am filled with faith.

Honor Your Inner Wisdom

You have wisdom inside of you, which springs directly from God's well of infinite knowledge. Your ideas come from exactly the same place as the wisest of all humans who have ever lived on this planet. You have the access to the same Source as everyone else.

We angels ask you to honor and trust your inner knowing today. You can see the best path for yourself, even if those around you don't understand it. Your insight is uniquely suited to your own situation, rather than other people's opinions.

If you're unsure about your ideas, you can always ask us angels for signs confirming that you're on the right track. The more you follow your own wisdom, the more opportunities you'll have to develop trust in God within, which is the basis for true happiness.

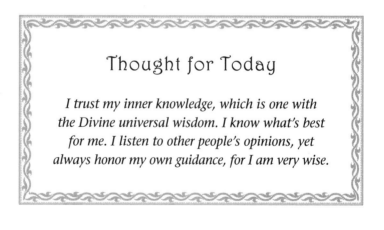

Thought for Today

I trust my inner knowledge, which is one with the Divine universal wisdom. I know what's best for me. I listen to other people's opinions, yet always honor my own guidance, for I am very wise.

Expect the Best

*Y*our expectations determine what you see and experience. If you anticipate problems, that's what you'll focus on and that's what you'll see. If you look forward to success, being attuned to this will lead you to see and experience it.

Your expectations are the steering wheel that determines the direction that you'll go. Hope for the best, and notice how positive your experiences are as a result.

Approach the day with the thought: *Everyone deserves the best. All people have greatness inside of them. I see and expect wonderful things, and that is what I experience.*

If you find yourself veering from this course at any time, simply stop, take a breath, and reset your compass toward a positive outcome. You're as strong as any human who's ever lived, and your bright outlook is very powerful. Anticipate good things today, and enjoy the rewards of this choice.

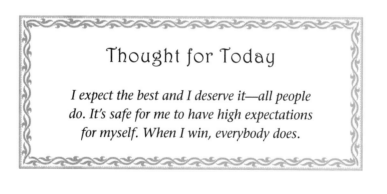

Thought for Today

I expect the best and I deserve it—all people do. It's safe for me to have high expectations for myself. When I win, everybody does.

Heal Regrets

Any regrets that you have about yourself or your past can be healed in order to help lighten your energy, mood, and outlook. Today we'll help you remove heavy coverings of guilt, shame, and regret.

The first thing you must know is that it's impossible for you to interfere with God's perfection. The love that's everywhere is constant and invulnerable. No one can disrupt infinite caring of the Divine, which exists within all people and things.

The only thing that needs healing is the illusion that you could bring anything but love to this planet—this emotion is who you are. As long as you carry hurtful feelings of regret in your mind or heart, you create a false sense of pain for yourself and those around you.

Today, switch off this dark impression of guilt and shame, and return to the light of understanding your spiritual truth and origin. This is forgiveness: first of yourself, and then spreading to all others.

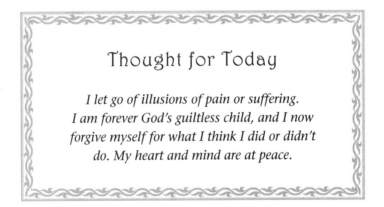

Thought for Today

I let go of illusions of pain or suffering.
I am forever God's guiltless child, and I now
forgive myself for what I think I did or didn't
do. My heart and mind are at peace.

Celebrate Your Uniqueness

*Y*our spirit is one with God and everyone else, yet in the physical world, you have unique qualities and talents in support of your personal life purpose.

Sometimes you feel at odds with other people—and you even feel alienated and misunderstood occasionally. Those are the times when you begin to question your self-worth. We angels are here to reassure you that your differences don't mean that anything's wrong with you . . . they're just part of your natural variation.

Today, celebrate your uniqueness. The more that you own your singular qualities, the more at ease you feel with yourself and others. The characteristic that people find most appealing is that sense of being comfortable in your own skin.

You don't need to change to fit in or belong. Celebrate being who you are!

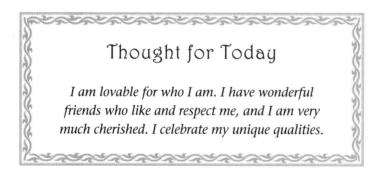

Thought for Today

I am lovable for who I am. I have wonderful friends who like and respect me, and I am very much cherished. I celebrate my unique qualities.

Ask for What You Want

It's part of your human spiritual-growth process to have dreams, and there's no shame in desiring something. The manifestation process allows you to practice your God-given creative abilities.

Everything that you have in your life is a product of your own wishes, including the seemingly undesirable elements. This is pointed out not to blame you, but to honor your incredible power to attract anything that you hold within your consciousness.

Today, ask for what you *really* want. Allow yourself to be outrageous in requesting and expecting your true desires to be fulfilled. Call upon God, us angels, and other people for the things that you wish for.

You'll be pleasantly surprised by how often the universe says yes to you—and all you had to do was ask!

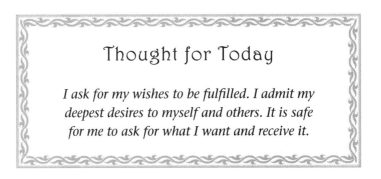

Thought for Today

I ask for my wishes to be fulfilled. I admit my deepest desires to myself and others. It is safe for me to ask for what I want and receive it.

261

Move Through Life Changes

The manifestation of your desires very often involves life changes. The old sometimes has to fall away to make room for the new. Your spiritual path has created a cushion around you, ensuring that the changes you make will be for the better.

Welcome novelty! It's the same energy as a beautiful sunrise on a perfect spring morning. The changes that you're encountering are answered prayers, even though you may not yet be able to see them that way.

We angels are with you throughout these transitions, holding your hand during every step. You can always ask us for guidance, courage, and direction at any time.

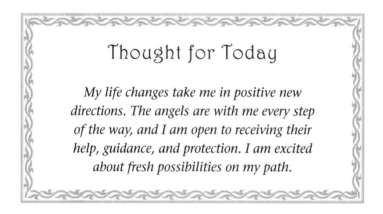

Thought for Today

My life changes take me in positive new directions. The angels are with me every step of the way, and I am open to receiving their help, guidance, and protection. I am excited about fresh possibilities on my path.

262

Take One Step at a Time

Every goal and change is accomplished one step at a time. We see your wonderful aspirations and desires, and we applaud you for reaching so high! We encourage you to continue along the path toward the realization of your dreams. Just remember that any road is traveled one step at a time.

Keep your focus centered on the current step that you're taking. Don't worry about the ones that you'll take next week, month, or year. They'll take care of themselves as you approach that time.

Put all your intention into making your present moment a magnificent one. It doesn't matter if it seems insignificant—just keep in mind that even the smallest action propels you forward.

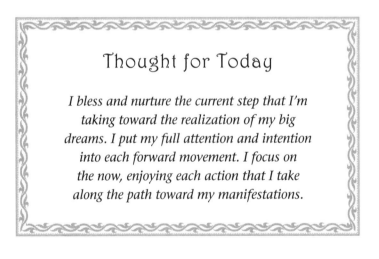

Thought for Today

I bless and nurture the current step that I'm taking toward the realization of my big dreams. I put my full attention and intention into each forward movement. I focus on the now, enjoying each action that I take along the path toward my manifestations.

263

Know That Everything Always Works Out

*Y*ou've had past experiences where you worried about the outcome, yet in the end everything turned out fine. Your current situation will also resolve itself perfectly, so relax your body and mind, knowing that there's nothing to fear.

God has never let you down in the past and won't do so in the future. Although the universe can't violate your free will if you choose to travel down a rocky path, love always surrounds you and everyone else. This cushions every experience and helps you always see the Divine order within all things.

Every episode of your life has helped you become stronger, wiser, more patient, and more evolved. Your current situation is also an opportunity to bring more light into your world . . . everything will work out fine. In the meantime, inhale deeply, and on the exhale, give any worries to God.

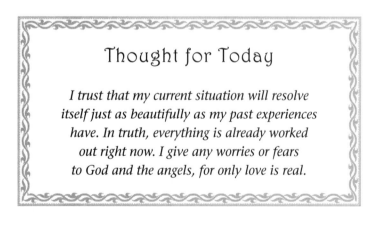

Thought for Today

I trust that my current situation will resolve itself just as beautifully as my past experiences have. In truth, everything is already worked out right now. I give any worries or fears to God and the angels, for only love is real.

Start in the Middle

Sometimes you might procrastinate about working on a meaningful project because you don't know where to begin . . . perfectionism has paralyzed you into nonaction. We angels suggest that you just jump right in. Start in the middle, at the end—anywhere. Just start.

Any step you take toward your goal will breathe life into it. Your project then takes on its own momentum, and it will guide you to the next appropriate action. Initially, though, you've got to take the first few steps.

Don't worry today about whether you're starting off "right" on your beloved project. Just perform any activity related to it, no matter how seemingly small or insignificant. Your heart will feel glad that you're investing time in meaningful ways.

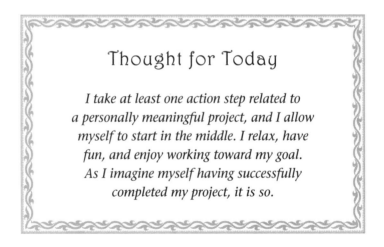

Thought for Today

*I take at least one action step related to
a personally meaningful project, and I allow
myself to start in the middle. I relax, have
fun, and enjoy working toward my goal.
As I imagine myself having successfully
completed my project, it is so.*

Enjoy Being Highly Focused

*Y*ou have a powerful mind, which is one with the Divine intellect of universal wisdom. You're easily able to focus and concentrate on whatever you desire, readily learning and retaining any information that you choose.

Today, honor the amazing power of your God-given mind. Say and think only positive thoughts about your abilities to focus, concentrate, and learn.

Your mind behaves exactly as you think it will, so expect the best from it, and notice how it delivers according to your expectations. Observe how natural and good it feels to allow your head to do what it does best: think, learn, and perfectly focus.

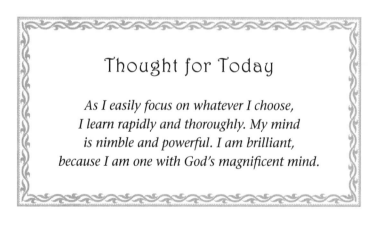

Thought for Today

*As I easily focus on whatever I choose,
I learn rapidly and thoroughly. My mind
is nimble and powerful. I am brilliant,
because I am one with God's magnificent mind.*

Appreciate Your Holy Self-Worth

You're worthy of everything, because you're a holy extension of the Divine. Everything within heaven is beautiful, fruitful, and blessed. Therefore, you share these qualities with all of your brothers and sisters.

Today, know that you deserve the best, just as everyone does. When you let yourself live beautifully, you're a portrait of heaven on Earth, and you inspire others with your joy and success. Allow your light to shine brightly today as your gift to the world.

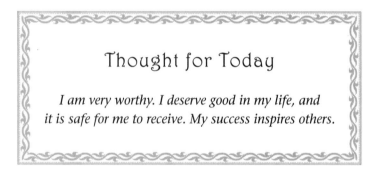

Thought for Today

I am very worthy. I deserve good in my life, and it is safe for me to receive. My success inspires others.

267

Enjoy Sacred Quiet Time

Today we angels would like to suggest that you create some quiet time to allow your mind and body to fully unwind and relax. Even five minutes spent in silence will nurture and revive your soul and spirit.

During this sacred time, turn off the phone, radio, television, and such. Sink into the quiet without trying to control your thoughts, emotions, or body—in other words, just be.

The moments that you spend alone in silence are a gift you give to yourself. Your inner self thanks you for your nurturing care.

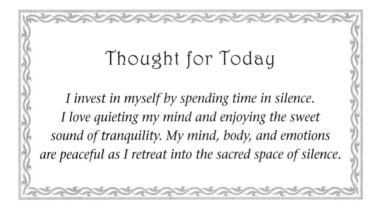

Thought for Today

I invest in myself by spending time in silence.
I love quieting my mind and enjoying the sweet
sound of tranquility. My mind, body, and emotions
are peaceful as I retreat into the sacred space of silence.

Notice Beauty

There's beauty all around and within you. The more you pay attention to it, the more life takes on a heightened, magical quality. You begin to notice your own radiance as a reflection of all that surrounds you.

Make it a point to see as much beauty as you can today. Witness it in the physical world through images of nature, as well as among people and their creations. Observe it in the realm of emotions as you feel affection from others and watch loving scenarios played out, and on the spiritual plane as you sense our angelic presence continuously by your side.

Today, affirm often that life is beautiful. Pause and drink in this fact, savoring each present moment.

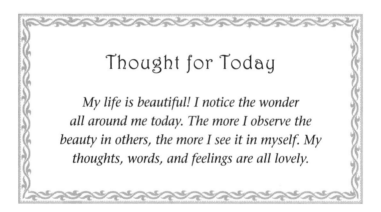

Thought for Today

*My life is beautiful! I notice the wonder
all around me today. The more I observe the
beauty in others, the more I see it in myself. My
thoughts, words, and feelings are all lovely.*

Know That You Live
in an Abundant Universe

The universe pulsates with giving energy in its ever-expanding growth. It sends endless amounts of love, which is the essence of every desirable experience. Anything that you wish for is fueled by this force.

Fear and worry close you off from experiencing the love and abundance of the universe, just as a kink in a hose slows the flow of water. Today, open yourself up to bathing in the steady stream of Divine love and supply, relaxing with the sure knowledge that all your needs are provided for.

Remind yourself that you live in an abundant universe. Look for examples of this, and be open to receiving the gifts that come to you. The more you rest in the certainty of this bounty, the more it will flow steadily through your life.

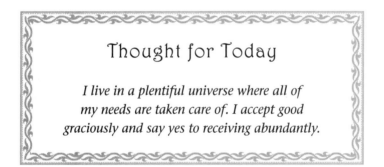

Thought for Today

I live in a plentiful universe where all of my needs are taken care of. I accept good graciously and say yes to receiving abundantly.

Daydream

aydreaming is often the catalyst for the imagination, where your mind reaches beyond the boundaries of logic and plumbs new possibilities. We angels often wonder why this activity is discouraged, since it's so vital to discovering novel ideas and inventions. We encourage you to sit in quiet repose today and let your thoughts run free as you daydream in peace.

Explore your wildest fantasies and the endless possibilities available to you. Imagine *What if?* scenarios, and visualize your wishes coming true.

Afterward, you may want to write down any ideas that came to you. Don't worry if they seem far-fetched. Remember that you just tapped in to the Divine, and there's something valuable and important within every dream.

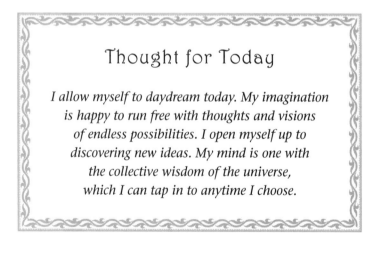

Thought for Today

I allow myself to daydream today. My imagination is happy to run free with thoughts and visions of endless possibilities. I open myself up to discovering new ideas. My mind is one with the collective wisdom of the universe, which I can tap in to anytime I choose.

271

Set Healthy Boundaries

*Y*ou're a sensitive, loving, and considerate person who would never want to hurt someone else's feelings. You're an angel on Earth—and we heavenly angels ask that you extend the same caring and thoughtfulness toward yourself that you do to others.

Today, we'd like to work with you on setting healthy boundaries for yourself. This doesn't mean rejecting or avoiding other people; you'll simply create a clear understanding of what is and isn't acceptable to you in any relationship.

This is especially important if you've felt used or as if you've been treated unfairly by others. While it's possible that people are deliberately taking advantage of you, it's more likely that they don't realize how you feel.

Setting healthy boundaries, then, involves being honest with yourself and those around you, which is an expected and normal part of any relationship. You can express your sincere emotions with the same sensitivity and love that you accord others right now. They'll respect your truthfulness, and you'll set a healthy example of how to take good care of yourself.

When you're straightforward with other people, you feel happier being in their company. Your increased joy is a true gift to yourself and your loved ones . . . it's a blessing to the world!

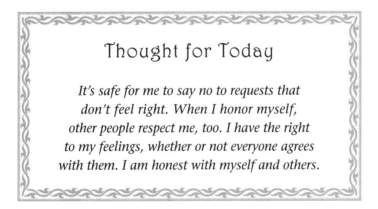

Thought for Today

It's safe for me to say no to requests that don't feel right. When I honor myself, other people respect me, too. I have the right to my feelings, whether or not everyone agrees with them. I am honest with myself and others.

Honor Your Compassionate Heart

All people are doing the best they can, including you. Remembering this can sometimes require a lot of compassion, but try to keep this thought in mind as you go about your day.

If you find yourself judging someone (including yourself), know that all people are doing the best they can. Allow yourself and others to occasionally stumble along the way. Instead of sending judgments, transmit prayers and warm feelings.

You have a compassionate heart, and love is your true nature. You feel better when you act in accordance with your authentic self, who is understanding, loving, and very gentle. Feel the joy of being who you are by seeing everyone through the lens of your caring heart.

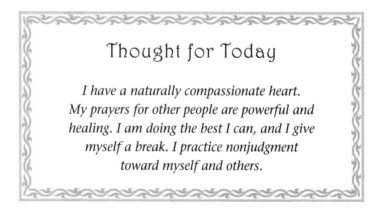

Thought for Today

I have a naturally compassionate heart.
My prayers for other people are powerful and
healing. I am doing the best I can, and I give
myself a break. I practice nonjudgment
toward myself and others.

Have Patience with Yourself

Akin to expressing self-compassion is the process of having patience with yourself. No one expects a baby to begin walking immediately: An infant's progress is gradual but steady, and your own growth is the same. We remind you to enjoy the path that you're on today, even if it seems to be taking longer than you'd like.

With patience comes progress. It brings a relaxed and open attitude that—coupled with faith—is always rewarded. Give us angels any concerns or anxiety that you have about the timeline of your progress. Focus completely on your action steps for today, and let tomorrow take care of itself.

Patience, then, is really another word for letting go of fear and worry. Remember that we're here by your side to help you release any tension or stress—just ask.

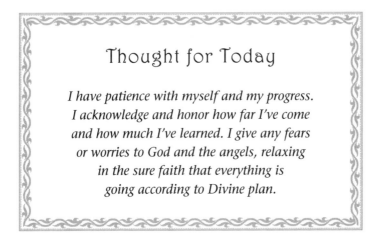

Thought for Today

*I have patience with myself and my progress.
I acknowledge and honor how far I've come
and how much I've learned. I give any fears
or worries to God and the angels, relaxing
in the sure faith that everything is
going according to Divine plan.*

Appreciate Your Body

*Y*our physical body is one of your most important tools to support your Divine life mission—it's your soul's dwelling during your time on Earth. And just as you care for the home that you live in, your body thrives on attention and appreciation.

Your physical self has a life force and intelligence of its own. This springs from its DNA, the connecting station between the spiritual and physical worlds that acts as a conduit between your oversoul (which is joined to the larger spirit world) and your inner self (the being housed within your body). The electrical balance of these receptors and conductors operates better when your body is well cared for.

The house of your spirit thrives on praise, appreciation, and other forms of care, just like any other living creature. The more you say kind things to and about it, the better it responds.

Today, love and appreciate your body. It will reward you in turn with increased energy and vitality as it shows its gratitude for your attention.

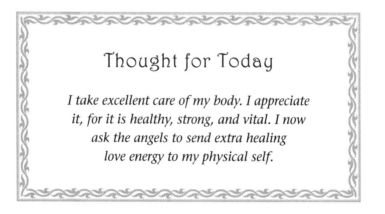

Thought for Today

I take excellent care of my body. I appreciate it, for it is healthy, strong, and vital. I now ask the angels to send extra healing love energy to my physical self.

Accept Compliments

Just as your body enjoys praise and appreciation, so does your soul. When you say words of love about yourself, this part of you shines extra brightly. When you speak this way about yourself to others, your soul warms and radiates—and this energy nurtures everybody.

Your appreciation acknowledges that everyone is equally lovable. Unlike bragging, there's no one-upmanship in love or appreciation (which is a common confusion).

When someone gives you a compliment, your soul longs to accept this gift, just as your body enjoys receiving sustenance from food or drink. Love and appreciation are the nutrients that feed your soul.

When others praise or acknowledge you today, accept the gift with openhearted gratitude. Don't deflect kind words—accept them. Enjoy the nourishment that appreciation brings you.

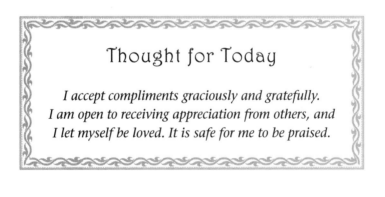

Thought for Today

I accept compliments graciously and gratefully.
I am open to receiving appreciation from others, and
I let myself be loved. It is safe for me to be praised.

Follow Your Divine Guidance

We angels communicate with you continually, answering your questions and giving you guidance. You hear us as gut feelings, tingles, goose bumps, dreams, intuitive words, and visions. You also notice repetitive signs in the physical world, and we want you to know that you really are communicating with us; these are real messages.

Much of our guidance is in answer to your prayers and questions about improving your life. Often we'll encourage you to take action that will support your peaceful happiness. Frequently this means that things will change—which is, after all, what you prayed for.

Change is entirely safe if you follow your Divine guidance. You'll notice that this is always very methodical and moves a single step at a time. Like a rhythmic dance, you make one motion, and we then lead you to the next. If you try to go faster than the universal music, you may trip and fall: This isn't the melody's fault; it occurs because you got out of rhythm.

Spend some time in quiet reflection today, recalling any repetitive thoughts, ideas, or feelings that you've been having. If these messages have asked you to make some positive changes, then this is the Divine guidance that we're referring to. Ask us to assist you in putting this into action. We can lend you courage, motivation, and other forms of support . . . just ask.

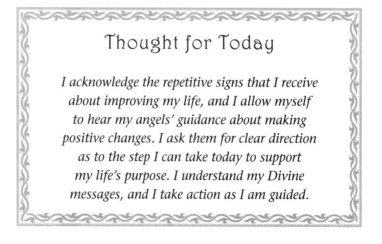

Thought for Today

I acknowledge the repetitive signs that I receive about improving my life, and I allow myself to hear my angels' guidance about making positive changes. I ask them for clear direction as to the step I can take today to support my life's purpose. I understand my Divine messages, and I take action as I am guided.

Trust Your Decisions

*Y*ou're a wise soul, and your heart is guiding you correctly. You feel the call for a major shift in your life, yet a part of you wonders if you can trust your intuition.

We angels are here today to counsel you to have faith in your decision-making abilities. Your heart knows best in this case, as it's a precise tool measuring your overall happiness. Trust and follow its direction.

Have confidence in your decisions today. Surrender any second-guessing to us so that we can filter fact from fiction. We'll help you distinguish fears of success from true cautionary feelings that should be heeded.

As you look back on your life, you can see the intricate pattern of decisions you've made. Many times your most seemingly illogical choices ultimately gave you the greatest satisfaction, and you're at a similar point right now. Heed the call of your heart . . . and trust.

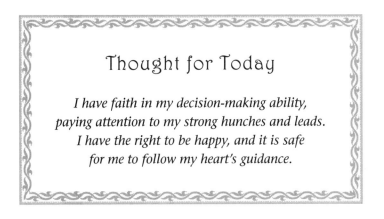

Thought for Today

I have faith in my decision-making ability,
paying attention to my strong hunches and leads.
I have the right to be happy, and it is safe
for me to follow my heart's guidance.

278

Ride the Energy Flow

*Y*ou have an uncanny knack for being in the right place at the right time. We angels are working with you today to further develop and polish this skill.

This begins with an understanding of energy flow, which operates exactly like a stream of water or air. You've learned that a physical object such as a rock can bend a river's currents but ultimately won't stop them.

In the same manner, Divine timing means trusting all the factors involved in answering your prayer. If you assume that there will be a problem, you erect an energy wall that's exactly like a boulder under the water: The flow doesn't go through the stone—it goes against and past it.

Today, hold the intention of letting the universe move you along. Don't resist the "push" that encourages you to expand and grow; instead, enjoy the ride that the current's flow provides.

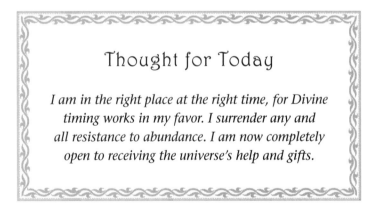

Thought for Today

I am in the right place at the right time, for Divine timing works in my favor. I surrender any and all resistance to abundance. I am now completely open to receiving the universe's help and gifts.

Know That You're Powerful

*Y*our source of strength is God within, Who is omnipotent. You're eternally connected to this force—you're powerful!

The only reason why you sometimes feel power*less* is because you become unaware of your source. Since you're continuously tapped in to Divine energy, and God is eternally strong, *your* might never leaves you or diminishes. Likewise, you could never abuse it, as it's fully governed by love's principles.

Today, remind yourself frequently that you're fully supported by God. This means that you can attract and manifest your every thought, so hold those that are desirable to you. . . . You have the power.

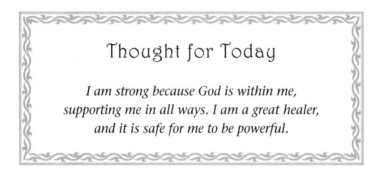

Thought for Today

I am strong because God is within me,
supporting me in all ways. I am a great healer,
and it is safe for me to be powerful.

Enjoy Your Youthful Spirit and Body

The spark of Divine fire in your soul is your spirit that never ages. Your body can reflect this eternal youthfulness if you allow yourself the freedom to act it out.

So what would a youthful spirit do to express itself? It would sing, dance, create, and explore its world. It would enjoy the exuberance of varied emotions and experiences, resting when needed and playing whenever it wanted to. There's no holding back.

Allow this side of you to come forth today. Notice the positive effects that such energy has on your body (including a fresher appearance). Youthfulness radiates aliveness, which translates into health at every level.

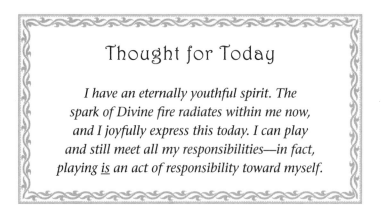

Thought for Today

I have an eternally youthful spirit. The spark of Divine fire radiates within me now, and I joyfully express this today. I can play and still meet all my responsibilities—in fact, playing is an act of responsibility toward myself.

281

Heed Your Calling

*Y*our Divine life purpose is calling you, asking you to breathe life into it. As the perfect child of the Creator, you have this capability of infusing life force into a potential situation.

Your calling is the activity or career that you frequently daydream about. You wonder about what your life would be like if you were to commit to it. This is called the "potential phase," and it's similar to holding an uninflated balloon.

When you investigate your pathway by reading about it, taking classes on that topic, or talking to other people in the field, you're partially inflating the balloon with your life force. This is when the calling becomes stronger—the more energy you put into it, the more forceful it becomes. Pretty soon you can no longer ignore it.

Heed your calling today, allowing yourself to fully recognize your desire to take up a journey such as a career, project, or volunteer activity. The more you invest your energy in this aspiration, the more life it takes on . . . until it finally shifts from dream to reality.

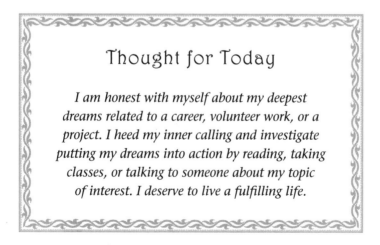

Thought for Today

I am honest with myself about my deepest dreams related to a career, volunteer work, or a project. I heed my inner calling and investigate putting my dreams into action by reading, taking classes, or talking to someone about my topic of interest. I deserve to live a fulfilling life.

Enjoy Harmonious Relationships

*Y*ou only experience difficulties in relationships when you fight the ultimate direction that they're headed. Each one sails along a different course, much like a ship upon the sea.

Ultimately, it's not about where you land at the end of the voyage; it's about the interactions among the people involved along the way. The most fruitful journeys occur when the crew members are heart centered and honest with one another.

Harmonious relationships are founded on mutual honesty, in a setting where both parties feel safe to share their true feelings. When you genuinely open up to one another, you then know that you're loved for who you really are.

Arguments occur when either person feels afraid or unsafe and becomes defensive, either verbally or through actions. We angels can help create a secure atmosphere by infusing love energy into both your hearts to aid you in selecting words that are kind and mutually respectful. Caring is the most powerful protective agent as you share your honest feelings with one another . . . this is how you bond and love.

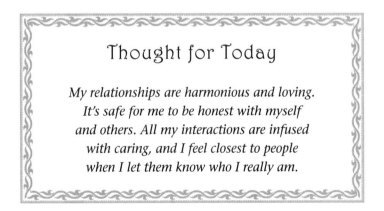

Thought for Today

My relationships are harmonious and loving.
It's safe for me to be honest with myself
and others. All my interactions are infused
with caring, and I feel closest to people
when I let them know who I really am.

Know That You're Lovable Just as You Are Right Now

*Y*ou don't need to change to earn God's love—you've always been cherished and adored just for who you are. Everything about you is lovable.

Of course, your compassionate and kind behavior is valued, but please know that you're appreciated no matter how you act. The more you can hold this kind of acceptance toward yourself, the more you'll relax and enjoy your experiences.

Life isn't about winning the approval of people's egos . . . it's about accepting the blessing that the egoless Spirit always extends to you. The former is a goal that can never be attained, and the latter has *already* been achieved.

Today, relax in the knowledge that we angels love you just as you are right now. Let go of any tension about yourself, and enjoy the gifts of today.

Thought for Today

I am loved just as I am right now, for God and the angels always value me unconditionally. I let down my guard and allow myself to feel at peace, knowing that I am lovable for being myself.

Connect with the Spirit of Nature

There's a reason why spending time outside refreshes you, regardless of the weather. It's more than the air, trees, and sunshine; it's the free spirit permeating the great outdoors that revives you, a force that's the very breath of nature.

This energy has a cleansing effect. A simple walk outside will remove any stale residue from stress, arguments, worry, and other emotional pollutants. The spirit of Mother Nature lovingly replaces lower energies with her higher vibration—it's similar to a laser beam zapping unwanted elements.

Today, connect with this spirit by going outside. Nature is everywhere, including city streets, so you don't need to delay this Divine assignment until you have time to drive to the countryside. These benefits are present wherever there's a direct connection to the atmosphere.

Step outside today, breathe deeply, and connect with the spirit of nature.

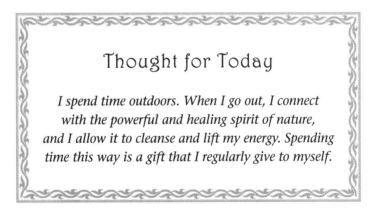

Thought for Today

I spend time outdoors. When I go out, I connect with the powerful and healing spirit of nature, and I allow it to cleanse and lift my energy. Spending time this way is a gift that I regularly give to myself.

Acknowledge That You Do Everything Right

How would your life be different if you knew that everything you did was foolproof and you could never make mistakes? Would you relax your mind and more enthusiastically pursue your dreams? Would you feel happier and more secure?

We angels are here to share with you a spiritual truth: You can't commit an error—all that you do is right.

In the universal sense, everything that God made is perfect, and that includes you. Since you're an extension of the Creator, then everything you do is also flawless. Human judgments may hold that both Divine and mortal creations are imperfect, but that doesn't change the spiritual fact of their perfection. Often human reason can't see the big picture that ties everything together in a logical way.

All that you do comes from God, because the Divine is all that exists. How could there be error in this creation?

Today, relax in the knowledge that your every decision and action is underwritten by the Creator's guarantee of perfection. All experiences bring growth, love, peace, and healing in the end, so you can't make a mistake.

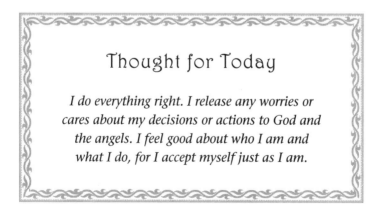

Thought for Today

I do everything right. I release any worries or cares about my decisions or actions to God and the angels. I feel good about who I am and what I do, for I accept myself just as I am.

Spread Your Wings and Soar

You have so many gifts to share with the world, beginning with your very presence on the planet. As the embodiment of God's love, you bring healing blessings just by virtue of being alive . . . yet you're itching to spread your wings and soar even higher. You want to experience the glow of joy and fulfillment more often. You long to feel free, unencumbered by the weight of worrying about money and other material issues. You'd like to devote your time purely to activities that make your heart sing.

The truth is that when you do occupy yourself with joyful pursuits, the energy involved elevates you like a bird catching a thermal updraft. Whether that activity directly pays you money isn't the point.

The residual benefits of your happiness are like a red carpet rolled out for new opportunities, friendships, business connections, and abundance. Those who are content are considered "lucky," but joy is the magnet that draws more of the same to you.

Invest in your happiness today by devoting time to your favorite leisurely pursuits. Remember that these activities are fruitful because they support you in spreading your wings.

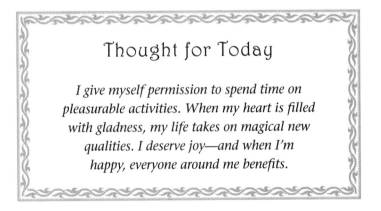

Thought for Today

I give myself permission to spend time on pleasurable activities. When my heart is filled with gladness, my life takes on magical new qualities. I deserve joy—and when I'm happy, everyone around me benefits.

Be Colorful

There's no safety or advantage in blending into the scenery. Your colorful side is much more fun and energizing for you and the people around you, so express this part of you today: Dress in bright hues; eat colorful foods; and display your vibrant nature by telling jokes, playing, having fun, and just being yourself.

Your glow inspires others to relax and be themselves. God created a wide variety of shades in nature, each of which carries a different and vital vibration. When you express yourself authentically, you emit a highly attractive rainbow of energy.

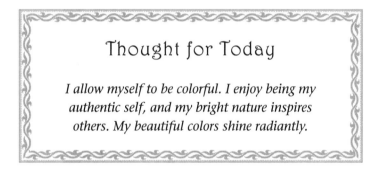

Thought for Today

I allow myself to be colorful. I enjoy being my authentic self, and my bright nature inspires others. My beautiful colors shine radiantly.

Trust That We're with You Right Now

There's never a time when you're alone, as we angels stand beside you continuously, watching over you at all moments. We're even with you while you sleep, as well as when you drive, work, eat, shop, love, argue, bargain, create, rest, and during every other activity. You can engage our assistance anytime you desire. We're also happy to give you reminders of our presence so that you remember to request our help—just ask.

We read these words alongside you right now. If you want, pause for a moment and specifically tune in to our presence. You'll know that we're here by the warm feeling you sense in your heart—that's the love we forever send your way.

You're always bathing in Divine caring, even when you're unaware of it. You're much like an unborn baby who isn't conscious of the source of nourishment supplied by the umbilical cord, but your connection to heaven, which constantly feeds you, can never be broken.

Today, do your best to remember our constant presence by your side. The more you ask for our help, the more we'll be able to deliver it to you.

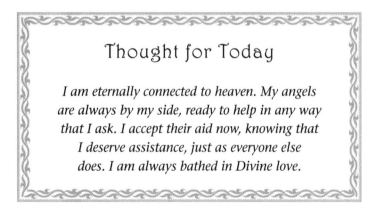

Thought for Today

I am eternally connected to heaven. My angels are always by my side, ready to help in any way that I ask. I accept their aid now, knowing that I deserve assistance, just as everyone else does. I am always bathed in Divine love.

Know That You Can
Never Ask for Too Much

We angels notice that at times you worry about asking for too much. You wonder if it's selfish or wrong to request help with material prosperity, healings, or the so-called small things in life. Today we'd like to address any fears that could cause you to hesitate in asking for and accepting our assistance.

This is a completely abundant universe, containing endless possibilities and the potential for every experience. There's no lack of supply, so your receiving could never take away from other people or prevent them from enjoying abundance.

We're unlimited beings, just as you are. We have all the time in the universe to help you—so never worry that you're bothering us with your requests or prayers. Our purpose is to support you.

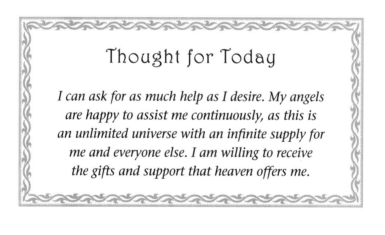

Thought for Today

*I can ask for as much help as I desire. My angels
are happy to assist me continuously, as this is
an unlimited universe with an infinite supply for
me and everyone else. I am willing to receive
the gifts and support that heaven offers me.*

Let Go of Self-Judgment

Ultimately, the only person you need to forgive is yourself. Any anger, resentment, or grudges that you hold toward others can always be traced back to feelings you have about yourself. This is why some of your attempts to forgive others have seemed unsuccessful. Until you forgive yourself, self-reproach will bleed into your relationships with those around you.

Self-forgiveness is different from accepting blame. Instead, it means first facing your feelings of guilt or anger. Admitting these emotions to yourself releases the power they had over you previously while they remained hidden secrets. Your self-candor will lead you to the understanding that you didn't do anything bad, because nothing wrong can happen in God's universe.

Today, forgive yourself for what you think you did or didn't do. Release the illusion of blame or self-contempt. Since you're 100 percent love, just like your Creator, you're only capable of cherishing yourself.

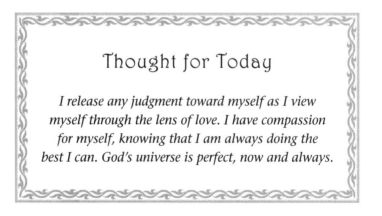

Thought for Today

I release any judgment toward myself as I view myself through the lens of love. I have compassion for myself, knowing that I am always doing the best I can. God's universe is perfect, now and always.

Know That You're God's Precious Child

*Y*ou're forever God's precious child. You were created as a gift of great love. Even during the times when you felt alone or unwanted, you've been entirely cherished by the Creator.

As you read these words, pause and feel the depth of love that embraces you right now. You may experience it even more intensely when you breathe deeply, drawing the energy into your conscious awareness.

Feel how much you're honored and revered. Every one of heaven's precious children receives this love and respect, for God looks past the surface and sees a perfect creation at all times. We angels ask you to try to do the same today.

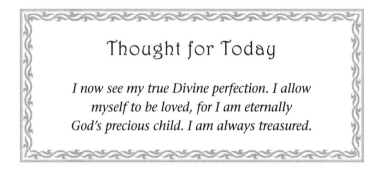

Thought for Today

I now see my true Divine perfection. I allow myself to be loved, for I am eternally God's precious child. I am always treasured.

Tap In to the Source of All Answers

*Y*ou have access to the most amazing database that provides counseling, guidance, and direction—it's located inside of you right now. The source of all answers is enabled and ready anytime you ask it a question, and there's no problem that it can't solve.

Sometimes this source will respond directly with words, thoughts, or visions; on other occasions, it will send synchronistic events as a reply. Each question is always accurately answered, provided that you're open to and aware of the responses as they come.

This wellspring of all information isn't some mysterious supernatural force. It's the most open and natural power in the universe: the infinite wisdom of God's mind, which is linked to your own.

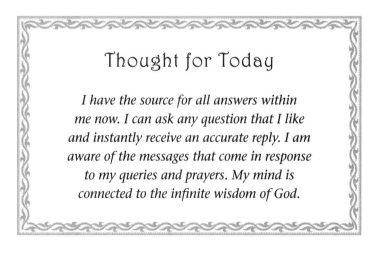

Thought for Today

I have the source for all answers within me now. I can ask any question that I like and instantly receive an accurate reply. I am aware of the messages that come in response to my queries and prayers. My mind is connected to the infinite wisdom of God.

293

Balance Play and Work

*Y*ou have an admirable drive to bring meaning to your own life and those of the people around you. You're exceptionally responsible in caring for others, and you do a good job of nurturing yourself as well.

Today we'd like to focus on the question of balance. Instead of looking upon this topic as one more addition to your "to-do" list, think of it as an equation for squeezing more joy, productivity, and energy out of each moment.

When your day is solely devoted to work, your expenditure of energy is unbalanced, which is what leaves you drained and hungry for food or drinks to boost your spirits. Electrical currents work in a loop of output and input—giving and receiving—and your own body operates in essentially the same way.

Playfulness completes your physical circuits, reenergizing you so that you have the fuel to give and create. When you enjoy yourself, your energy is naturally elevated, which is why play is just as productive and essential as work.

Together, the two activities are the negative and positive poles that keep powerful currents moving. Spend time today playing as well as working, and enjoy the rewards that come from this balance.

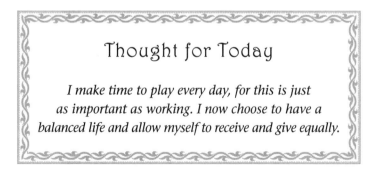

Thought for Today

I make time to play every day, for this is just as important as working. I now choose to have a balanced life and allow myself to receive and give equally.

⤦ 294 ⤧

See Your World Through Fresh Eyes

Sometimes daily routines can blur your ability to notice the fine details of your world, yet those little things are what make life fun and meaningful. One way to reawaken your sensitivity is to imagine that you're seeing everything through someone else's eyes.

Today, imagine that a person who's brand-new to your life is walking beside you. This individual is entirely loving, so you needn't worry about being judged—yet it's interesting to imagine how he or she would view your day. This novel perspective may shed light on some unconscious routines that are no longer serving their purpose. You may decide to make some improvements after seeing your world in this new way.

You'll also probably feel grateful for how blessed you are to have such amazing friends and family in your life. You'll have more appreciation for all the gifts that you have after seeing them with fresh eyes.

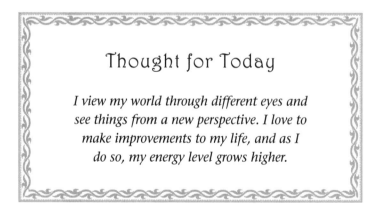

Thought for Today

I view my world through different eyes and see things from a new perspective. I love to make improvements to my life, and as I do so, my energy level grows higher.

295

Script a Happy Ending
to Your Personal Movie

Sometimes you worry about your future and whether everything will
turn out okay. It's similar to the feeling you may have during an intense
movie: The plot is so complicated that you have no idea how the issues
could be resolved, yet ultimately the lead characters are at peace because
they've grown from all that they've faced. All is well and ends happily.

Your own worrisome situations are already taken care of on the
spiritual plane. We angels have fast-forwarded to the conclusion of your
"movie" and seen that it has a happy ending. Every seeming problem
resolves itself—usually in creative ways.

We won't spoil things for you by giving away what we learned in our
sneak preview. Besides, much of your life remains unscripted and awaiting
your personal direction. What we *can* tell you is that your story definitely
ends very happily, with many heartwarming and uplifting scenes along
the way.

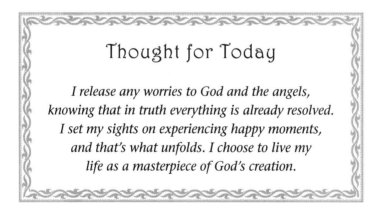

Thought for Today

I release any worries to God and the angels,
knowing that in truth everything is already resolved.
I set my sights on experiencing happy moments,
and that's what unfolds. I choose to live my
life as a masterpiece of God's creation.

Make Time for Yourself

You've been working hard and giving a lot to others. So we angels are here to gently remind you to take some time for yourself. The moment has come for *you.*

Just as you give to others, you also deserve to receive. Treat yourself as well as you do the people you care about. They merit loving attention, and so do you.

Allowing people to assist you benefits them: You let them experience the satisfaction of giving. When you graciously accept others' offers of help, they feel wonderful about their abilities.

Today, wear the hat of both the giver and the receiver. They're really reverse sides of the same thing, and are equally important.

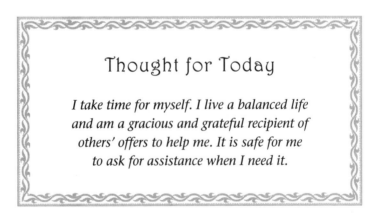

Thought for Today

I take time for myself. I live a balanced life and am a gracious and grateful recipient of others' offers to help me. It is safe for me to ask for assistance when I need it.

297

Trust That You're on the Right Path

We angels applaud you for the path that you're on, and we encourage you to keep going. Your recent decisions to make positive life changes are the result of our teamwork. You requested our help, we gave you guidance, you listened to it, and the adjustments were implemented. Congratulations!

We love you unconditionally, no matter how your life is going or what actions you take. Our joy for you is also without reservation, and we bask in the glow of your contentment.

Since happiness is the closest earthly energy to God, this emotion is our highest state—and yours. It's a form of pure love, so when you're joyful, we're *all* on the same wavelength with God. Your gladness is a key that opens many wonderful doors in your life.

You're on the right path of happiness, so keep going.

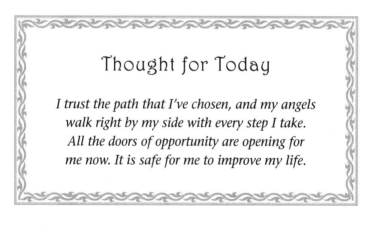

Thought for Today

I trust the path that I've chosen, and my angels walk right by my side with every step I take. All the doors of opportunity are opening for me now. It is safe for me to improve my life.

Meet New Friends

We angels can help with your friendships, both old and new, if you ask us to. We can support you through misunderstandings, help you with communication, and provide you with ideas to celebrate the love between you and those you care about.

We're also happy to usher in new friends for you. As you've grown in your spirituality, your relationships may have shifted. Some people whom you once considered yourself close to are drifting out of your life, and you seem to have different interests from a few of your loved ones. But have no fear . . . these transitions and changes will balance out very soon.

Ask us to help you with your friendships. Know that some of the new people you've met—and will soon meet—are answers to your prayers. Hold expectations of having wonderful, harmonious connections, and that result is inevitable.

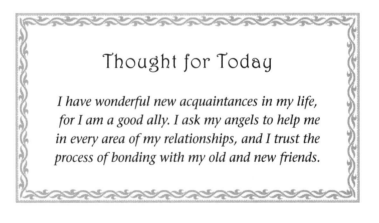

Thought for Today

I have wonderful new acquaintances in my life, for I am a good ally. I ask my angels to help me in every area of my relationships, and I trust the process of bonding with my old and new friends.

Feed Your Heart

You may wonder how to satisfy your desire for more fulfillment and meaning in your life. Sometimes these spiritual and emotional longings are confused with physical cravings for food or other substances. They have similar roots, as they're all a signal that your heart is in need of love.

Today, feed your core the emotional nutrient that it craves. Gently talk to your heart, reassuring it and asking it to open up to the love that continuously encompasses you. Ask it to trust that you will protect it, with the help of us angels.

Nourish yourself with extra doses of caring and compassion, and understand why your heart may have closed up out of a well-meaning desire to protect itself. Feed yourself with fun, friendships, sunsets, and the fragrance of flowers today.

As you care for your heart, you're able to feel the pleasure of giving and receiving love.

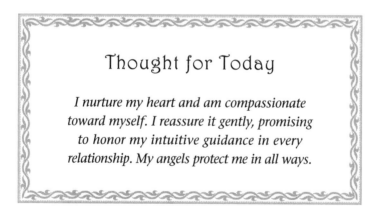

Thought for Today

I nurture my heart and am compassionate toward myself. I reassure it gently, promising to honor my intuitive guidance in every relationship. My angels protect me in all ways.

300

Believe in Your Ideas

Many of your ideas are answers to your prayers. When you pray for Divine assistance, we angels often answer by whispering suggestions into your ear that you hear as thoughts, feelings, visions, or actual words. For instance, if you pray for financial help, we might send you an insight that could increase your income.

As with the other gifts that you receive, our messages are to be opened, used, and enjoyed. Never doubt your capacity to breathe life into a concept. You're God's wise child and have the same capabilities as any other person.

Today we ask you to believe in your ideas. Begin by writing them down; then consult with us frequently, and we'll help you develop a plan of action. The energy that you put into this process now brings great blessings in the future. Nurture your idea and it will care for you after it's developed.

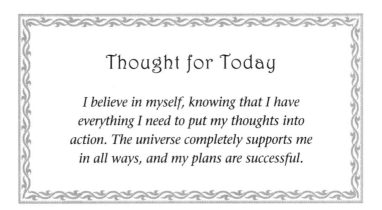

Thought for Today

I believe in myself, knowing that I have everything I need to put my thoughts into action. The universe completely supports me in all ways, and my plans are successful.

Celebrate Yourself

Instead of waiting for a holiday, anniversary, or birthday, why not celebrate today? You have much to appreciate about yourself and your life. Although you have the desire to make improvements, there are so many reasons for you to rejoice.

A celebration sends the powerful energy of your gratitude out into the universe, where it reverberates and grows, bringing more blessings as it returns to you.

Whether you simply want to rejoice with us angels, or choose to do so with your loved ones (who can also celebrate their own blessings), spend some time toasting everything that you're thankful for.

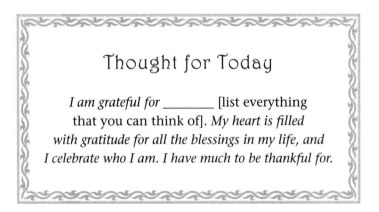

Thought for Today

I am grateful for _____ [list everything that you can think of]. My heart is filled with gratitude for all the blessings in my life, and I celebrate who I am. I have much to be thankful for.

302

Enjoy the Measurement of Love

Sometimes people measure their progress in life by their income or clothing size, yet what truly matters is how much you've loved during your time on Earth. This is all that counts.

When you open your heart to feel, receive, and send affection, you're truly heroic. The voyage to the frontier of love is the most important journey of them all. You have everything you need to ensure a safe and fruitful time as you allow your heart to open wider to permit more affection to be given and received. The key is to let go of any blocks to love, the chief of which is judgment.

When you judge yourself or someone else, you then affirm a separation from God and other people. This gulf could never be true, but believing in it creates the illusion that it exists and elicits a feeling of alienation from Divine affection.

Today, allow yourself to care more. Look past the superficial aspects of other people, and know that you are one with them . . . united by love.

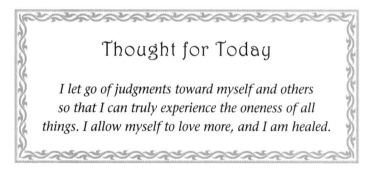

Thought for Today

*I let go of judgments toward myself and others
so that I can truly experience the oneness of all
things. I allow myself to love more, and I am healed.*

303

Pass Along Smiles

We angels have been focusing on expanding the love that you feel, give, and receive. Today we'll work on showing affection in the form of smiles.

You already know that this facial expression is contagious in the best sense of the word. Your smile inspires gladness in others.

Today, see how many grins you can inspire with your own. Like lighting candles from your own flame, you'll brighten the day for many people (including yourself) by passing along your cheer.

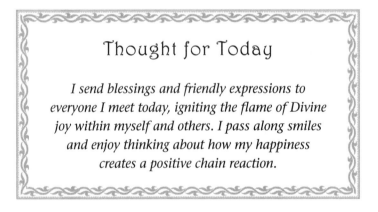

Thought for Today

I send blessings and friendly expressions to everyone I meet today, igniting the flame of Divine joy within myself and others. I pass along smiles and enjoy thinking about how my happiness creates a positive chain reaction.

Focus on the Best That Could Happen

Sometimes you allow your imagination to dwell on the worst-case scenario, allowing this fear to stop you from making positive life changes. We angels would like to offer another perspective: Instead of brooding over the worst that could occur, put your whole focus on pondering: *What's the best that could happen?*

Allow your imagination to run free as you think about the wonderful possibilities. Keep your thoughts anchored on positive outcomes, and feel your excitement as you consider all these options. Know that the actual result could even exceed everything that you're dreaming of.

With each action you take in the direction of your desire, anticipate the best. Your positive expectations shine a bright light on the step that's before you. Your illuminated path then takes on a magical quality, which helps you attract and manifest the very best possibilities.

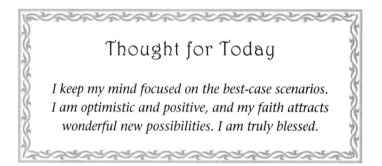

Thought for Today

I keep my mind focused on the best-case scenarios. I am optimistic and positive, and my faith attracts wonderful new possibilities. I am truly blessed.

Make It a Good One

When you first begin working on a new goal, the end can seem a long way off. We angels want to remind you that every important journey begins with a first step, which in many ways sets the tone for the entire trip—so make it a good one.

Take that initial action with enthusiasm and a high regard for yourself. Put your entire focus and energy into the path before you. Stay positive about the outcome, without investing any fear into your vision of the future.

You'll soon enjoy the steps along the way as though they were a fun game that you play with yourself. Your progress is amazing when you make each part of the process count.

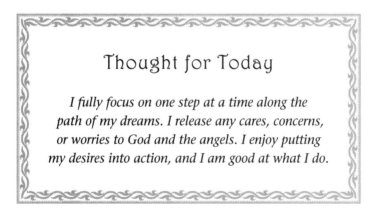

Thought for Today

I fully focus on one step at a time along the path of my dreams. I release any cares, concerns, or worries to God and the angels. I enjoy putting my desires into action, and I am good at what I do.

Try On Your Future

When you come to a fork in the road and can't decide which path to take, you can always "try on" your future as you would clothing that you're considering purchasing. In that way, you can sense the choice that feels best to you.

First, close your eyes and think about the alternatives before you—including the option of nondecision, where everything remains as it currently is. Then imagine the consequences of each option as if you'd already made it, and pay attention to how your body reacts. Do you notice any scenarios where your gut tightens or relaxes? Which choice feels the most natural to you? What do you prefer in your heart? If all excuses were removed (such as believing that you need more money, time, talent, and so on), which road would you take?

All of these considerations will help you make a clear choice, which is essential to fully committing to the course that you pick. Your complete dedication allows you to put more energy into your decision, rather than just making a tentative selection. The greater effort you put into any project, the more powerful its outcome, since the energies of giving and receiving always balance each other.

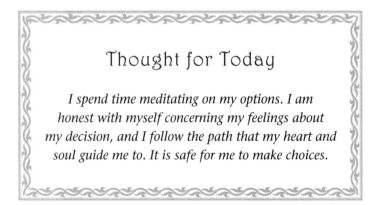

Thought for Today

I spend time meditating on my options. I am honest with myself concerning my feelings about my decision, and I follow the path that my heart and soul guide me to. It is safe for me to make choices.

307

Enjoy a Sense of Belonging

If you ever feel as though you don't fit in with other people, remember that you're always in harmony with us angels. A sense of belonging comes from sharing common interests and habits with others, so sometimes this means joining a club or class related to your favorite sports or hobbies as a way of reaching out to make new friends.

You do belong on this earth, because you have a life purpose that the world needs. You're unique, just as all beings are, yet you share a lot in common with others (including us), which we'll explore today.

To find your similarities, you'll need to put a filter on your thinking that says: *Notice the traits that I share with other people.* Once you set this intention, you'll begin to see commonalities that you might have overlooked if your mind-set had been focused on finding differences between you and others.

Today, remember that we're always with you. We're your loyal companions and friends—and just as *we* love being in your company, so are there people on Earth who will benefit from your friendship.

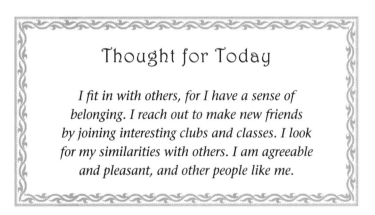

Thought for Today

I fit in with others, for I have a sense of belonging. I reach out to make new friends by joining interesting clubs and classes. I look for my similarities with others. I am agreeable and pleasant, and other people like me.

Accept Our Love

Although there are moments when you doubt your lovableness, we angels cherish you continuously. We never judge or withhold affection, because as reflections of God, we're only capable of love.

Yes, of course, we see your human behavior and know that at times you don't feel good about some of your patterns—yet they serve an important purpose for you, or else you wouldn't continue to repeat them. It's more helpful to hold compassion for who you are than berate yourself for some conduct that you regret.

Think about examples of this in your own life. Which was a more helpful learning experience for you: when a person criticized or punished you for an action that you took, or when someone patiently listened to your reasoning and then offered to show you another way?

Consider how this applies to your relationship with yourself. Gently embrace who you are and all your patterns of behavior. Don't discard any part of you, because it's all essential in the process of reclaiming your holy and loving identity.

Guide yourself tenderly (with our help, if you so desire), like a newly sprouted plant growing in the direction of the sunshine.

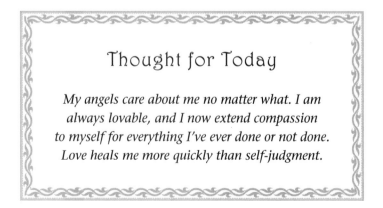

Thought for Today

My angels care about me no matter what. I am always lovable, and I now extend compassion to myself for everything I've ever done or not done. Love heals me more quickly than self-judgment.

Be True to Yourself

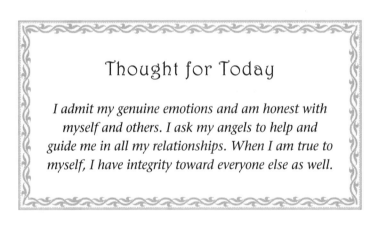

You already know you_____rs, and you must follow their direction. If you defy yourself, y____ ____comes blocked in a holding pattern that's disruptive to many are____ ____ysical, emotional, financial, and spiritual health.

Although many people att_____ _____press their real feelings to please others, eventually these em_____ ____ce and make themselves known—for instance, they might be _____ s physical symptoms of illness or as financial blocks.

While deferring to someone else migh_ seem like a way to be caring, it actually denies you and the other person authenticity. We angels can help you have the courage to voice and act on your feelings while maintaining love, thoughtfulness, respect, and harmony within your relationship.

Thought for Today

I admit my genuine emotions and am honest with myself and others. I ask my angels to help and guide me in all my relationships. When I am true to myself, I have integrity toward everyone else as well.

310

Know That You Deserve
Love and Support

*Y*ou deserve to receive God's love and support as much as anyone. Yes, it's true that you're strong and capable, yet there's no need for you to deny yourself or suffer. Pain isn't the route to enlightenment.

When you push away the help that we angels offer you, we know that it's because you're afraid that you don't deserve it. We have complete compassion for you, so we don't judge your feelings. We do, however, hope that you'll consider our perspective: We were so happy when God appointed us as your guardian angels. Our assignment was to love, support, and guide you throughout your physical life.

Loving you is easy and doesn't require your permission because of our soul-to-soul connection. However, supporting and guiding you can only occur with your approval. When you forget to ask for our help or the answers to your prayers, our mission is delayed. Since we have all the time in the world, we don't become frustrated under these circumstances—we love you, whether or not you accept our aid.

Today, please remind yourself that you merit heaven's help. This isn't the same as entitlement; it's the natural process wherein we support and guide you as part of God's plan.

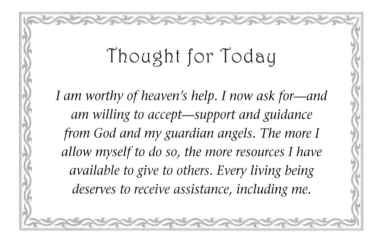

Thought for Today

I am worthy of heaven's help. I now ask for—and am willing to accept—support and guidance from God and my guardian angels. The more I allow myself to do so, the more resources I have available to give to others. Every living being deserves to receive assistance, including me.

Hold On to Your Dreams

*Y*our dreams, goals, ambitions, and intentions are very personal. They belong to you because they're part of your soul's path. Only you know what your heart and spirit are guiding you to do and become.

No matter what circumstances arise in your life, how you feel about yourself, or what other people say or do, you must hold on to your dreams. They're an essential component of why you were incarnated on Earth at this time—they're a part of you, as well as the building blocks of your creations.

Today, embrace your desires. Revive them if you haven't thought about them for a while, and ask us angels to help you put them into action. We'll open doors for you, and even motivate you to walk through them.

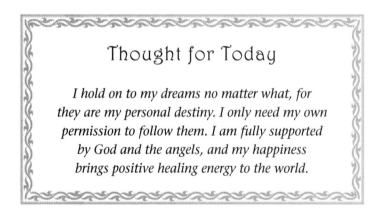

Thought for Today

I hold on to my dreams no matter what, for they are my personal destiny. I only need my own permission to follow them. I am fully supported by God and the angels, and my happiness brings positive healing energy to the world.

Savor the Sweetness of Life

*Y*our life is meant to bring you sweet enjoyment, even as you're fulfilling your purpose and other responsibilities. Joy doesn't just come during moments of leisure—much of your greatest satisfaction occurs while you're performing a service for someone else.

You can enjoy more sweetness simply by noticing it. The rich textures of your relationships and the fine details of humor, drama, playfulness, love, and so forth are all a part of your wonderful life.

Play a game with yourself today, seeing how much delight you can extract from every situation. Find the richness within each interaction and experience that you have. Savor the sweetness that today (and every day) brings you.

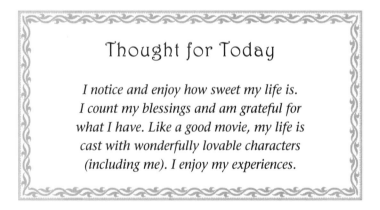

Thought for Today

I notice and enjoy how sweet my life is.
I count my blessings and am grateful for
what I have. Like a good movie, my life is
cast with wonderfully lovable characters
(including me). I enjoy my experiences.

Do Something Nice for Yourself

*Y*ou're always doing considerate things for others, both loved ones and strangers alike. Today, give yourself the same caring treatment—do something nice for yourself. You already know what it is you'd like; it's the first thing that entered your mind as you read this paragraph.

Perhaps you want to buy a special gift that you've been longing for, or make time for some pampering treatments. Whatever you do, your inner self always appreciates loving attention. The form that your self-care takes is secondary; what's most important is simply the fact that you're being kind to yourself. You deserve it.

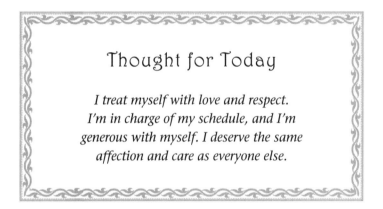

Thought for Today

I treat myself with love and respect.
I'm in charge of my schedule, and I'm
generous with myself. I deserve the same
affection and care as everyone else.

Enjoy Unwavering Faith

*Y*ou already know the importance of staying filled with faith as far as manifestations and healings are concerned. We angels are here today to teach you some methods to gather and boost your power of belief.

Faith is the ability to stay focused on love no matter what, trusting it to bring about wonderful solutions and miracles. This belief counts on love to provide all the answers. Distrust, on the other hand, is the opposite: It makes you believe that you have to do everything by yourself; and all things in life are won through struggling, worrying, and competing. Of the two feelings, which do you believe is happier and healthier?

Remember that when you ask for a prayer to be answered, you can also request to have your faith elevated.

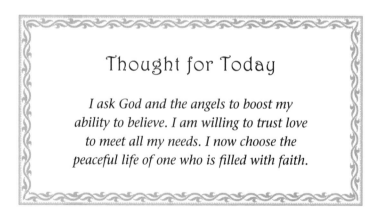

Thought for Today

I ask God and the angels to boost my ability to believe. I am willing to trust love to meet all my needs. I now choose the peaceful life of one who is filled with faith.

Release Fear and Indecision

There's nothing to fear. This emotion is merely an echo reverberating from the far reaches of your memory, from the time when the human ego tried to separate from God. Of course, such a feat could never be accomplished, so the decision was made to create "race-mind consciousness" to diminish awareness of the Divine. In other words, a mass amnesia about love occurred in an attempt to mimic independence from heaven. This is when free will was born.

The way out of this trap is to always remember that you're one with God and everyone else. This simple yet profound fact will remind you that every fear is based on illusion . . . so affirm your oneness with heaven often today. Feel the tension leave your body and consciousness as you recognize the spiritual truth within yourself and every situation.

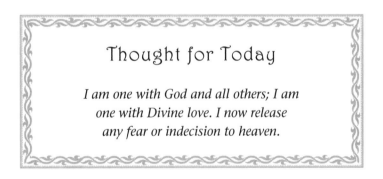

Thought for Today

I am one with God and all others; I am one with Divine love. I now release any fear or indecision to heaven.

Enjoy Clear Focus and Thinking

*Y*our mind works perfectly. You're intelligent, wise, and able to focus and concentrate at will. All your mental gifts stem from the fact that you're linked with the infinite wisdom of the Creator, Who made and knows everything in the universe.

Your mind is always working, even when it appears to be asleep or at rest—it gathers information from the ether and your physical surroundings. You can ask it any question, and it will always deliver an accurate response. You know much more than you're consciously aware of.

Today, enjoy your special wisdom. Ask yourself questions throughout the day and listen to the answers. The more you're aware of your mental gifts, the better they'll serve you.

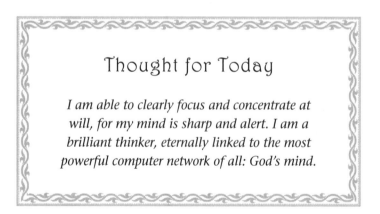

Thought for Today

I am able to clearly focus and concentrate at will, for my mind is sharp and alert. I am a brilliant thinker, eternally linked to the most powerful computer network of all: God's mind.

Be Lighthearted

A happy heart is healthy, both physically and emotionally. There's no such thing as being "*over*joyed," since everyone contains unlimited amounts of happiness. However, we angels have noticed that some people distrust feeling pleasure, and this is what we'd like to focus on today.

Contentment is the safest state of being because it's the most natural one. When you're joyful, you're truly being yourself—it's the act of being lighthearted, which means bringing "light" into your "heart." You do this by visualizing breathing in healing energy, by sending love to another person (including someone in the spirit world), or by thinking carefree thoughts.

Throughout the day, hold the intention of being lighthearted, consciously drawing God's illumination into your core. Allow this radiance to feed and nourish your soul. Emit it wherever you go through your eyes, breath, and the words that you speak so that everyone will receive your gift of joy.

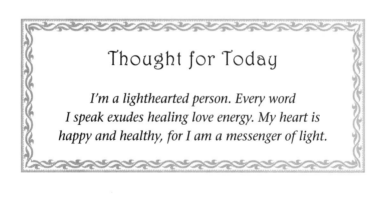

Thought for Today

*I'm a lighthearted person. Every word
I speak exudes healing love energy. My heart is
happy and healthy, for I am a messenger of light.*

318

Hold Yourself in High Esteem

We angels sometimes watch you struggle with feelings that you're not liked or loved. We want you to know that although this is a universal concern among humans, it's not based in reality. The truth is that you *are* likable and lovable. People do appreciate you . . . and you know that *we* cherish and adore you.

If you ever feel alone, misunderstood, or unloved, stop and call upon us to help you. We'll immediately send extra doses of caring Divine energy to fuel you.

You're love itself and can never be apart from your spiritual source. You're eternally wrapped in our wings—which is an expression of God's magnificent reverence for you. Hold yourself in high esteem, for you're truly worthy of all the great affection that heaven bestows upon you.

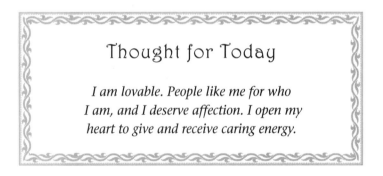

Thought for Today

I am lovable. People like me for who I am, and I deserve affection. I open my heart to give and receive caring energy.

Know That You're Qualified

At times, your ego tries to dissuade you from pursuing your spiritual purpose and practices. If you were to listen to this voice, you'd feel disheartened and confused about yourself and the meaning of your life. Today we angels will work with you to lower the volume of the ego. You have the ability to tune out the sound of fear and focus on the universal voice of love.

The first step is to recognize negative messages as they occur. You can do this by noticing your physical reactions to distressing thoughts. When your muscles tighten and you feel tense, this is a sign of the ego's interference. Divine intervention, in contrast, leaves you feeling blissful, safe, and lighthearted.

Once your body signals that it's been affected by your ego, the next step is to realize that love prevails over all fear. You already know this, yet you can forget such a basic truth in the face of conflict. Call upon us to remind you of your powerful Divine nature, which drives all negative emotions away.

You're qualified to perform the job that you came to Earth to do. You have monumental skills and talents that you inherited directly from God, the Creator. Enjoy these abilities, as they're gifts from heaven.

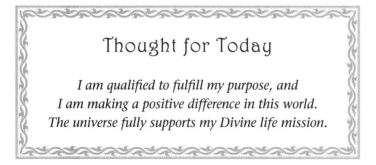

Thought for Today

I am qualified to fulfill my purpose, and
I am making a positive difference in this world.
The universe fully supports my Divine life mission.

Recapture Wonder and Awe

Children naturally see the world through innocent eyes. They're delighted and entertained by their environment, and this sense of wonder and awe doesn't have to fade with time. You can become entranced with your life simply by stating that this is your intention.

Boredom occurs because of the belief that repeated stimuli become uninteresting. You find things dull when your life seems static and routine. Yet everything is always changing in the physical world: Colors, lighting, and other nuances are constantly shifting. It's impossible for anything to stay the same on Earth due to the function of time—this is the opposite of the realm of Spirit, which stays identical throughout eternity.

By training your senses to seek out these subtle (and sometimes not-so-subtle) alterations and differences, you recapture some of your youthful excitement about life. Today, notice the rich variations that run through every experience.

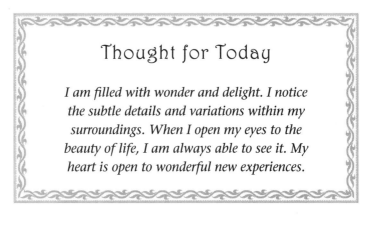

Thought for Today

I am filled with wonder and delight. I notice the subtle details and variations within my surroundings. When I open my eyes to the beauty of life, I am always able to see it. My heart is open to wonderful new experiences.

321

Retreat and Rejuvenate

When you're feeling low or tired, we angels can prop you up so that you return to your naturally high state of awareness and vitality. Spend some time reclining with your eyes closed, and we'll work with you to revive your energy levels. Simply rest your eyes, breathe deeply, and call upon us to assist you.

This is the equivalent of going to a spa and asking for a treatment. Anytime you wholeheartedly allow yourself to receive help—whether from a loving person or us—you'll feel your energy increase. Tiredness comes from too much unidirectional giving. Every being needs to recharge after making so many contributions.

Allow us to give to you, replenishing and rejuvenating your spirits.

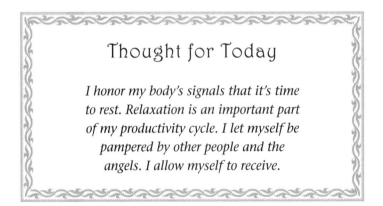

Thought for Today

I honor my body's signals that it's time to rest. Relaxation is an important part of my productivity cycle. I let myself be pampered by other people and the angels. I allow myself to receive.

Be Easy on Yourself

Of course you want to be happy, healthy, prosperous, and fulfilled, but the route to these goals is gentleness. You actually detain yourself when you try to go faster or judge yourself harshly. When it comes to your spiritual path, pain doesn't equal progress—peace does.

We angels ask you to be easy on yourself today. Treat yourself with tenderness, even while you're meeting your responsibilities and goals. Think of how a horse responds to loving care and wise coaching versus tyrannical prodding. Don't you deserve the same respect that you'd give another living being?

There's no racecourse for you to run. Your path is beautiful and so much more enjoyable if you meander slowly enough to notice the people, flowers, trees, birds, and other lovely details along the way. Enjoy the day!

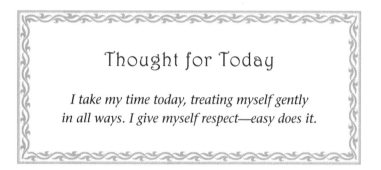

Thought for Today

I take my time today, treating myself gently in all ways. I give myself respect—easy does it.

Know That You're Already Perfect

God created you perfectly. You needn't strive for more greatness, as you're flawless in every way right now. Your health, spirituality, emotions, relationships, and purpose are already ideal.

The only reason why you might not view your life this way is if you're looking for faults. Whatever you seek, you will find. Imperfections are impossible in God's world, yet you have the free will to see and experience whatever you desire.

Today, seek out the wonder within yourself, others, and all situations. See the shining light that rises like the dawn, casting away the darkness.

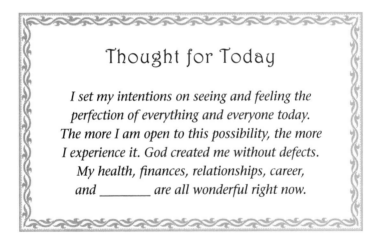

Thought for Today

I set my intentions on seeing and feeling the perfection of everything and everyone today. The more I am open to this possibility, the more I experience it. God created me without defects. My health, finances, relationships, career, and _____ are all wonderful right now.

Trust Your Ideas

Many of your ideas are Divinely inspired answers to your prayers. For example, you wish for a more meaningful career or a better relationship, and we angels—the messengers of God's teachings—show you how to create these conditions for yourself. And when you finally take action, the results are Divine.

First, you must trust your ideas so that you can put the full weight and energy of your convictions behind them. Believe in yourself because you have faith in God's wisdom, which is infallible. Know that you have the support of the entire universe behind you. Move forward confidently as you breathe life into your Divinely inspired ideas.

Trust in the thoughts you receive today that emphasize serving, loving, healing, and inspiring. The focus of these ideas is giving, and when they're manifested, they always yield great rewards.

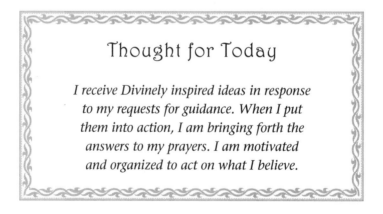

Thought for Today

I receive Divinely inspired ideas in response to my requests for guidance. When I put them into action, I am bringing forth the answers to my prayers. I am motivated and organized to act on what I believe.

Trust Your Feelings

*Y*ou primarily hear messages from us angels through your physical and emotional sensations. Our guidance comes to you as gut feelings, intuition, warmth in your chest, tightening of your muscles, goose bumps, and so forth.

Since we sometimes see you dismiss such feedback as "just a feeling," we're asking you to trust yourself. Think of the many times when you ignored your instincts, only to have them confirmed later—you've certainly regretted some instances when you didn't listen to yourself. You're also occasionally afraid of the intensity of what you feel, and you confuse your own emotions with those of others.

Don't worry about dealing with these issues, beloved one, as we have answers available to you around the clock. Check in with us if you ever have doubts about the validity of your impressions. We'll give you concrete signs and guidance to help you benefit from the beautiful messages that are delivered through your feelings.

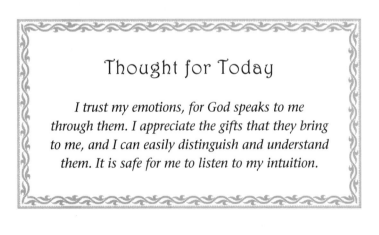

Thought for Today

I trust my emotions, for God speaks to me through them. I appreciate the gifts that they bring to me, and I can easily distinguish and understand them. It is safe for me to listen to my intuition.

Set Down Your Burdens

You've been carrying your cares on your shoulders, weighing yourself down with burdens that interfere with your peace and happiness. We angels ask you to set down your load today and give your worries to us.

When you hand us your concerns, your mind and heart are freed from fear, giving you more access to creativity and wisdom. Solutions come more easily to those who are unafraid.

Right now, take a deep breath and allow us to lift the weight from your shoulders. Once your heart is liberated from fear and anxiety, it's open to receive the help that we always offer you.

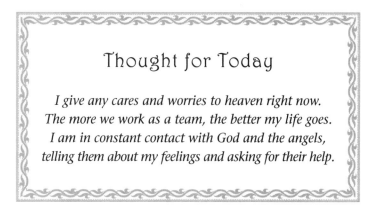

Thought for Today

I give any cares and worries to heaven right now.
The more we work as a team, the better my life goes.
I am in constant contact with God and the angels,
telling them about my feelings and asking for their help.

Know That We're Proud of You

Throughout your life, we angels have stood at your side, experiencing everything along with you. In some instances, you asked for our help, which we gladly provided; other times, you were more comfortable going it alone.

Through it all, we've always been proud of you. We're impressed right now with all the ways that you've stayed committed to your truth. You've grown, learned, given, and received—and we're as eternally pleased as we could be.

Today, stand tall and know that you're a valuable individual. You deserve respect and honor from yourself and other people. You're a blessing to the world.

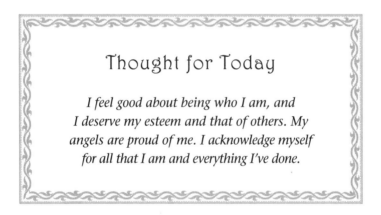

Thought for Today

*I feel good about being who I am, and
I deserve my esteem and that of others. My
angels are proud of me. I acknowledge myself
for all that I am and everything I've done.*

Open the Gates of Abundance

*Y*ou have the keys to the gates of abundance right now. They consist of an open heart and mind that are ready to receive. Receptivity comes from the ability to see the possibilities and potential within yourself, others, and all situations. It means noticing and capitalizing on the Divine ideas that we angels send you, as well as allowing other people to help you.

Everything you need is yours for the asking. You begin with a simple request, which can be made in any number of ways: through prayers, affirmations, visualizations, and such. Any method is sufficient to set the wheels in motion.

Your receptivity is the next part of this process. The universe will transmit messages to guide you in the direction of your desired outcome or send what you want directly to you. This requires alertness and a willingness to receive help and gifts.

In following this path, you aid many people besides yourself. You serve as an inspiration to all those who need a reminder of the importance of asking for assistance and accepting it when it comes.

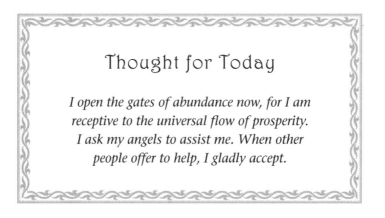

Thought for Today

*I open the gates of abundance now, for I am
receptive to the universal flow of prosperity.
I ask my angels to assist me. When other
people offer to help, I gladly accept.*

Have Patience with Yourself

*Y*ou're making progress along your chosen path. Everything that's brought you to this point has been a learning experience. You have hard-won knowledge and wisdom that will help you with all your future endeavors.

It's important to have patience with yourself. You may not be able to see how far you've come until you can look back on this moment from some point in the future. You've made monumental strides and gained a great deal of practical wisdom—and all this learning took time.

Today, have patience with yourself and your progress. Know that whenever you worked, played, loved, and rested, there was a reason you did so. All of those experiences have culminated in the wonderful person you are today, so enjoy yourself, beloved one . . . relax.

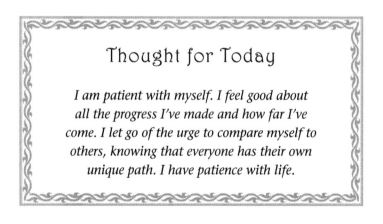

Thought for Today

I am patient with myself. I feel good about all the progress I've made and how far I've come. I let go of the urge to compare myself to others, knowing that everyone has their own unique path. I have patience with life.

Focus on Similarities

When you're newly in love with someone, you naturally focus on everything that you both have in common. This energy of caring is shared by everyone. As you concentrate on your similarities to the people in your life, you bring loving understanding to every relationship.

The ego relishes making you compare yourself to others and focus on all your differences. This is a device to support the illusion that you're separated from God, us angels, and other people.

Your higher self, in contrast, is centered on the true nature of love, so look for the features that you share with others today. Notice the tender feelings that this inspires within you and your relationships. You may find that you have more in common with the people in your life than you'd ever have thought possible.

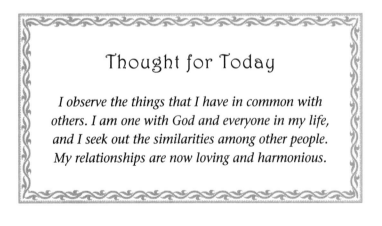

Thought for Today

I observe the things that I have in common with others. I am one with God and everyone in my life, and I seek out the similarities among other people. My relationships are now loving and harmonious.

Rise above Illusions

Every seeming problem is built upon an illusion that something could go wrong in God's world. When you realize that there's Divine order behind everything, you relax into the arms of the universe, which really does know what it's doing. Its mathematical precision and love are the foundation for everything that happens. So any difficulties that you encounter come from an assumption that something is amiss or out of order, and this is impossible.

Today, we angels will work with you to look past false impressions to the true symmetry underlying all people and things. By doing so, you make a great contribution, similar to what your physicists call the "observer effect," which states that your very presence changes whatever you're looking at. In the same way, when you see beyond the appearance of chaos and notice orderliness instead, you help others do the same.

The more people are able to rise above illusions, the more God's universe is revealed to be an infinite and vibrant paradise. It's heaven on Earth for those who are observant.

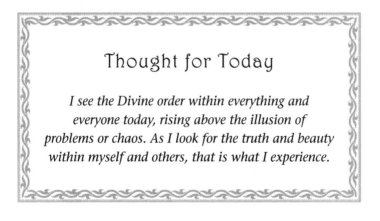

Thought for Today

I see the Divine order within everything and everyone today, rising above the illusion of problems or chaos. As I look for the truth and beauty within myself and others, that is what I experience.

Decide What Kind of
Day You'd Like to Have

*Y*ou have the ability and power to set the tone for your day. You do this by determining the type of experience that you'd prefer. Ask yourself now: *What kind of a day would I like to have?* Only allow yourself to visualize and feel the highest energies. If you find yourself focusing on negative scenarios, ask us angels to transmute this fearful energy into love.

You're the director of your day. In any situation, there's a best possible outcome, and you move to that higher level through your commitment to have extraordinary experiences.

You deserve all the greatness that life can offer. Collect your bounty today, and decide to have a wonderful time.

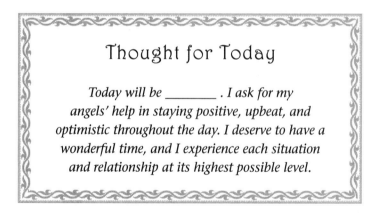

Thought for Today

Today will be _____ . I ask for my angels' help in staying positive, upbeat, and optimistic throughout the day. I deserve to have a wonderful time, and I experience each situation and relationship at its highest possible level.

Relax Because It's All God

God is omnipresent, which means that the Divine is everywhere and within each person and thing. All that you see is God. It's impossible for anything or anyone to be apart from heaven, no matter how it might appear.

Cling to this knowledge today. In any situation where you feel fear or stress, tell yourself, *This is God.* This reminder relaxes away the worry that something could be out of order. You'll recall that you're safely guided in all circumstances and need only listen to and follow that guidance with faith.

Today, remember that the Divine is within you and every person—it's all around you. As you focus on the fact that it's all the Creator, you experience heaven's enveloping love. Apparent problems begin to vanish through undreamed-of solutions.

Relax right now, because it's all God.

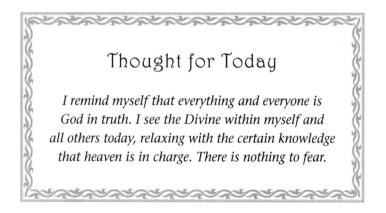

Thought for Today

I remind myself that everything and everyone is God in truth. I see the Divine within myself and all others today, relaxing with the certain knowledge that heaven is in charge. There is nothing to fear.

Put This Situation in God's Hands

The best way to resolve a situation that stirs worry or anger in you is to give it to God. Today, put what's bothering you into the Creator's ready and able hands. You don't need to go through it alone—ever.

Stewing over a situation only makes it more combustible. Releasing the situation to God means that it will be settled in a miraculously harmonious way. It also frees you from the toxic effects of stress or rage.

If you need help in letting go, please call upon us angels. We'll never interfere with your free will, but we can aid you in seeing the light of all the peaceful options that are available to you.

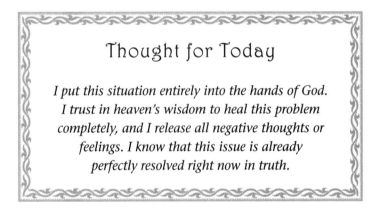

Thought for Today

I put this situation entirely into the hands of God. I trust in heaven's wisdom to heal this problem completely, and I release all negative thoughts or feelings. I know that this issue is already perfectly resolved right now in truth.

Bless Your Past

*Y*our prior experiences and relationships have given you many gifts of wisdom, learning, strength, patience, and the like. Now is the time to make peace with your past and know that everything happened for a beautifully Divine reason. Have no regrets about what's occurred, for it's made you the wonderful person you are today.

Bless your past and anything within it that you feel needs healing. Whatever weighs on your mind or body will benefit from your loving intentions today.

Send healing energy to your life—in every direction of time. Honor your mother, father, and anyone else who comes to mind from your personal history. The more blessings you bestow upon your past, the more gifts you'll receive in the present.

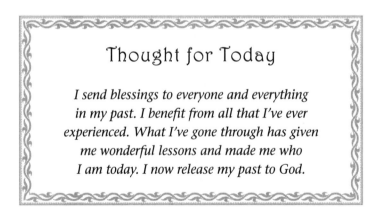

Thought for Today

*I send blessings to everyone and everything
in my past. I benefit from all that I've ever
experienced. What I've gone through has given
me wonderful lessons and made me who
I am today. I now release my past to God.*

Know That Your Divine Power Works Perfectly

As a child of God, you inherited spiritual gifts from your Creator, and they work perfectly all the time. Since your power is an extension of God, there could never be a time when it's blocked or reduced—it's always radiating at full intensity, ready to be harnessed.

Your power puts your thoughts, feelings, and wishes into action. Since it's like a laser beam, you must be cautious about where it's pointed. Use care in selecting only thoughts that mirror your heart's desires, and don't put energy into fears, lest you manifest them into form.

You're Divinely guided in all that you do with your God-given gift. Today, use it to amplify your caring thoughts and feelings. In a single day, you can greatly increase the amount of love that you experience in your life. Your heavenly power can magnify anything for you, so allow it to be directed toward love.

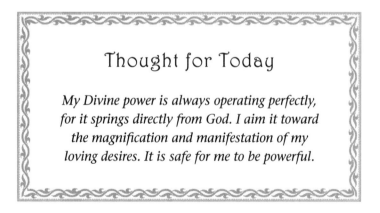

Thought for Today

My Divine power is always operating perfectly, for it springs directly from God. I aim it toward the magnification and manifestation of my loving desires. It is safe for me to be powerful.

Celebrate Your New Beginnings

This is a time of positive change for you. It's important to focus on what's coming up, instead of worrying about what you're letting go of. You're in a growth cycle, so you may feel overwhelmed as many life lessons come at you at once. However, know that things are starting to calm down for you now.

Today we angels want to herald and celebrate the new beginnings in your life! You're venturing into uncharted water, so it's natural to feel nervous or even afraid. We're holding your hand through each step, and we won't let you fall. It's safe for you to move forward—just keep checking in with your inner guidance, which is the system of communication directly connected to the Divine.

Recast any nervousness into feelings of excitement about all the wonderful possibilities that lie before you. You're on the threshold of spectacular new opportunities that will enrich your life in undreamed-of ways.

Celebrate your new beginnings today, beloved one. They're the start of something wondrous and beautiful.

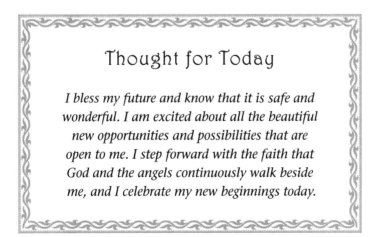

Thought for Today

I bless my future and know that it is safe and wonderful. I am excited about all the beautiful new opportunities and possibilities that are open to me. I step forward with the faith that God and the angels continuously walk beside me, and I celebrate my new beginnings today.

338

Enjoy Eternal Love

The affection that you've shared with another person or animal is a bond that can never be broken. Even in relationships that later soured, the love remains intact—it brought you together for a purpose. The caring that you shared created a magic that lifts you both up eternally, even after the relationship is over.

Love is an everlasting energy that can never dissipate, but will grow and take innumerable forms. Today, ride on the crest of the wave where this emotion has elevated you. Give thanks for the affection that you've shared in every relationship . . . it is a sacred and lasting gift from God.

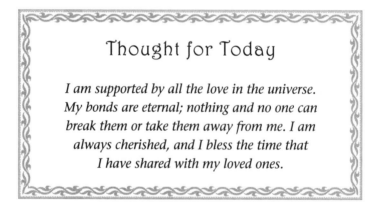

Thought for Today

I am supported by all the love in the universe. My bonds are eternal; nothing and no one can break them or take them away from me. I am always cherished, and I bless the time that I have shared with my loved ones.

Walk Through Open Doors

$\mathcal{E}$very door of opportunity is open to you right now—there's nothing that you're barred or blocked from. The question is which one you wish to enter, since it's entirely your choice.

Sometimes you might feel overwhelmed by having too many options available, or you may question your ability to walk through a particular door. Today we angels will help you see the possibilities that are open to you, lending you the clarity and courage to enter the dreams that you desire. Give us any fears, questions, or reservations about this process.

Sometimes moving forward means leaving something behind. We'll safely guide and support you through this change.

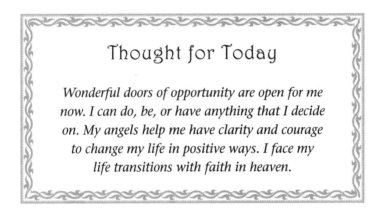

Thought for Today

Wonderful doors of opportunity are open for me now. I can do, be, or have anything that I decide on. My angels help me have clarity and courage to change my life in positive ways. I face my life transitions with faith in heaven.

Trust That Your Prayers
Are Being Answered

Although you may not see the results, your prayers are being answered. The universe is currently working behind the scenes on your behalf, and the manifestation of your desire is imminent.

Your role in the meantime is to maintain faith and follow your inner guidance; the rest is up to God and us angels. We're very happy to work to support you in the name of love and peacefulness. As you ascend in happiness, we're elevated right along with you, so is it any wonder that we work diligently to boost your joy?

God's will is radiated like beams of the sun, ensuring elation for all. As we guide you along the warm pathways of love, your answered prayers spring up before you like flowers.

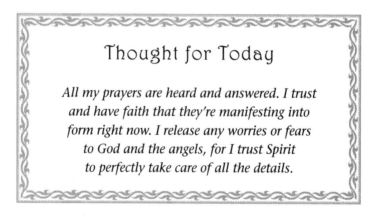

Thought for Today

*All my prayers are heard and answered. I trust
and have faith that they're manifesting into
form right now. I release any worries or fears
to God and the angels, for I trust Spirit
to perfectly take care of all the details.*

Embrace Happiness

*Y*ou needn't strive or struggle for happiness, as it's your natural state of being. God is entirely joyful, and as the Creator's offspring, you share this eternal trait. You only seem to be down when you turn away from the light and stare into the illusion of darkness. Look toward the radiant Source today; focus on the Divine in all that you think, say, and do; and know that all is well.

Happiness is your natural state of being—in fact, it dwells inside of you right now. To reveal and enjoy it, simply be honest with yourself and others. We angels will lend you the courage and strength to do so, if you ask us for assistance.

You have the right to be happy, just as all of God's children do. The Creator's will for everyone is joy, and our assignment is to put this into action. Today, allow us to help you feel the contentment that is your birthright and spiritual essence.

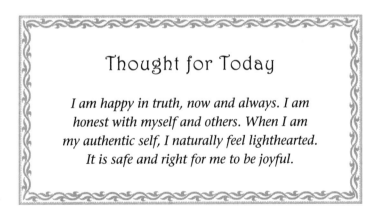

Thought for Today

I am happy in truth, now and always. I am honest with myself and others. When I am my authentic self, I naturally feel lighthearted. It is safe and right for me to be joyful.

Trust That Your Loved Ones Are Safe

Give us angels any concerns or worries about your loved ones, and know that they're truly safe. We're guarding them with God's infinite care and wisdom, and your love also ensures their protection.

Nothing can harm a being who's created by the Divine, as that soul is eternally happy, healthy, and alive. We watch over the people you care about—just as you and God asked—and we send blessings and guidance to help them all along the way.

Continue with your beautiful prayers for your loved ones' well-being. Trust that they're spectacularly well cared for each and every moment, safely cradled in heaven's tender embrace.

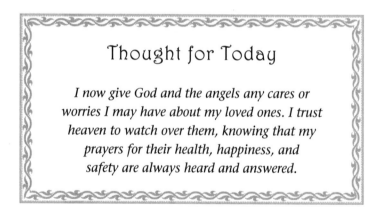

Thought for Today

I now give God and the angels any cares or worries I may have about my loved ones. I trust heaven to watch over them, knowing that my prayers for their health, happiness, and safety are always heard and answered.

Trust Your Decisions

There's a decision that you're wondering about, and you wrestle with yourself regarding the pros and cons of each side of it. You already know which direction you're leaning toward, yet you fear the unforeseen negative consequences of your choice.

We angels are here today to help you make peace with your decision. Resolve not to think about the various options that you're grappling with, shelving the entire topic right now. During this incubation period, your mind is more relaxed and open to the creative Divine input that you've prayed to receive.

Let go of any sense of strain. The more you ease your mind about the issue, the clearer and more apparent your choice becomes. At that point, it's not even a decision—the answer is so obvious to you that it becomes an awakening.

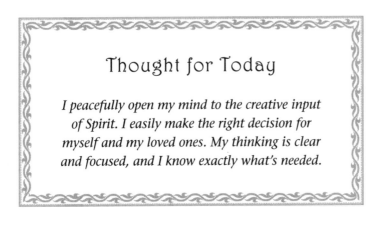

Thought for Today

I peacefully open my mind to the creative input of Spirit. I easily make the right decision for myself and my loved ones. My thinking is clear and focused, and I know exactly what's needed.

Let Ideas Come to You

The universal mind has infinite ideas that you can always tap in to. You receive them in response to a question that you've posed to the universe with a clear and quiet awareness. Today, ask Spirit about any topic that you need help or guidance with. You can think your question or voice it aloud.

Sometime today, sit quietly and notice the ideas that come to mind after each query. All that you need to do to hear the answers is spend time listening in silence. These ideas are gifts to you from the universe. You're qualified and ready to act on them, and all of creation fully supports your doing so.

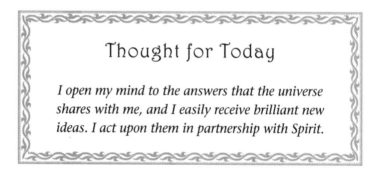

Thought for Today

I open my mind to the answers that the universe shares with me, and I easily receive brilliant new ideas. I act upon them in partnership with Spirit.

Enjoy Infinite Abundance

Everything that you need for your Divine life purpose is continuously offered to you. What would you like to have more of? Anything you can think of is provided for you—the key is to stay in steady contact with Spirit through prayer and meditation, and then take action as you're guided. This partnership program allows you to relax, and focus on doing service with joy.

Please don't worry about any earthly details of how you'll have enough time, money, ideas, and so forth. Those needs are provided for you as you go along.

Today, rest in the faith that your world is infinitely abundant. All things are forever being born, growing, and regenerating. The universe is constantly giving to you and everyone who teams up with the heavenly flow.

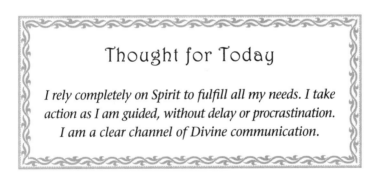

Thought for Today

I rely completely on Spirit to fulfill all my needs. I take action as I am guided, without delay or procrastination. I am a clear channel of Divine communication.

Honor Your Sensitivity

*Y*our sensitivity is a gift that allows you to hear Divine guidance, feel your own and others' emotions, have compassion, and respect nature. Treasure this part of you, beloved one.

Honor your gentleness by avoiding harsh energies today. We angels will protect you and steer you away from negative situations and relationships. We'll guide your eating and drinking choices so that your diet nurtures your sensitivity as well.

As you treat yourself with the respect and care that you deserve, your self-appreciation and love automatically increase. Trust that everything you feel is a blessing, and be glad for your gift of sensitivity.

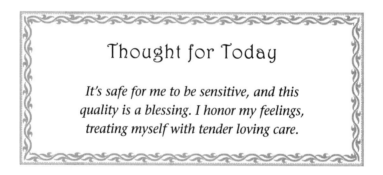

Thought for Today

It's safe for me to be sensitive, and this quality is a blessing. I honor my feelings, treating myself with tender loving care.

Uncover Your Peaceful Nature

eloved one, you don't need to do anything to become peaceful . . . you already are. If you don't feel this way right now, call upon us angels to help you.

Fear doesn't keep you safe, nor does it solve problems. Only a tranquil mind can clearly hear the voice of the Divine, which calmly guides you toward the solutions you seek.

Regardless of the situation at hand, the answer is always found through your inner peace. Today, be an explorer who ventures inward. Make serenity your target—not as something that you must acquire or earn, but as a treasure lying in wait for you to find.

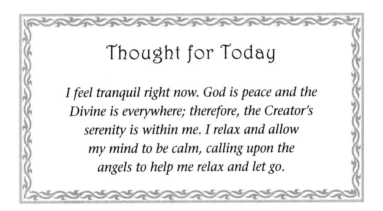

Thought for Today

I feel tranquil right now. God is peace and the Divine is everywhere; therefore, the Creator's serenity is within me. I relax and allow my mind to be calm, calling upon the angels to help me relax and let go.

Embrace Your Prosperity

As you count your blessings, more are revealed to you. The route to prosperity is paved with gratitude and the awareness of abundance. Today's guidance is very simple and direct: Notice all the examples of bounty in your life. There are many varieties, such as a profusion of time, choices, love, energy, beauty, and so forth.

As you notice prosperity in one area of your life, you begin to attract it into others.

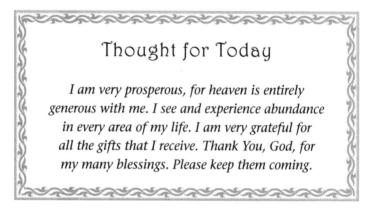

Thought for Today

I am very prosperous, for heaven is entirely generous with me. I see and experience abundance in every area of my life. I am very grateful for all the gifts that I receive. Thank You, God, for my many blessings. Please keep them coming.

Embrace Your Health

As with prosperity, health is a viewpoint that's chosen. The more you focus on well-being within yourself and others, the more you experience it. Today, look past any earthly appearances of illness or injury, and see the wellness inside of each person (especially yourself).

Give us angels any concerns that you have about health, doing your best to concentrate on the light that resides within you and everyone. The more you focus on this illumination, the more brightly it glows. The radiance of the Divine within each person is a beacon that banishes darkness. In its place is the perfect grace and stillness that God created inside all beings.

You're already healthy, and so is everyone in your life. Affirm this frequently today, and feel the truth of it in your body. You find exactly what you seek, so today, set your intentions on looking for health. If you only see wellness, that's what you experience as a result.

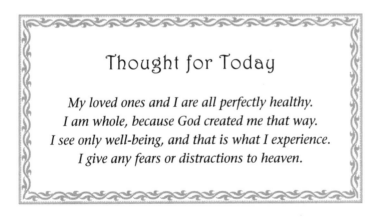

Thought for Today

My loved ones and I are all perfectly healthy.
I am whole, because God created me that way.
I see only well-being, and that is what I experience.
I give any fears or distractions to heaven.

Expect Everything to Go Well

Put your entire focus on anticipating that whatever you're concerned about will go well. Your positive expectations about your situation will steer it in the desired direction.

Remember that worries are influential energies that are perceived as wishes by the universe. When you're troubled, you draw your anxiety into your experiences. Don't allow yourself to give in to fears—deliver them to us angels instead.

Holding positive or negative expectations takes the same amount of time and effort. The outcome of your current situation is guaranteed to be good, yet your experience of the process of getting to that point is influenced by what you think will happen. If you foresee problems, you'll come across them along the way; on the other hand, if you anticipate harmony, then that's what you'll experience. Either way, everything is going to turn out just fine—but which path would you prefer to take? Your expectations set your course.

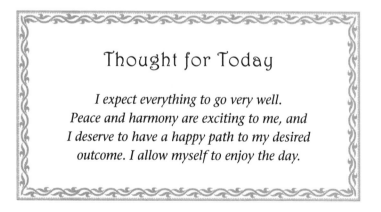

Thought for Today

I expect everything to go very well.
Peace and harmony are exciting to me, and
I deserve to have a happy path to my desired
outcome. I allow myself to enjoy the day.

351

Listen to Your Inner Child

No matter how old you are, the child within you still needs attention, care, and love. All children thrive on praise and wish to express themselves. Today, we angels encourage you to listen to this part of you.

If your spirits or emotions lag, it's very likely a sign that your inner child requires some attention. When you listen to its needs, the reward is increased energy and joyfulness. Take a moment right now to become still and quiet, think about the little one within you, and notice any feelings that result. Ask it: "How can I care for you today?"

Listen to the response that comes to you as a thought, sensation, vision, or words. Your inner child is glad when you listen and feels even better when you take action based on its requests.

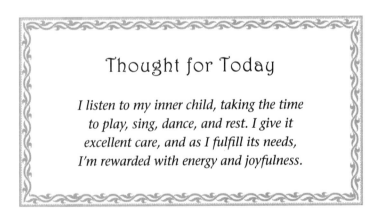

Thought for Today

*I listen to my inner child, taking the time
to play, sing, dance, and rest. I give it
excellent care, and as I fulfill its needs,
I'm rewarded with energy and joyfulness.*

৩৩৯ 352 ৩৩

Take Charge of Your Schedule

*Y*ou have wonderful dreams, ambitions, and intentions for yourself. We angels are here to help you take charge of your schedule so that you're able to act on these desires.

You don't need large chunks of time in order to accomplish lofty dreams. Most are manifested in small steps, so you could devote even 30 minutes a day toward your goal and still make amazing progress.

Watch out for the ego's tendency to hold up your aspirations and ambitions with unrelated activities. We call these "delay tactics," as they're unconscious schemes that detain you from working toward your purpose and dreams—addictive behaviors are common ones.

If you find yourself sidetracked by distractions of your own making, call upon us for help. We'll assist you in focusing on the small steps that are before you now. Manage what's on your agenda, and in so doing, take charge of your life.

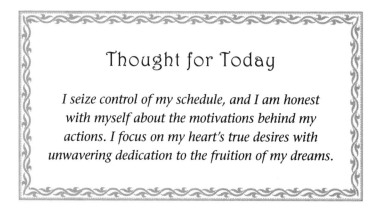

Thought for Today

I seize control of my schedule, and I am honest with myself about the motivations behind my actions. I focus on my heart's true desires with unwavering dedication to the fruition of my dreams.

Be Honest with Yourself

What are some feelings that would be helpful to admit to yourself today? This question will probably trigger answers that come through your thoughts or feelings.

Self-honesty is the process of being your own best friend. Just as close confidants share everything with each other, so is a healthy relationship with yourself based on truthful communication.

Sometimes you fear looking at your real desires because you wonder if it's safe to make changes in your life. On such occasions, it feels more secure to keep your emotions hidden away so that even you aren't aware of them. However, unexpressed feelings always find a way to make themselves known, and the healthiest route is to simply admit them to yourself. Know that we angels are supporting you through this process, and we're also by your side if you decide to make some life improvements.

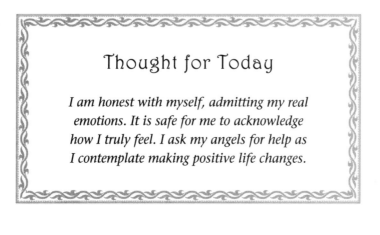

Thought for Today

I am honest with myself, admitting my real emotions. It is safe for me to acknowledge how I truly feel. I ask my angels for help as I contemplate making positive life changes.

Acknowledge the Genius Within You

*Y*our inner self is wise beyond limits. You're tapped in to the universal Source, which has access to all knowledge. Your wisdom comes from the same place as any genius who's ever lived—directly from God's mind. This is why it's important to think and speak about yourself lovingly. When you discuss your intelligence, you're talking about the Creator.

You have a genius within you, just like everyone else. The people who appear to be most brilliant are those who listen to their inner wisdom and put it into action. We angels can assist you in harnessing this part of your store of knowledge. We can help you hear, trust, understand, and act upon it—all you need to do is ask.

Today, revel in the certainty that you're wise. Even if you don't currently know something, you can always tap in to the information that you seek. Just quiet your mind, think of a question, and listen to the answer that comes to you.

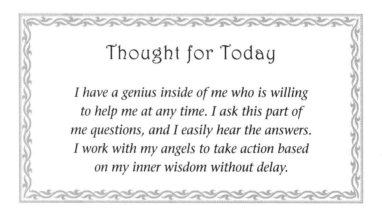

Thought for Today

I have a genius inside of me who is willing to help me at any time. I ask this part of me questions, and I easily hear the answers. I work with my angels to take action based on my inner wisdom without delay.

355

Trust Your Inner Knowing

You already know the answer to questions about your current situation. In stillness, you hear the inner wisdom that guides you, and today we angels counsel you to trust this source. You already know what to do, so your query isn't a request for new information or even guidance; rather, it asks whether you can trust that your decision will lead in positive new directions.

We're here today to reassure you of the validity of your inner wisdom. Whatever you're facing calls you to act on faith, without knowing very much about your future. That's why it's doubly important for you to hold positive expectations about the outcome.

All results are always beneficial in the ultimate sense, because only good things can happen in God's universe. Even the most seemingly dire circumstances bestow blessings on the souls involved.

Your positive expectations help bring about the greatest possible outcome, elevating your experience as you travel toward it.

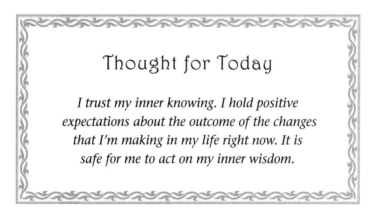

Thought for Today

I trust my inner knowing. I hold positive expectations about the outcome of the changes that I'm making in my life right now. It is safe for me to act on my inner wisdom.

Give Your Cares to God and the Angels

What troubles or worries you, beloved one? Don't hold on to those feelings single-handedly. Give them to us angels!

Take a deep breath right now, feeling our loving presence. On the exhale, blow out your cares, and we'll catch them and take them to the light for healing. Once these concerns are released, you'll feel the freedom of living carefree. This doesn't entail being irresponsible, as some people mistakenly believe; rather, it means moving through your duties with love, passion, and enthusiasm. Worries drags down your responsibilities, turning them into chores.

Today, be lighthearted by giving us any cares as soon as you become aware of them. Deliver them all to us, and rest easy with the knowledge that heaven is helping you along the way.

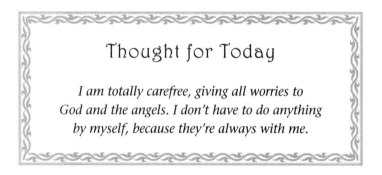

Thought for Today

I am totally carefree, giving all worries to God and the angels. I don't have to do anything by myself, because they're always with me.

Move Forward Fearlessly

*Y*ou can move forward fearlessly on the path of your dreams, without anxiety or reservation. In everything you do, you're always protected—as long as you ask us angels for help and then follow the guidance that we give you.

Today, boldly take one step in the direction of your dream. Do so with complete confidence that we walk by your side. You won't fall, and if you become afraid, we'll catch you.

Remember to work with us as eternal teammates, checking in before making decisions or taking action. We won't tell you what to do; however, we will give you guidance and helpful suggestions that are always based on love and respect for you. We're by your side, cheering you on toward the happiness that belongs to you.

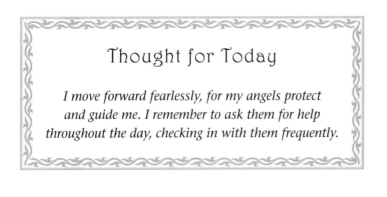

Thought for Today

I move forward fearlessly, for my angels protect and guide me. I remember to ask them for help throughout the day, checking in with them frequently.

Embrace Us as Your True Friends

Throughout your life and during every circumstance, we angels cherish and adore you. We never waver from the pure affection that we feel for you, because we always see the goodness and beauty that God created—we never look at the illusory surface. Instead, we focus on the brilliant light that radiates within and around you. If you could witness this illumination, you'd see why we love you so much.

Today, know that through everything we're your true friends. We trust, admire, and respect you for who you are. We're your constant companions, and we'll never leave your side.

Throughout your entire life, you can always be certain that we love you.

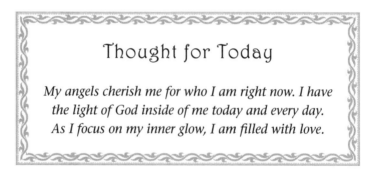

Thought for Today

My angels cherish me for who I am right now. I have the light of God inside of me today and every day. As I focus on my inner glow, I am filled with love.

Remember to Ask for Our Help

We angels are ready and able to help you with everything today. Never worry about overdoing your requests for our assistance. We're unlimited beings who can perform multiple tasks simultaneously, so you can ask for as much support as you'd like.

We prefer that you request our aid at the outset of anything that you do. In this way, we can be involved from the very beginning to ensure smooth operation from start to finish. However, if you forget to call upon us for help, that's perfectly fine. We're able to jump in whenever you ask, even if things have escalated. Anytime is good to request our assistance. We're always here for you—that's our purpose.

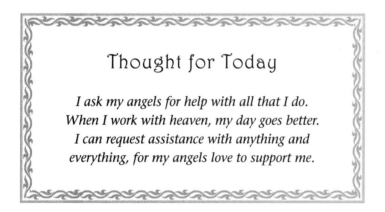

Thought for Today

I ask my angels for help with all that I do.
When I work with heaven, my day goes better.
I can request assistance with anything and
everything, for my angels love to support me.

Enjoy Your Unlimited Nature

Throughout this year, we angels have discussed how we're unlimited beings who can help you with anything. Today, we'd like to focus on the fact that *you* also possess unbounded potential. The only restrictions you have are those that you've decided on. Sometimes such choices come from personal beliefs, which—once you adopted them—resulted in your experience of limits.

How could God, the infinite and boundless Creator, make anything that did not share these qualities? Everything and everyone that comes from the Divine is also without constraints.

You have a wide range of abilities that haven't yet been discovered or explored. Basically, you're capable of anything that you can conceive of doing, because all activities are governed by the imagination. In time, you'll learn to capitalize on this fact, but for today, let's focus on shedding one restricting belief so that you can experience your infinite nature.

Think for a moment about an area of your life that you feel is missing something. The impression of lack signals a belief in limitations. Anytime that you begin a sentence with, "I don't have enough . . ." you're uncovering a self-imposed restriction.

Look for these ideas in your thoughts and words today, and counteract them with positive affirmations such as: "I have plenty of . . ." and "I possess unlimited . . ." As we've discussed, words are your starting point for manifestation and creation. Affirm your limitlessness, and notice how soon you experience this freedom for yourself.

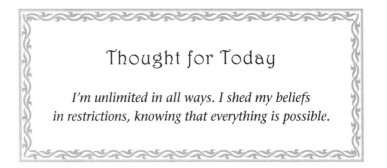

Thought for Today

*I'm unlimited in all ways. I shed my beliefs
in restrictions, knowing that everything is possible.*

Explore New Avenues

Part of your limitlessness comes out of the infinite number of choices available to you. You can do anything that you desire. Sometimes these options may overwhelm you in their scope, and that's when you retreat into comfortable routines. This is fine as long as you realize that *you've* chosen them. If you ever feel as though you're a victim or prisoner of your habits, it's time to reassess your decisions.

You always have options about how to spend this day. If you feel otherwise, then you've forgotten the original choices that led you to your current situation, so take a moment to remember why you made some of them. This will help you see that you've always been the decision maker in your life, even if you elected to let someone else choose for you. Remember that ultimately you don't have to do anything that you don't want to. You always have freedom in every matter.

Today, feel gladdened by all the alternatives that are before you, and explore some new avenues for yourself. You might begin by researching something that you'd like to try for the first time in the coming year. Choose a path that excites your passions, reigniting them with the youthful energy contained within all possibilities.

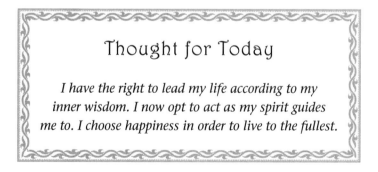

Thought for Today

I have the right to lead my life according to my inner wisdom. I now opt to act as my spirit guides me to. I choose happiness in order to live to the fullest.

362

Cherish Each Moment

Every moment of this day is a precious gift. Within all circumstances, no matter how things appear, you can find the beautiful light of Divine love shining brightly. Allow that radiance to warm you today.

Your tenderness has a healing effect on those around you. Others may not understand why they feel better in your company, yet they feel drawn to you—they're attracted to your light, which reminds them of their heavenly home.

Appreciate each moment today, even if some of them seem ordinary or painful. As you love right now, you extract the maximum amount of joy from your life, since happiness can only be experienced in the present.

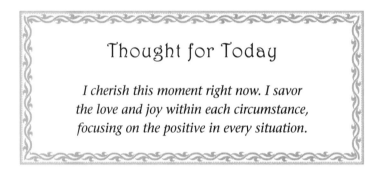

Thought for Today

I cherish this moment right now. I savor the love and joy within each circumstance, focusing on the positive in every situation.

363

Review Your Year

We angels would like to spend today reviewing the past year with you. What stands out in your mind when you think about it? What did you learn? What are some of your favorite memories? What would you like to change and experience in the coming year?

We can help you prepare for the future by taking an honest look at the past. Every situation offers opportunities for you to learn and grow—sometimes the most painful times inspire the greatest changes and improvement in your life.

Regret nothing about the past months. Each moment was a masterpiece, since you lived it as God's magnificent child. Use your memories as a catalyst to prepare and propel you into an even more amazing future.

We angels are with you through every day of every year, ready to help you upon request.

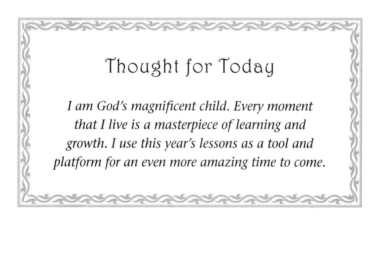

Thought for Today

I am God's magnificent child. Every moment that I live is a masterpiece of learning and growth. I use this year's lessons as a tool and platform for an even more amazing time to come.

364

Affirm the New Year

What would you like to experience next year? What do you want to change? If you knew that everything were possible and available to you, what would you ask for?

Now is the time to invest your energy in the coming months by affirming what you desire. As we angels have emphasized, anything that you wish for is manifested through the words that you speak, think, and write.

Today, put together a mental or written list of your dreams for the coming year. Turn every goal into an affirmative statement, asserting that your wish is already fulfilled. Thank the universe for the manifestation of these desires, expressing gratitude that the answers to your prayers have exceeded your expectations.

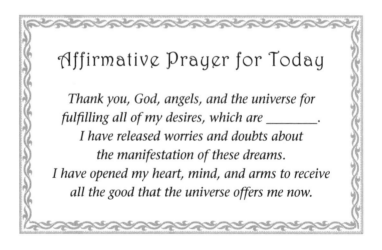

Affirmative Prayer for Today

Thank you, God, angels, and the universe for
fulfilling all of my desires, which are _____.
I have released worries and doubts about
the manifestation of these dreams.
I have opened my heart, mind, and arms to receive
all the good that the universe offers me now.

Know That Love Is the Key

In everything that you do or desire, love is the key. Your heart is the portal through which God's energy flows into you, so keep it open, and allow yourself to feel. When you do so, it's like a larger gasoline tank carrying more fuel for a vehicle. A receptive heart experiences life at a richer and deeper level, noticing the subtle details in every situation.

Ask us to help you open yourself up further today. As you stand on the brink of another year, take this gift with you across its threshold.

Of all the New Year's resolutions that you could make, the greatest of them is this: to love more often and deeply, and to feel and experience caring in every way.

Affirmative Prayer for Today

God and angels,
I ask for your assistance in opening my heart.
Please help me be aware of my soul, mind, and body.
Guide me to leave behind any old pain, anger, or hurt
and enter the new year with a clean and open heart.
Assist me in loving fearlessly, with grace and acceptance.
Help me love like an angel.
Thank you.

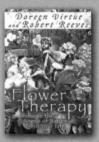

ABOUT THE AUTHOR

Doreen Virtue is the author of the *Healing with the Angels* book and oracle cards; *Archangels & Ascended Masters;* and *Angel Therapy,* among other works. Her products are available in most languages worldwide.

A doctor of psychology who works with the angelic realm, Doreen has appeared on *Oprah,* CNN, *The View,* and other television and radio programs. For more information on Doreen and the workshops she presents throughout the world, to subscribe to Doreen's free e-mail angel-messages newsletter, to visit her message boards, or to submit your angel healing stories, please visit **www.AngelTherapy.com**.

You can listen to Doreen's live weekly radio show, and call her for a reading, by visiting **HayHouseRadio.com**®.

NOTES

NOTES

NOTES

NOTES

∽ Hay House Titles of Related Interest ∾

ASK AND IT IS GIVEN: *Learning to Manifest Your Desires,*
by Esther and Jerry Hicks (The Teachings of Abraham)

BORN KNOWING: *A Medium's Journey—*
Accepting and Embracing My Spiritual Gifts,
by John Holland, with Cindy Pearlman

THE DISAPPEARANCE OF THE UNIVERSE: *Straight Talk about*
Illusions, Past Lives, Religion, Sex, Politics, and the Miracles of Forgiveness,
by Gary R. Renard

THE GOD CODE: *The Secret of Our Past, the Promise of Our Future,*
by Gregg Braden

MENDING THE PAST AND HEALING
THE FUTURE WITH SOUL RETRIEVAL,
by Alberto Villoldo, Ph.D.

PRACTICAL PRAYING: *Using the Rosary to Enhance Your Life,*
by John Edward
(published by Princess Books, distributed by Hay House)

SACRED CEREMONY: *How to Create Ceremonies*
for Healing, Transitions, and Celebrations,
by Steven D. Farmer, Ph.D.

SPIRIT MESSENGER: *The Remarkable Story of a*
Seventh Son of a Seventh Son, by Gordon Smith

ॐ

All of the above are available at your local bookstore,
or may be ordered by contacting Hay House
(see info on next page).

ॐ

We hope you enjoyed this Hay House book. If you'd like
to receive our online catalog featuring additional information
on Hay House books and products, or if you'd like to find out
more about the Hay Foundation, please contact:

Hay House, Inc., P.O. Box 5100, Carlsbad, CA 92018-5100
(760) 431-7695 or (800) 654-5126
(760) 431-6948 (fax) or (800) 650-5115 (fax)
www.hayhouse.com® • **www.hayfoundation.org**

Published and distributed in Australia by: Hay House Australia Pty. Ltd.,
18/36 Ralph St., Alexandria NSW 2015 • *Phone:* 612-9669-4299
Fax: 612-9669-4144 • www.hayhouse.com.au

Published and distributed in the United Kingdom by: Hay House UK, Ltd.,
Astley House, 33 Notting Hill Gate, London W11 3JQ
Phone: 44-20-3675-2450 • *Fax:* 44-20-3675-2451 • www.hayhouse.co.uk

Published and distributed in the Republic of South Africa by:
Hay House SA (Pty), Ltd., P.O. Box 990, Witkoppen 2068
Phone/Fax: 27-11-467-8904 • www.hayhouse.co.za

Published in India by: Hay House Publishers India, Muskaan Complex,
Plot No. 3, B-2, Vasant Kunj, New Delhi 110 070 • *Phone:* 91-11-4176-1620
Fax: 91-11-4176-1630 • www.hayhouse.co.in

Distributed in Canada by: Raincoast, 9050 Shaughnessy St.,
Vancouver, B.C. V6P 6E5 • *Phone:* (604) 323-7100 • *Fax:* (604) 323-2600
www.raincoast.com

Take Your Soul on a Vacation

Visit **www.HealYourLife.com®** to regroup, recharge,
and reconnect with your own magnificence. Featuring
blogs, mind-body-spirit news, and life-changing
wisdom from Louise Hay and friends.

Visit **www.HealYourLife.com** today!

Free e-newsletters from Hay House, the Ultimate Resource for Inspiration

Be the first to know about Hay House's dollar deals, free downloads, special offers, affirmation cards, giveaways, contests, and more!

 Get exclusive excerpts from our latest releases and videos from *Hay House Present Moments*.

 Enjoy uplifting personal stories, how-to articles, and healing advice, along with videos and empowering quotes, within *Heal Your Life*.

 Have an inspirational story to tell and a passion for writing? Sharpen your writing skills with insider tips from *Your Writing Life*.

Sign Up Now!

Get inspired, educate yourself, get a complimentary gift, and share the wisdom!

http://www.hayhouse.com/newsletters.php

Visit www.hayhouse.com to sign up today!

HAY HOUSE

HAYHOUSE RADIO
radio for your soul

HealYourLife.com ♥